CAREER IN TOURISM

CAREER IN TOURISM

Geetanjali

CENTRUM PRESS
NEW DELHI-110002 (INDIA)

CENTRUM PRESS
H.O.: 4360/4, Ansari Road, Daryaganj,
New Delhi-110002 (India)
Tel: 23278000, 23261597, 23255577, 23286875
B.O.: No. 1015, Ist Main Road, BSK IIIrd Stage,
IIIrd Phase, IIIrd Block, Bangalore-560085 (INDIA)
Tel: 080-41723429
Email: centrumpress@gmail.com
Visit us at: www.centrumpress.com

Career in Tourism

First Edition, 2010

PRINTED IN INDIA

Printed at Mehra Offset Press, Delhi

Contents

PREFACE

Tourism is travel for recreational, leisure or business purposes. The World Tourism Organization defines tourists as people who "travel to and stay in places outside their usual environment for more than twenty-four (24) hours and not more than one consecutive year for leisure, business and other purposes not related to the exercise of an activity remunerated from within the place visited". Tourism has become a popular global leisure activity. In 2008, there were over 922 million international tourist arrivals, with a growth of 1.9% as compared to 2007. International tourism receipts grew to US$944 billion (euro 642 billion) in 2008, corresponding to an increase in real terms of 1.8%.

These service industries include transportation services, such as airlines, cruise ships and taxis, hospitality services, such as accommodations, including hotels and resorts, and entertainment venues, such as amusement parks, casinos, shopping malls, various music venues and the theatre. The World Tourism Organization (UNWTO) forecasts that international tourism will continue growing at the average annual rate of 4%.

With the advent of e-commerce, tourism products have become one of the most traded items on the internet. Tourism products and services have been made available through intermediaries, although tourism providers (hotels, airlines, etc.) can sell their services directly. This has put pressure on intermediaries from both on-line and traditional shops.

There is now a demand for a better quality products, which has resulted in a fragmenting of the mass market for beach vacations; people want more specialised versions, such as Club 18-30, quieter resorts, family-oriented holidays or niche market-targeted destination hotels. The developments in technology and transport infrastructure, such as jumbo jets, low-cost airlines and more accessible airports have made many types of tourism more affordable. WHO estimates that up to 500,000 people are on planes at any time. The book paves way for many students to shape their career in tourism industry.

Author

Chapter 1

The Emergence of Alternative Forms of Tourism

The latter half of the twentieth century has been marked with amazing changes in technology, transportation, and communication and, in varying degrees, a spread of geo-political stability that has accompanied economic affluence for many citizens in industrialized and developing countries throughout the world. These changes have triggered the development of a number of new industries and the substantial evolution of existing industries to address the needs of increasingly prosperous, educated, and sophisticated post-industrial societies. One of these industries, tourism, has quietly emerged to become an important force in many societies and economies in various parts of the world.

Though not usually thought of as a single cohesive industry, the growth of tourism since World War II has nonetheless been dramatic. Higher discretionary incomes, smaller family size, changing demographics, lower transportation costs, improved public health standards, infrastructure development, and hospitable environments for tourists in many destinations have made tourism, especially long-distance tourism, an activity within the reach and desires of many members of many nations.

Furthermore, developments in marketing, management, vertical and horizontal integration, pricing, and tour packaging, as well as capital investments in physical facilities — "bricks and mortar" — and public infrastructure, have provided tourism with the necessary framework to allow the tremendous growth it has experienced over the past half century. Thus, tourism has indeed emerged as an "industry" which, according to the World Tourism Organization, in 1989 gener ated approximately 74 million jobs in its direct and service-related industries, such as airlines, hotels, travel services, and publications.

Table. International Travelers: Volume and Expenditure Patterns.

Year	*Arrivals (millions)*	*Per cent Increase*	*Expenditures (U.S. $ billions)*	*Per cent Increase*
1950	25.3		2.1	
1960	69.3	173.9	6.9	229
1970	158.7	145.0	17.9	159
1980	204.8	29.0	102.4	472
1990	425.0	107.5	230.0	125

Source: World Tourism Organization Secretariat 1991

At least at the international level, the growth and extent of tourism activity can be appreciated by examining the volume and expenditures of international travelers; data from the period 1950 to 1990 are presented. Though these data include many who are traveling for other reasons, a good portion of the growth is attributable to tourism.

Many countries and regions which have possessed the necessary resources for tourism development have chosen, either consciously or otherwise, the path of developing large scale tourism as a major national or regional activity. Tourism has become a major employer, taxpayer, and physical and political presence in many jurisdictions. As a result, tourism has often altered the very nature of social, political, and economic interaction that occurs in these places. Frequently, the transformation has been no less dramatic than the shifts that took place generations before, as agrarian ways were pushed out by industrialization.

Now, in industrialized countries, tourism is frequently

pushing out (or more correctly, replacing) manufacturing, distribution, or extractive industry as the economic mainstay. In developing countries, the shift typically has been from an agrarian economic base to a touristic economic base, bypassing an industrial phase altogether.

The reasons for this explosion of growth in tourism are many and interrelated. At one level, transportation systems, especially with respect to the automobile and commercial air travel, have opened new opportunities for potential tourists by making transport from home to destination less expensive (in real terms), more convenient, quicker, and safer.

Increases in real incomes since 1950, especially in the industrialized countries of Europe, North America, and Australasia, have expanded the numbers of potential long distance tourists from solely the upper classes to virtually all social strata.

Shortened work weeks, increased leisure time, earlier retirement age, and extended life expectancies have provided many more people with the discretionary time and opportunities to undertake frequent holidays, or "get-aways," or to pursue lengthy exploratory excursions.

Improved communications and information dissemination, ranging from travelogues on television, to movies filmed in exotic locations, to extensive word-of-mouth networking, have familiarized potential tourists with the far corners of the globe long before they consider visiting them.

The desire to see famous natural or man-made sites, to experience new or familiar adventures, different cultures, or one's own historic or ethnic roots, or just to change one's environment from the cold chill of winter to the warmth of sun-drenched beaches has been enhanced and stimulated by the marketing efforts of such various components of the tourism industry as airlines, destination resorts, and tourism authorities in their efforts to increase volumes of business or visitorship to specific locations.

On the supply side, various improvements have been made which have catered to the tastes and preferences of potential tourists. No longer is long distance air travel considered a major ordeal. With the combination of increasingly experienced travelers and customer sensitive airlines, trips that would have been considered extremely demanding only one or two generations ago are now taken in stride by all but the most fickle of travelers.

The uncertainty of the availability or quality of accommodations that may have prevailed in the past has been replaced by worldwide reservation services, hotel franchises that guarantee quality standards and potable water, and the familiarity and assurances generated by prior visits, visits by friends, or observations by travel writers.

However, tourist development has not progressed without controversy. Disillusionment with "mass" tourism and the many problems it has triggered has led many observers and researchers to criticize vociferously the past methods and directions of tourism development and to offer instead the hope of "alternative tourism," broadly defined as forms of tourism that are consistent with natural, social, and community values and which allow both hosts and guests to enjoy positive and worthwhile interaction and shared experiences.

To date, however, such reactions have been more notable for their harsh judgments against mass tourism than their positive contributions as to what "alternative tourism" means. As many of the articles in this volume point out, it is easier to grasp and speak against the negative results of mass tourism than it is to formulate a realistic and cohesive view of what "alternative tourism," however defined, can reasonably offer.

The flurry of research and publication concerning mainstream and alternative tourism in the past two decades can be placed in historical perspective. Most analysts recognize that tourism takes on forms appropriate to an era, and therefore historic styles develop consistent with population size, economic status, available modes of transport, and geographical habitats of home in comparison with destinations abroad.

Public participation creates mainstream tourism, usually in several variations at any given time; and the needed infrastructure develops accordingly. In addition, the existence of "alternatives" to mainstream tourism is not new.

Sigaux documents the history of tourism from the time of the early Greeks to the period after World War II, and this chronology clearly shows both mainstream and "alternative" tourism for more than two millennia. According to Casson, for example, during the Empire the seven hills of metropolitan Rome supported an estimated 1.5 million people, many of whom must have shared modern motivations for travel including the need for fresh air and a change of scene.

Wealthy Romans traveled to Naples, where their vacation homes were constructed on piers built over the water, providing a fine view of Mt. Vesuvius reflected in the Bay. A fragment of etched glass depicting this salubrious scene may well be the first known tourist souvenir. Around this cluster of superior accommodations, lesser folk rented lodging in small rooms on side streets.

The rich traveled by chariot from Rome to Naples and built private villas (*diversoria*) for their overnight stops along the highway. Even though used only three or four nights per year, these en route accommodations were elegantly furnished and maintained by a permanent staff of servants. Their gardens were filled with fruit and flowers, but water was so scarce in the hill country that it was necessary to "water" the plants with wine!

To house the commoners who also toured, farmers whose land fortuitously fronted the Roman highway built *tavernas* to provide lodging, meals, and stables and soon were in business as innkeepers.

Not all Romans could travel so far. Early in the Imperial era Tivoli (originally *Tibur*), only a few miles outside Rome, became a popular holiday centre noted for its gardens and waterfalls. "Second home" tourism also dates at least to Roman times in the many villas and spas constructed outside every major city of the Empire.

Near Rome, Hadrian's Villa, built between 125 and 135 AD, is still a much-visited attraction.

Tourism became a major industry in the nineteenth century. The *Dictionnaire universale du XIXe siécle* of 1876 (quoted by Sigaux 1966:7) defines tourists as "people who travel for the pleasure of traveling, out of curiosity and because they have nothing better to do" and "even for the joy of boasting about it afterwards."

Construction of railroads and the innovations of Thomas Cook and George Pullman created new forms of "mainstream" tourism such as group tours. In his first nine years in business (1857-1866), Thomas Cook alone handled more than a million customers, building an economic empire in mainstream tourism with his hotel vouchers, rail tickets, traveler's cheques, and a global travel agency network.

As Dennison Nash (1979b) details, European aristocracy (together with the gamblers, ne'er-do-wells, and voyeurs who followed them) created at Nice the first European winter resort where a cluster of palatial hotels with ballrooms and adjoining concert halls provided annual recreation for some 60,000 *hivernants* (winter visitors) amidst opulence, indoor toilets, and a discriminating hotel staff. And tiny adjacent Monaco attained its fame with the establishment of a resplendent casino to serve the so-called "international set."

But "alternative" forms of tourism also developed in Europe during this same period, as reported in the 1985 Special Issue: The Evolution of Tourism, of the *Annals of Tourism Research*. Noteworthy is the article on "tramping" by members of the British working classes for whom these "tramp trips appear to have become rites of passage to full male adulthood".

The similar French *Tour de France* and the German *Wanderpflicht* provided European journeymen with an opportunity to gain work experience away from home, and thereby served to "regulate competition by geographically dispersing workers and delaying entrance to master craftsman status" for as long as four to five years. *Compagnonnage* as a rite of passage into manhood is said to have been one of the most powerful working class institutions ever developed in France. For domestic tourism, Fichtner and Michna (1987) trace the rise of Europe's famous amusement parks, the forerunners of today's theme parks.

In the twentieth century, the first passenger jet service in 1958 is credited with inaugurating modern mass and charter tourism, with all its attendant problems of overcrowding and pollution. Thus mainstream tourism in subsequent decades has used airplanes for long-haul travel and autos on the local scene.

The railroad which reigned supreme during the nineteenth century fell quickly into decline, as Martinus Kosters documents in this volume. Mainstream tourism in this century has been primarily north-south because of climate and, as Hall observes (1984:540), "destination countries represent a much wider spread than originating countries, reflecting a spatial diffusion of tourists from the developed world across the globe, with fastest growth in the more remote regions of the Third World."

Rapid development of resort infrastructure to receive and accommodate airborne guests in favored spots was responsible for the Miami Beach/Waikiki atmosphere, advertising sun, sea, sand, and sex on beaches from Antigua to Zihuatanejo.

Alternately sun, ski, snow, and sex have become winter sports attractions in resorts from the Arlberg to Zermatt, with the attendant gridlock on mountain access roads. By the 1990s, there is a sense that the public has become "tired" of the crowds, weary of jet lag, awakened to the evidences of pollution, and in search of something "new."

Innovative but rapidly gaining in popularity as "alternative" vacations for this decade are walking tours (some of which are very costly because of the level of accommodations and cuisine provided), barge and canal tours (many of which are also deluxe and expensive), bicycle tours, home and farm stays (as discussed by Pearce in this volume), and, at least within the United States, an increase in domestic tourism.

Youth tourism has also taken many forms over time, most of which seem to have been a simple expression of youthful energy and curiosity about the world beyond their bounded society. Their travels were usually a form of "alternatives" to prevailing tourism. Historically, these have involved travels to medieval universities and such institutions as the "Grand Tour," with its year abroad for young scholars and their tutors.

In recent years, the youth hostel movement encouraged "hitchhikers" and the 1960s generated the "hippies," followed by what Riley now terms the "long term budget traveller". This last group is to be distinguished from the "drifters" first described by Cohen whose deviant, drug-related behaviour and counterculture still persist in some locales such as Thailand and Sri Lanka.

Thus, to seek "alternatives" to the tourist mainstream is a contemporary but by no means a novel theme. The history of tourism is replete with centuries of parallel examples.

ECONOMIC TRENDS AND BYPRODUCTS IN MAINSTREAM TOURISM

Because of the growing awareness of tourism as an activity, an industry, and a catalyst for economic growth and development, competition for the tourist and for tourism expenditures has been significant in recent decades. One result has been market segmentation and a considerable broadening of the perceived and actual opportunities available for potential tourists. Thus tourists can choose from "sun and sand" holidays, "adventure travel," "theater tours," "shopping sprees," summer or winter sports vacations, cultural immersion, historic re-enactments, and various other tourism experiences.

An interesting illustration of product identification and market segmentation is offered by two of the fastest growing tourism destinations in the United States: Orlando, Florida and Las Vegas, Nevada.

Both of these tourist-dominated cities offer predominantly artificially created tourism experiences: Orlando with the presence of Disney World, Epcot Centre, and MGM and Universal Studio "Hollywood"-themed parks; and Las Vegas with its variety of themed "must see" casino-hotel resorts such as The Mirage, Caesars Palace, and Excalibur, along with high-technology showroom extravaganzas and unparalleled convention facilities, all framing a wide variety of gambling opportunities.

Both Orlando and Las Vegas offer escapism and fantasy in highly artificial environments and have been tremendously successful in doing so. It is no accident that Las Vegas is often referred to as providing an "adult Disneyland" for its visitors, whereas Orlando provides the "real" Disney experience. With the exception of the slot machines and gambling tables, there are strong similarities between these two rapidly growing tourism destination cities. Indeed, it may not be so farfetched to call Orlando, with all of its thrilling but nonetheless artificial attractions, an "adolescent's Las Vegas."

It is worth noting that the economic success of both Las Vegas and Orlando has led to many recent attempts to emulate them; legalization or attempted legalization of casino-style gambling has been widespread in the United States, Canada, and Australia over the past fifteen years, and Mickey Mouse has gone abroad to France and Tokyo to found new Disney Worlds to conquer.

However, in spite of the many forms it has taken, not all tourism industries in the developed or the developing world have been beneficial. Success in attracting tourists and tourism-related investments has sometimes led to overexploitation of tourism resources, which has deteriorated the tourism experience for visitors and hosts alike.

Conflicts have arisen between natural and constructed tourism resources as governments and entrepreneurs have cooperated in competition with those of other locations to attract the economic benefits and prestige that popular destination resorts could bring. Sheer numbers of tourists have altered the "pristine" or "natural" experience that some regions initially offered.

The development of high volume tourism facilities, such as high-rise hotels and tourist-oriented strip retail centers, with inadequate attention paid to traffic patterns, urban planning, infrastructure needs, or aesthetic considerations, has created more than a few "tourism disasters." It is clear in retrospect that, in many cases, the benefits linked to tourism development were quickly dissipated, either due to inadequate or inept planning or because of short-term, shortsighted exploitation.

Disillusionment with mainstream or mass tourism is reflected in the retrospective disappointment of many locals and tourists alike with the ultimate results of tourism developments. An interesting illustration is provided by the case study of Maui, Hawaii, written by Farrell in this volume. For the locals — the hosts — the concerns may be of promises unfulfilled, destruction of an older and simpler way of life, inadequacy of employment opportunities, or dissatisfaction with other economic changes which came with tourism development.

For tourists the view is often summarized with statements such as "This used to be a nice place, but now it is ruined" because of overcrowding, overcommercialization, or overdevelopment. The "mass tourism," the tackiness, and the variety of problems experienced in such places as Niagara Falls, Waikiki, Spain's Costa Brava, and Australia's Gold Coast have too often created eyesores alongside beautiful natural settings; herded large numbers of tourists as if they were so many cattle; disrupted traditional cultures and occupational patterns by creating a pervasive tourism industry characterized by low-paying service jobs and manipulative values; and ignored the needs of local citizens and the community values that were inconsistent with pragmatic economic requirements of the tourism industry.

The decade of the 1990s has been predicted to become the "Decade of Eco-Tourism," and the travel industry is becoming sensitized to mounting global concern about the social costs and environmental damage created by too much tourism. In the past, planners in the private and public sectors have relied heavily on short and intermediate term economic and investment criteria for decision making and for resource allocation considerations regarding tourism projects.

This has often led to problems of overdevelopment accompanied by rapid decline in a destination's general appeal to more upscale tourists. Select coastlines in Florida, Spain, and Mexico provide a variety of examples of this pattern of development.

One reason for this short-sightedness is that the market pricing mechanism and other economic processes do not always provide a full and complete accounting of all costs and benefits associated with tourist developments. In instances where important resources are held as the property of "all the people," or where individual property rights are poorly defined, externalities — defined as costs (or benefits) resulting from transactions undertaken between buyers and sellers but falling on otherwise uninvolved third parties — can and frequently do arise.

Pristine beaches and alpine settings, for example, are usually perceived as complementary resources for tourism development projects. Yet the attempt of too many projects to capture the common benefits from such shared resources can lead to congestion, pollution, and a general degradation of the value of such resources for tourism purposes.

Thus local residents at tourist destinations, as well as the general public, often bear the costs of overdevelopment through diminished aesthetic or use value of the resources;

by paying for mitigation, abatement, or clean-up efforts through private endeavors or increased taxes; or with lower wealth through foregone opportunities, diminished incomes, or depressed property values.

There is also the socially destabilizing issue of redistribution of income and wealth that invariably follows rapid economic change. Tourism development creates "winners" and "losers" among the local residents, often without a common acceptance as to the equity of such redistribution.

Alternatively, many of the "winners" might be outsiders who are then viewed as exploiters of the native population and rapists of the land. Furthermore, the changes in income and wealth are often viewed in light of the long term depletion of an area's resource base; the ability of such destinations to capitalize fully on their tourist resources in the future may become permanently impaired because of rapid tourism development.

Good decision making procedures should take all such externalities and their costs fully into account in planning for tourism development and in directing the evolution of existing tourist industries. Private market forces by themselves cannot rectify such external costs and often ignore altogether — or treat amorally — the income and wealth redistribution issues. When such situations occur, policy makers should structure government intervention to stimulate more desirable outcomes. Regrettably, such enlightened planning is often not realized in practice.

Awareness of such resource and social conflicts, however, and their relationship to the health of a tourism industry is growing. Antonio Savignac, Secretary-General of the World Tourism Organization, was the keynote speaker at the International Travel Industry Expo 1990, held in Chicago. Among his comments delivered to some 3,000 travel agents and 400 industry suppliers were: "if the destination deteriorates, so do the profits."

This conference dealt with "green tourism," or tourism

in the context of man's stewardship with nature, with the development of rural tourism, and with the need to develop responsible tourism policies. It was emphasized that industry and tourism planners need to establish criteria which would determine carrying capacities, both physical and social, for many tourist destinations.

Those criteria then require implementation to insure a more enjoyable and lasting experience for the guest and an economically and psychologically more rewarding environment for the hosts. This volume's article by Bryan Farrell provides discussion and a case study of the aspects and pitfalls of this process. In short, the direction of tourism planning in the 1990s should be toward enlightened self-interest and the value of preserving the quality and stability of both natural and human resources in tourism destinations.

CONCEPTUAL BASIS FOR MAINSTREAM AND ALTERNATIVE TOURISM

The concept of mainstream and alternative tourism needs to be reviewed in theoretical perspective. Although European guidebooks date to the fourteenth century and European scholars began to write about the phenomenon of tourism as early as 1899, serious interest in tourism as an institution spans only two decades.

Analyzing the literature to date, Jafar Jafari (1989a:20) has aggregated the individual opinions and writings about tourism into four groups, each with "a distinctive position or consolidated platform on tourism." The four platforms appeared in chronological order but are not mutually exclusive. One has not replaced the other, and all four platforms are still being individually used:

- The Advocacy Platform includes both private and public interests that "focus on tourism's importance to the economy" as a labour-intensive industry that generates foreign exchange, preserves environment, revives traditions of the past, and actively promotes cultural performances. This viewpoint became a strong voice in the 1960s as nationalism swept many countries into independence, heightening their need for funds, and is still prevalent. It was recently expressed as the route to success "with mass tourism as a ticket to development" *Economist.*

- The Cautionary Platform grew out of research and case studies largely undertaken in the 1970s by social scientists who questioned the validity of the benefit claims as contrasted to the realities of commoditization of culture and other negative impacts on a host society. An extensive literature supports the voiced concerns and challenges the Advocates.
- The Adaptancy Platform, benefiting from the arguments raised by its predecessors, seeks new strategies for tourism such as indigenous tourism, soft tourism, green tourism, sensitized tourism, responsible tourism, appropriate tourism, alternative tourism, cottage tourism, local level tourism. However, as Jafari has noted, "the Adaptancy Platform has emerged as a partial remedy, but strategies have not been fully developed to accommodate the mass tourism generated globally. Tourism's forms and practices can be influenced but its volume cannot be curtailed".
- *The Knowledge-Based Platform* is the most recent development and "aims at positioning itself on a scientific foundation which simultaneously maintains bridges with other platforms...the many studies are intended to contribute to a holistic study or treatment of tourism; not just its forms or consequences. The main goal is the formulation of a scientific body of knowledge on tourism."

As with many other aspects of modern life, tourism has brought with it benefits and costs, blessings and curses. Reflecting people's inherent curiosity, hedonism, desire for adventure and excitement, or just a need to change the pace and setting of everyday experiences, tourism has opened the door to many to seek out and fulfill their vacation needs. Furthermore, tourist industries have been the willing suppliers of the demanded services.

But all of this has not come without dissatisfaction. Perceived difficulties with mainstream tourism have encouraged planners, researchers, and social critics to rethink the logic of traditional tourist development, to examine the alternatives to mainstream or mass tourism, and to begin formulating better ways to integrate tourism into a broader range of values and social concerns that traditional tourism development has somehow put at risk.

Fully understanding the benefits and costs of tourist development in terms of their sources, possibilities for mitigation, and implications of "alternatives" will we hope play a major role in correcting the mistakes of the past.

Every body of scholars, working in a particular time span, develop an explanatory mode appropriate to their frame of reference. Just as Jafari has developed a typology of tourism literature (as discussed above), most of the members of the International Academy for the Study of Tourism have been involved in tourism research and/or as consultants to various facets of the travel or transportation industry.

As noted earlier, in the early 1960s the new self-rule of former colonies mandated an immediate search for new sources of foreign exchange and domestic employment. The World Bank and the United Nations recognized the potentials of tourism to meet those needs and negotiated loans and support for new resort developments, for modern airplanes, and for tax benefits for investors.

The pace of this type of development has not yet slowed, both because of the development of new overseas destinations such as Boracay in the Philippines and because of the mounting interest in increased domestic tourism in virtually every country on the globe, including many Third World nations.

Of necessity, government planners and policy makers

throughout the world are seeking direction for the management of their tourism industries. In many ways this book provides such direction.

The contributors to this volume and the members of the Academy are mindful, however, of the intellectual and ideological alternatives to a tourism management perspective: the emerging interest in eco-tourism, in local level and privatized development, and the concerns and implications suggested in dependency theory and in ecumenical edicts.

To a degree these issues are addressed here, but the body of data to test and verify theory in many of these areas is not yet at hand or is in need of refinement. Meanwhile, development goes forward, sometimes scarcely keeping pace with demand, and the need for direction and greater understanding by and for policy makers remains a most significant challenge. The pragmatic issue that can be useful to policy makers -understanding the broad implications of the various choices confronting them — constitutes the philosophical organizing core for many of the articles in this volume. It is hoped that this will serve as a major building block in the accumulation of knowledge of tourism and its various effects on societies.

Chapter 2

Scope in International Tourism Reconsidered

On the eve of the third millennium, the quest for "alternative" models is urgent; today this urgency is gaining power within the field of tourism. Many authors identify with this question. Seminars and symposia proliferate in opposing the problems of unchecked tourist growth. Alternative Tourism has become a symbol of the "Tourism of the Future."

In choosing "Theoretical Perspectives on Alternative Forms of Tourism" as the topic of its first seminar, the International Academy for the Study of Tourism invited academics and other scientists to consider all aspects of this theme. As social scientists, we must be concerned with Alternative Tourism in all its facets, actual or potential. It is the contention of the authors that the popularity of this new concept should itself be analyzed as a symptom.

The alliance of the two words "tourism" and "alternative" should alert us. It has a paradoxical resonance, an incongruity stimulating further enquiry. In this chapter, we intend to squeeze the meaning out of these words and to question the underpinnings of their use over the past two decades. Thus, ours is an essay in the sociology of knowledge and praxis.

THE PHENOMENON AND ITS CONCEPT

At several recent meetings, we have noted the perplexing

nature of the term Alternative Tourism. Whenever speakers were asked to define it, their embarrassment became clear. At the International Round Table organized by URESTI, Georges Cazes (a French geographer) and Linda Richter (an American political scientist) presided over the debate on the problematics of alternative tourism in local societies. Cazes was irritated by what he considered a confusing notion and Richter proposed replacing Alternative Tourism with the term "appropriate tourism."

At Zakopane, the academicians concluded by condemning the "imprecise character of the term Alternative Tourism [as] ambiguous and hardly congruent with scientific work." Finally, at the World Tourism Organization Seminar on Alternative Tourism, the participants voted to replace the term with Responsible Tourism, purposefully defined as "relating to all forms of tourism which respect the host, natural, built, and cultural environment, and the interests of all parties concerned: hosts, guests, visitors, tourist industry, government, etc."

How can we understand the success of the term Alternative Tourism in spite of all the reservations about it?

"Alternative Tourism" has a nice ring to it. It is alliterative like an advertising gimmick. It is dynamic and provides a rallying cry. It sounds like an appeal: "Let's make the improbable a reality!" It connotes quality, responsibility, and respectability. It suggests a sensitivity that wins over the world. Yet, though attractive, the label is deceiving.

From the beginning there has been a problem of definition: where to draw the line between various kinds of tourism. The many meetings on Alternative Tourism have spawned a "discourse of good intentions." In this chapter we hope to reveal the ideological pressures behind the discourse.

There is a danger of oversimplification of the complexities of tourism: in order to avoid the dilemma of having to decide whether to reject tourism completely or accept it unconditionally, people have latched onto the easy idea of Alternative Tourism.

UNCERTAIN ORIGINS

The emergence of the word "alternative" allied with tourism throws light on its *ideological* nature. The Ecumenical Coalition on Third World Tourism (ECTWT) claims paternity. Since its establishment in Bangkok, it has aimed "to explore possible models of alternative tourism in the Third World."

In 1980, a precursor group of militant Christians gathered just before the World Tourism Organization Conference on Tourism in Manila to denounce economic imperialism, domination by transnational corporations, political exploitation, organized prostitution of women and children, the degradation of traditional cultures, and other ills.

The Tourism European Network (TEN) was soon formed in Stuttgart in collaboration with ECTWT and, in 1984, held a seminar on Alternative Tourism in Asia. In 1986 a similar international conference took place at Bad Boll, West Germany. This called for the different sectors — tourists, hosts, businesses — to participate in building a New Tourism Order. But there were broader forces and other groups also promoting Alternative Tourism.

ALTERNATIVE TOURRISM

One could also link these calls for Alternative Tourism with various "Alternative Movements" that arose in Germany or the West Coast of the United States in the 1960s. These movements wanted to promote a counterculture by rejecting consumer society. Alternative Tourism, in rejecting mass tourism, is a similar radical attempt to transform social relations and is thus part of the larger movement. Is tourism a new kind of development strategy or, more powerfully, a prime force within a new strategy of international relations? A recent congress was called "Tourism — A Vital Force for Peace." This issue of "alternatives" penetrates all domains, and tourism is but one entrée.

Thus one could envisage a sociology of "Alternative Tourism as a social movement": a force aimed at social change; a movement of people in the process of mobilizing ideas; a series of acts and speech diffused in many segments of social life, where the actors are not totally aware of their real motives.

It is only with the hindsight of history that we can speak about a real change of strategy. One should be able to analyse the actors, the channels of communication, the ramifications, and the different forces of the movement. But the believers in Alternative Tourism belong to various social groups and the issue is still unclear.

The whole question is complex. In the 1980s everybody started to talk about Alternative Tourism, but with scattered meanings and heterogenous or contradictory interests.

Alternative Tourism encompasses a wide range of connotations: tourists characterized by particular motivations; touristic practices; a touristic product; levels of technology; solutions to planning; local, regional, national, or international politics; a strategy for development.

In the last case, Alternative Tourism is the application to tourism of Alternative Development in regions where tourism has been chosen as a factor in economic development. Finally, Alternative Tourism expresses the concept of a "New order of Tourism." The multiplicity of these meanings is both a great source of confusion and a rich opportunity for in-depth study.

PROFILES OF CONCEPTUALIZATION

We may approach the problem in two ways. There is a difference between the emergence of a practical concept and the construction of a scientific concept. The analysis must go further than surveying the various meanings and denouncing the confusion, even in order to clarify them. Listing the different uses of the term and coming up with an approximate definition is easy but insufficient.

Using the methods of structural linguistics, we analyse

the structure of meanings underlying the discourse of Alternative Tourism — the discourse of the tourists, professionals, politicians, scientists. We deconstruct this discourse in order to lay bare the conceptual operations from which it derives its power of persuasion. This is only a much needed preliminary step.

The expression Alternative Tourism can be baffling; to one businessman interviewed in the French Alps it meant "that the roads, the hotels, the whole place, is periodically filled and emptied!" The word "alternative," taken literally, engenders such images as ebb and flow, going and returning, leaving and arriving! But to the initiated, "alternative" (as in Alternative Tourism) is a special kind of qualifier. The whole phrase is an "autonomous syntagm"; the words are bound together like a single noun.

Using the methods of structural analysis, we look at the opposing pairs in which Alternative Tourism is used in speech. We find that Alternative Tourism always has an antithesis: commercial, conventional, mass tourism. It arises as the contrary to whatever is seen as negative or bad about conventional tourism, so it is always a semantic inversion, found at all levels of discourse.

For instance, some tourists are motivated to think that Alternative Tourism is individualized or selective, expressing their good taste, as opposed to mass tourism, which is seen as plebeian, organized, gregarious, and allowing little individual choice.

As lodging, Alternative Tourism refers to human scale, small and medium sized local, family, or community enterprises, well integrated into the area. Anything other than the usual concrete tourist establishments qualifies. Alternative Tourism connotes local artisanship, with wood and fine materials and typical local architecture.

As a tourist product, Alternative Tourism is expensive, sold by travel agents to a wealthy clientele or social leaders. "Cultural tourism" is the key word. Paradoxically, it also claims to be free of commercial circuits and capitalist profits.

It appeals to advocates of "social tourism" and independent tourists alike.

As activity, it favors physical well-being acquired by good health habits, competitive sports, or strenuous outings. It implies intellectual and aesthetic attitudes, trips to far regions with unexplored cultural or natural treasures appealing to the socially mobile. It opposes mass tourism for its comfort and repetition of the "four S's" (sun, sand, ski, sex) of the average middle classes.

Finally, as planning, Alternative Tourism appears to express local wishes to bring together tourists and host communities and thereby enters into endogenous development policies concerned with local interests. Some claim that this "new model" of tourism will replace mass tourism as "old fashioned" or out of date. Thus for some, "alternative" is not just another kind of tourism, but aspires to become *the* tourism in the promotion of a new order.

THE PRINCIPLE OF THE ALTERNATIVE

In logic, an alternative is based on a judgment that there are only two possibilities. Two contemporaneous terms are placed in mutual exclusion, with an "excluded middle," that is, no other possible course is open. It is either one or the other. Thus the promotion of Alternative Tourism relies on a series of value-laden judgments: devaluation/valuation, negation/affirmation, neutralization/idealization.

Emerging from such a series of discriminating processes between"reference tourism" and Alternative Tourism, logically Alternative Tourism becomes *the* tourism.

After analyzing many texts referring to tourism, an unending repetition of these mental processes can be noted. We idealize what we promote and reject what we disapprove of.

ALTERNATIVE TOURISM AND THE CHALLENGE OF INTERNATIONAL TOURISM

To situate the Alternative Tourism movement, we must

compare its goals with those of International Tourism. Within the discourse, Alternative Tourism can be seen as an opposite of International Tourism, which is itself multidimensional. Some major characteristics of International Tourism include the following.

THE PRIMACY OF ECONOMICS

International Tourism is generally defined as a particular aspect of Tourism (with a capital T), as the extension into international geographical space of a mobility originally confined within national limits in opposition to internal (or domestic) tourism.

There are, however, many ways to define international tourism. In the literature, modern international tourism is commonly linked with the Grand Tour, which began in the eighteenth century among young British aristocrats making an initiatory trip to the Continent.

As other classes were emancipated in the nineteenth and early twentieth centuries, the idea was generalized as a "vacation." In this way, the ideas of tourism and vacations are interchangeable. Thus international tourism is seen as an irrepressible seasonal mobility which crosses frontiers, as "a tidal wave, a North-South invasion, or a stampede to the sun."

Seen historically, this is a one-sided view, that of the industrialized nations. But international tourism is an "international social fact" in the sociological sense. "Not all social facts are amenable to internationalization...there are some phenomena which reflect more precisely the characteristics of one group, people, or nation; other phenomena are seen to better advantage as *exchanges* between different peoples; they surpass national territories,...they live a kind of supra-national life."

THE DUALITY OF THE CONCEPT

In the 1930s, countries in the League of Nations were aware of the assets and liabilities of international travel on the balance of payments, "petty things" which can amount to considerable sums. At that critical period, some governments protected their balance of payments by limiting travel abroad.

The League's Economic Commission, however, took a position in favour of International Tourism, with the important argument: "It is ultimately wrong to consider domestic tourism to be something essentially different from international tourism, just as it would be to forget that the economic activity of a country is indissolubly linked to its external trade".

Thus tourism is divided into international and domestic but, though linked, they refer to different networks of meaning.

Domestic tourism is seen as a cultural habit increasingly widespread in industrial societies, but International Tourism has become an import/export activity reckoned in terms of international monetary exchange.

Thus International Tourism is implicitly reduced to its economic and commercial aspects, which take preference over cultural aspects. Whereas domestic and national tourism are seen as inherently cultural, International Tourism is seen as prospectively economic. Needless to say the notion of Alternative Tourism bears the consequences of this cleavage.

POLITICAL WILL: THE GROWTH OF INTERNATIONAL TOURIST MOVEMENTS

Thus tourism became first and foremost an "economic fact" for decision makers, who take this as a given in considering tourism within their overall planning. The opening of an area to foreign tourists is seen as a market phenomenon and is calculated as a matter of foreign exchange by international organizations. Countries are measured by their performance, and regions are urged to enter into this "competition." The development of tourism is seen as axiomatic.

Tourism is not just a matter of national growth, but must be conceptualized as part of international relations.

TOURISTS IN THE GLOBAL FLOWS

Reading economic forecasts gives one the impression that tourism is constantly in danger of collapse. The discourse of officials is preoccupied with signs of weakness, decrease, or loss. Thus international tourism always appears to be on the brink of a crisis, one which it in fact anticipates and resists.

The constant growth of international tourism is not spontaneous, but reflects a supernational institutional will. In the Universal Rights of Man Charter the liberty to circulate freely in the world is fundamental.

The worldwide expansion of international tourism is the subject of massive propaganda. In this regard it is noteworthy that the International Union of Official Organizations of Tourism (IUOTO), which became the World Tourism Organization in 1974, was originally founded at the Hague in 1925 as the International Union of Official Spokesmen of Touristic Propaganda.

In spite of variations during economically or politically sensitive periods, tourism has enjoyed an average growth rate of 8 per cent per annum since World War II. In 1950, 25.3 million people crossed borders as international tourists. This number reached 390 million in 1988 and is projected to grow at 4 to 5 per cent per annum through 2010. The World Tourism Organization forecasts that tourism will take first place among world economic activities, and no decline is in sight before 2000.

The question is not so much whether or not there is an alternative to tourism but whether major new emerging forms of tourism will remain within the frame of reference of the dominant model or break away from it.

A POINT OF DOCTRINE

International tourism makes money **and the**

industrialized nations are the main benefactors. Yet as early as the 1960s Kurt Krapf (1961), one of the pioneers of the economic theory of tourism, advanced a then-revolutionary idea that the developing nations should also benefit from international tourism. Soon thereafter the United Nations Conference on Tourism and International Travel proclaimed, "Tourism makes a vital contribution to the economic development of Developing Nations" (United Nations 1963).

This theory came to the fore at the very time when affluent nations decided to help "needy" societies by announcing a "Decade of Development," just when many former colonies gained their political independence.

It was reasoned that, though planting a luxury industry in such poor countries might appear shocking, the developing nations had few other resources, but they did have an abundance of natural and cultural riches and a cheap, underemployed workforce.

Tourism, a frivolous activity, could become a useful instrument in economic development. But this doctrine contains a condensation of meanings which must be untangled to avoid the pitfalls into which the doctrine of Alternative Tourism also risks sinking.

The imposition of international tourism on the developing nations suggests not only a change of scale but a turning point. International tourism is not just an international extension of domestic tourism, nor just a major contribution to foreign exchange, but is also a "transmission belt" connecting the developed and the underdeveloped worlds.

Tourism policy has become part of a global project which lumps together seemingly contradictory economic interests: the organization of vacations (an idea originating in rich countries) and the aspirations for development of economically weak societies. Thus "free time" resulting from the exploitation of the surplus value of capital is put back into the calculation of economic productivity.

Societies inexperienced with industrialization are re-oriented toward "touristification"; tourism comes to be judged by economic and political criteria within the international framework, a vector for global integration. It becomes a factor in the North-South dialogue and a component of the much-discussed New World Economic Order.

THE OPENING OF DEVELOPING NATIONS TO INTERNATIONAL TOURISM

Since the 1960s, the developing nations have been persuaded to open themselves to international tourism, to give tourism a favored place in their economy, to welcome foreign capital, and to make fiscal concessions.

Many countries have responded enthusiastically, hoping to solve their problems of endemic poverty. Between 1969 and 1979 the World Bank supported twenty-four projects in eighteen countries. Immense resort projects were started on the Costa Brava and the Costa del Sol in Spain, on the Bulgarian and Romanian shores of the Black Sea, in Tunisia, the Antilles, the Caribbean, Mexico, Thailand.

Tourist resorts form a world apart, a delimited area on the fringe of ordinary life. Tourists are grouped into a hotel or complex containing all the services necessary for maintenance and pleasure, following the needs of the notorious "4 S's."

Architecturally and technically modern buildings are erected in spaces in the process of desertification or overpopulation. It sometimes happens that the local population must leave or nomads can no longer traverse the area, the land is abandoned or remodeled, or new fresh water supplies sought, all for the reception of vacationers from rich countries. Touristic mobility is an unprecedented "delocalization" movement.

TOURISM, A FACTOR IN ECONOMIC DEVELOPMENT ON A WORLD SCALE

At times of crisis, even the developed nations see tourism as a primary "export activity" worthy of subvention. In addition to the multiplier effect and offsetting foreign debts, tourism becomes one of the few remedies for never ending unemployment. According to Organization for Economic Development and Cooperation (OEDC) experts, tourism is moving from an accessory to a major and necessary economic activity.

Rich countries are adopting policies first intended for the poor, and tourism has become a development factor in post-industrial societies. Almost all nations promote tourism development as a producer of profit, leading to envy and stiff competition for foreign exchange and tourists.

TRANSNATIONAL COMPANY NETWORKS

The tourist industry's system of production is now considered one of the world's most powerful driving forces. Through mergers and concentrations, these companies have become agents of an interconnected network penetrating many sectors.

The transnationals of tourism are the avant garde for strategies of capital internationalization. The system of tourist production has evolved into network-companies, models for transnational companies in the world economy.

Decisions for whole regions or countries are made inside one company. Yet the states or communities involved may have no veto or even influence in this "Dialogue of Monopolies and Countries". Competition is reduced by collusion, for profits grow best in homogeneous spaces. Thus culture, society, and identity become mass products when International Tourism enters a country.

These network-companies operate in an almost centralized system in which power stems from negotiations and meetings in search of consensus. This efficient organizational system, with its savoir faire and its capacity to manage behaviour and technology, is what Galbraith called "technostructure." The system relies on experts who often bring identical solutions to contrasting local conditions. Growth is external to and independent of local conditions of production.

This system also aids the integration of regions and communities into the international whole. To accept international tourism is not only to welcome foreign vacationers and their currency, it means access to international planning, technology, and finance, entering the world economy and approaching world modernity. One cannot understand Alternative Tourism without this view of reality.

THE ROLE OF THE STATE IN THE PROMOTION OF INTERNATIONAL TOURISM

It is often difficult to draw the line between the state and industry. By internationalizing tourism, the structure of the state is transformed by the arrival of officials trained in commercial technology and marketing at all levels of administration, an evolution obvious in France and many other countries.

The training of government authorities integrates local business into higher echelons. In January 1990, meetings on local development were exhorted to "think local, act global/ think global, act local". Thus international tourism is one domain where the public-private dichotomy is misleading.

FROM SECTORIAL PLANNING TO GLOBAL PLANNING

International tourist planning has to do with the introduction of rational thought into management practices. Since the 1960s it has enlarged its range, from purely sectorial choices to the opening of the developing nations to international tourism.

As tourism moved from a secondary activity to a primary force in national economies, intersectorial comparisons of profitability became crucial. In addition, as tourism is inscribed in national development plans, it is justified not only by profit, but for its contributions to political aims of development. It becomes the axis on which other sectors rely, and national intersectorial planning gives way to global planning.

At the instigation of international organizations or Western, formerly colonial, powers, Third World countries cooperate and endeavor to finance their investments within a long-range set of programs. National tourist offices depend on international data.

Tourism becomes one of the vectors of internationalization and thus attempts to become a generating principle for the whole society, enabling the instruments and goals of the world economy to penetrate and weave transnational bonds.

GEARING UP A SOCIETY FOR TOURISM

Marketing, long an essential tool of international tourism promotion, articulates supply and demand within a market economy, and societies embracing international tourism are plunged into this international system. Unlike other industries, the "products" of the tourist industry are a pastiche of formerly heterogeneous elements amalgamated by advertising for tourist consumption.

Combined symbiotically, they include services (lodging, dining, transportation, recreation), culture (folklore, festivals, heritage, monuments), and less palpable things such as hospitality, ambiance, and ethnicity. At last this "product" incorporates the society itself, its culture, its identity.

International tourism promotion, aimed at economic development, requires every location to offer something unique. By this logic, each country or region must produce and publicize its unique identity, with a "name recognition" that signifies its superiority.

All over the world there is a fantastic incorporation of identifying signs into touristic products: nostalgic places, historic monuments, traditional and rural heritage, the skills of ethnic groups. Populations are solicited to attract foreign attention with their talent and creativity.

Everyone plays himself or herself and acts out a performance. Widespread marketing research determines what this image should be, matching aspects of local identity with the desires of potential clients. This fabrication of identity defines the seductive attributes and crystallizes them in an advertising image such that even the locals may eventually recognize themselves in it (cf. Carpenter 1973)!

TOURISTIC RESTORATION/APPROPRIATION

In the analysis of the creation of "tourist attractions," cultural heritage is exploited as a "mineable resource." It must be "put to good use" by changing its purpose, and hence its meaning. It is restored along rational lines for commercial promotion and may end up looking like one in a series of reproductions rather than its own historic self.

In Europe, for example, historic landmarks and properties were often preserved by philanthropy derived from a sense of community pride. Now, however, every city restores its historic ramparts, church, or castle to attract tourists, and funding is solicited from art dealers, from cultural sponsors, and from the tourist arms of the state.

Tourism promotion is allied with marketing, and uses the quick functional "cultural engineering" perfected in the United States. Heritage, transformed into productive capital, is renovated and the profit used to repay the cost rather than for safeguarding. Tourism therefore ensures renewal.

Goaded by European unification in 1992 and the prospect of additional millions of tourists, France is now turning itself into a vast "theme park." Compared with the new EuroDisneyland near Paris, other cities and villages will appear authentic!

Castles, cathedrals, old villages, prehistoric sites, and public gardens appeal increasingly to the public. The new ecomuseums have also met with great success, as they look to older people to explain the activities and tools displayed. In disused factories, on canal towpaths, or in historic urban areas we might just meet the last person who has the skill for these obsolete phenomena or the last memories of their working past.

RESURRECTION CREATION OUT OF NOTHING

Much time and money is now devoted to the "remaking of memory" (Jeudy 1986) to create new marketable identities. Thus we restore, regenerate, conserve, and preserve works and events as identities for a touristic society. Things long resigned to decrepitude are resuscitated as heritage or "collectibles." The obsolescent and the obsolete once more become profitable. We extract the old from fragments of collective memory or, better still, from rare survivals still found in daily life.

Anything can become a tourist product as long as it can be given value. We invent new deposits to be mined: forgotten folklore, buildings in ruin, the sites of ancient cities. We move monuments from one place to another, change their meanings, and make new springs gush. Thus even the "natural" regional distribution of tourist attractions may become obsolete.

NEW CONSECRATION

MacCannell (1976) first analyzed the process of the transformation of things into tourist products. In order to become an attraction, the phenomenon must be "baptized"; it must be named and become associated with a recognizable sign or "marker" bringing it to the attention of the tourist, guaranteeing its "uniqueness," and making it worth seeing.

To display this object, we frame it, elevate it, light it up, mount it like a jewel, and mark it off from ordinary objects. Detached from the ordinary world, it becomes "sacred" within the ritual of tourism. Its old meaning as heritage is stripped, and it is given a new one appropriate to its role within the tourist system. Thus marked, it becomes a signifier of the identity of the society for foreign visitors.

THE NEW SETTING

The requirements of commercialism join with the moral goals of international organizations: to use tourism for the promotion of mutual understanding and to maintain, preserve and respect cultural identities. This accords with modern humanistic ecumenical and universalist ideals whereby each culture is supposed to make a special contribution to "universal culture."

Through the will of these organizations, patrimony and the extant traditions of archaic societies are placed in new relationships and come to constitute a common cultural foundation for all humanity. The chosen markers represent the identity of the place and its rank within the panoply of world heritage. Thus we can see that international tourism acts as a powerful force in the universalization of culture and society.

THE DILEMMA OF TOURISM

The modern concept of tourism as a factor in economic development is pivotal and is the only way to understand the contradiction between the economic and the cultural. Though first aimed at the Developing Nations, this doctrine has recently been adopted by nearly all countries in response to internal challenges.

The key document is Kurt Krapf's paper, presented to the Association Internationale d'Experts Scientifiques du Tourisme (AIEST) in 1961.

TREATED AS AN INFANT

In bringing together developing nations and consumer societies in one global vision, Krapf embraced Rostow's theory of development, by which societies are classified into five stages: (1) traditional; (2) pre-take-off; (3) take-off; (4) push to maturity; and (5) mass consumer. This theory of economic growth has encouraged rich countries to aid poor ones. It imitates child development theory and, though naive, provides criteria for the distribution of aid according to what economists call "the coefficient of capital."

Using this vocabulary, developing nations are "still in their infancy" and need to be pushed to maturity where citizens are assured a "stable consumption economy." The "immature" countries are labeled by their inability and have to accept the paternalistic aid of scientific experts in tourism. They are shown that it is "tourism or nothing." But nothing is not just nothing in this case, it is "the image of death appearing on the horizon".

ECONOMIC DEVELOPMENT

Krapf's argument conceals a paradox: "No one needs imagination to know that a developing country presents the characteristics of an economic take-off." In the terms described above countries have attained stage (2) or (3). As for "traditional society," Rostow's first stage, it is, according to Krapf "doomed to disappear." The economists' death sentence provokes us, for they assert that without tourism a society turns its back on development. In this theory, the gap is accentuated between those developing societies veering toward modernization and isolated traditional societies sliding back into decline.

Yet "traditional society" keeps haunting the imagination. Put aside in the economic order it is stored in the symbolic order, and tomorrow it may reemerge, promoted as a touristic product. Threatened with "imminent death," "traditional society" must be conserved, as a haven of tradition and infancy, in order to sustain the argument for development. Tourism promotion often concentrates on destinations that are virgin, intact, and distant in space.

THE IMAGE OF DEATH

Let us recall some of the debate of the 1960s about the ruinous effects of tourism on culture and environment.

Davydd Greenwood, a U.S. anthropologist studying agriculture in the community of Fuentarrabia in the Spanish Basque country in 1968-69, turned his attention to the Alarde, a lively local festival that drew many tourists. It was a Basque ceremony to celebrate the victory of their ancestors over the French in 1638.

To attract more tourists, the municipality decided to

perform the Alarde twice in the same day. The inhabitants not only refused to cooperate with this commercial masquerade but lost their will to participate in the event. For Greenwood "tourism killed the Alarde."

Many similar cases probably exist. Just as the economic benefits emerge, tourism is discredited by the transformation of culture into market value, desecration of ceremonies, debasement of culture and the arts, falsification of traditions, and the loss of identity. The opposition of the economic and the cultural is revealed; here we are faced with the "dilemma of tourism."

In logic, a dilemma is reasoning where the major premise contains an alternative and the minor premises lead to the same conclusion. In practice a dilemma occurs when there are two contradictory possibilities, yet the subject making the choice finds that either way leads to the same consequences.

The discourse of tourism decision making and management is rife with this figure of speech. Actors, whose interests should converge but are in fact opposed, face a dilemma: to develop or contain tourism, to restore culture or celebrate it, leads to the same result. To reject tourism is death, but to accept it is also death.

"The touristic dilemma is clear: to freeze or not to freeze, to maintain boundaries or to remove them...the sword cuts both ways".This double-edged sword underlines the break between tourism as seen by outside agents and by the local society, placing visitors and the visited in a reciprocal extermination.

For a developing nation not to choose tourism amounts to eventual death according to economists, but to choose tourism is also death according to anthropologists. To choose in favour of tourism is the outcome of a double bind, the requirement to make a choice between two impossibilities.

The figure of this dilemma is a leitmotif in the discourse on tourism: "blessing or blight," "trick or treat," "boom or doom," "panacea or a new slave trade," "mirage or strategy for the future." There is always the same disjunction between the economic and the cultural which governs the problematics, be they alternative or dominant. This is still the dilemma which underlies the argument for Alternative Tourism, wherein the word "Alternative" gains its force.

Three Examples

1. The dilemma of tourism pertains to actual situations. The 1989 WTO Seminar on Alternative Tourism in Tamanrasset took place at a symbolically loaded site, which could have been the source of the love of Uranus and Gaia, in the heart of the Sahara Desert. Here at the gates of Ahaggar the difficulties are magnified because of the barrenness of the place. Yet decisions had become urgent; every year the tourists were coming in greater numbers. Algeria, which previously had no tourism policy, had decided on large scale projects, with perhaps 100,000 beds. Ahaggar was targeted as exemplifying the touristic image of the nation.

   But the desert is an extremely fragile environment, with diminishing ancient water sources. Vegetation is sparse but includes unique local species. Garbage is not degradable. The desert people, adapted to the severe environment, have become guides, serving the tourists but anxious about uncontrolled growth. The experts were conscious of the risks and felt the proximity of total destruction. The government was perplexed when some seminar participants prophesied the end Ahaggar within twenty years if mass tourism develops.

2. In Australia's Northern Territory, the management of the National Parks faced another classic dilemma. This is a special case applied to the Aborigines who at the turn of the century were seen as one of the most "primitive" groups on earth. Survivors of these "totemic societies" are scattered throughout the vast territory. The Australian Government has chosen the

National Parks of this region as a "pole of growth," a plan also favored by the White residents of Darwin and the nearby mining camps. The area is highly valued by some for its nature resources and its primitive life. Here we must ask who speaks about the dilemma and whose dilemma it is.

For the Aborigines, the policy gives them the poignant choice of "to be or not to be." Already decimated and chased away by military maneuvers, their numbers are greatly reduced. These lands, ceded to them in the early 1960s, were temporarily retracted by the regional government without extinguishing Aboriginal rights. For the state as well as for the industry, the Aborigines provoke ambivalent attitudes. On the one hand they are inconvenient inhabitants, an obstacle to the development of the parks; on the other, they are a positive presence, certifying the original character of the place and its preservation from the ravages of civilization. From this point of view, Aborigine society is valued precisely because it is near extinction. One can weigh the tensions between international tourism promotion and a "traditional society." It is not just for economic reasons that the Aborigines are valued; they also possess unique skills, especially in hunting and fishing.

Thus we can see the dilemmas of both the parties involved. For the Aborigines to reject tourism is to remain welfare recipients. But to choose tourism and participate in it they would have to learn the industry's skills and become "servants," and thereby be evicted from their welfare status. They might be ready to say, "Anything other than Tourism!" In addition, the state risks making investments from which it would not reap a profit, as the land belongs to the Aborigines who, without spending any capital, might in twenty years become an economic power.

Thus each of the participants might be tempted to reject the option of tourism. Do the problematics of the alternative find meaning in this kind of case?

3. The Statement on Responsible Tourism propounded by the 1989 Seminar on Alternative Tourism at Tamanrasset is fraught with paradoxes. It amounts to a paradoxical injunction when it supposes symmetrical behaviour between the partners involved, within the framework of relations defined as complementary. Proponents of Alternative Tourism favour the lodging of tourists in the houses of local people, some of whom respond: "When someone comes to my home because I have invited them, I receive them as a friend. But when they are imposed on me from the outside, they are an occupier!"

   Yes, tourism produces many situations where the imperative of the double bind traps the recipients of the message of development. To escape, it is not enough to reverse the terms of the alternative; one must break away from the frame of reference.

MISLEADING ARGUMENT

In 1970 the American anthropologist P. F. McKean thought about the possible consequences of mass tourism in Bali, where it had not yet developed. The Indonesian government, following the usual plans of the World Bank, included a focus on tourism in Bali in its first Five Year Plan for Economic Development.

The experts invited by the government drew up a Master Plan for Balinese Tourism with a somber prognostication: Bali risked the destruction of its well conserved traditions which would be devastated by the advent of mass tourism; the very attractions of Bali, its artistic creations, were at greatest risk.

To these experts the Balinese were a poor and isolated agricultural population. It was a "traditional society" where temple festivals, shadow puppetry, and sacred dances were integrated with village life. The experts proposed that, for the protection of the Balinese, tourists should be restricted to enclaves on the southern coast, for ordinary seaside tourism.

But the Balinese adopted a contrary policy. They wanted tourists spread throughout the island so that all villages could benefit. They came up with their own idea of "cultural tourism" and wanted to offer the tourists their best. McKean agreed: "Far from destroying, ruining or spoiling the culture of Bali, I am arguing here that the advent and increase of tourists is likely to fortify and foster the arts."

ECONOMIC DEVELOPMENT/CULTURAL INVOLUTION

McKean admits that by opting for cultural tourism as a means to modernization a country consents to transform its culture into a tourist product, its heritage into profit-making capital. Thus such a society undergoes what McKean calls "cultural involution."

In such cases, every society must construct its future by clinging to its past. This implies that the society turn back toward its past in order to construct out of its heritage touristically recognizable symbols of identity. The society has to prove that it is truly unique.

To choose one's heritage as a symbol of identity leads to ambivalence. Should one restore it to the original state in which it was handed down by ancestors? Should one set it apart as an attraction for foreign tourists?

For in this case, its restoration would follow the procedures of cultural engineering rather than of historical methods or subjective memorizing.

Heritage would have to be managed by new criteria in order not only to be profitable but also to be added to the catalogue of world heritage. For this to happen, though, is to pass out of genuine cultural filiation.Here is a potential source of tension.

A CHANGE OF COURSE

Since the 1960s the euphoric promises of tourism — return to nature, the noble savage, the peaceful co-existence of peoples — have been called into question by a long list of acts which have aroused indignation:

- Violent expropriation and occupation of territory, pollution and destruction of forests, landscapes, and coasts;
- Dominating financial interests, provoked bankruptcies, real estate speculation, the puffery of "straw men";
- Tourist ghettos, private squads of armed guards, expulsion of locals and marginals, segregated residential ethnic reserves;
- Violation of sacred places, appropriation of arts and crafts, manipulation of collective memories and heritage;
- Indecent behaviour, organized prostitution of women, adolescents, young children.

These aggressive accusations worry the authorities who try to stifle them, but their numbers continue to mount. The attacks come from many directions: from the tourists who scorn each other, from host populations whose hostility is organized in their own interests, from some sectors of the governments involved, and from experts employed by the World Bank to research the impacts of tourism.

By the 1970s these converging critics could not be avoided, and tourism developers realized that the time for impact evaluations had arrived.

Rising competition, increasing marginal costs, the burden of tourism and the degradation of the environment shook the faith of the tourism experts: "Tourism can destroy tourism; tourism as a user of resources can be a resource destroyer and, through destroying the resources which give rise to it, make resource-based tourism short-lived".

EVOLUTION OF THE OFFICIAL DISCOURSE

Let us examine how experts and international

organizations responded to these criticisms, partially explaining the rise of "alternative" solutions, following this evolution through seminars and meetings because there the ghost of the dilemma mentioned above underlies many of the attempted solutions.

Actually, organizations like the World Bank, the World Tourism Organization (WTO), and UNESCO were from the start attentive to the results of their efforts. From Washington to Tamanrasset by way of Manila, one can see the same guiding thread.

In 1976 the joint World Bank-UNESCO seminar on The Social and Cultural Impact of Tourism responded to concerns about the economic functions of tourism in the Third World and their sociocultural effects. This highlighted the double cleavage between the local host societies and the foreign economic powers, and the growing antinomy between the economic and the cultural.

Analyses since that era have worried about surmounting these dilemmas which permeate the social fact of tourism. How can the local and international join together again; how can we surmount the split between the economic and the cultural? These are key questions in the analysis of the problematics of the alternative.

The World Tourism Organization World Conference on Tourism held in Manila was a major event in changing directions, as can be seen in both the papers and the recommendations.

The latter contained two convergent themes: (1) an insistence on the perpetual advance of tourism through the growth of "national tourism" in the better-off countries and, in contrast to the earlier WTO focus on "international tourism," the promotion of these "national tourisms"; and (2) raising the awareness of nations and organizations of the spiritual values of tourism.

"Tourism...a vital force for peace...a moral and intellectual basis for mutual understanding and the interdependence of nations...suitable for the foundation of a new economic order which will narrow the gap between the developed countries and the underdeveloped...a means to promote the lessening of international tensions and to develop a spirit of friendly cooperation, with respect for human rights...within the equality of societies and nations.

This was a vast ideological movement toward a new conception of tourism, surpassing the still important economic factors by linking nations with the noblest aspects of "tourism in the service of humanity" in the social, educational, political and cultural arenas.

The WTO was attempting to reverse the prior order of causality by asserting that tourism is "primarily a cultural phenomenon." This is highly meaningful if we bear in mind that up to this point international tourism was seen as an economic phenomenon and domestic tourism as a cultural problem.

In light of this change of course, the aims of the Seminar on Alternative Tourism organized nine years later by the WTO in Tamanrasset became clearer.

One can thus understand how the evidence of the social and cultural impacts of tourism from the 1976 Washington seminar led the decision makers and government representatives to first take into account the social and cultural dimensions of tourism (Manila) and convincing all the parties concerned — hosts, guests, tourist industry, and governments — to respect the social and cultural resources on which the sustainable development of tourism was seen to rest (Tamanrasset).

Here the organizers managed to use the mobilizing force of this concept to obtain consensus among the various parties present. The assembly, having been captivated by the words Alternative Tourism, finally chose to endorse "responsible tourism."

The problematics of the alternative were founded on the reversal of the terms opposed in the discourse. But to understand this, one must again pass through the labyrinth of economics. This is critical to the continuing research on the break between Alternative Tourism and International Tourism.

Since the late 1960s, World Bank experts have been sent to evaluate the effects of the introduction of tourism. At first the evaluations were purely economic — foreign exchange generated, jobs created, changes in the standard of living. But increasingly, sociocultural impacts were included alongside and later came to infiltrate the economic model. To the sociologist this is an interesting epistemological jump.

The question of sociocultural impact opens the economics to social analyses. The economist wants to integrate sociocultural data into his evaluation schemes, and therefore turns to the sociologist or anthropologist. One must understand that the goals of the process are to optimize the aims of tourism development.

Economists want to quantify these elusive sociocultural factors into their cost-benefit analyses. This involves choosing "sociocultural indicators" which are then evaluated dualistically as "positive" or "negative" for the purposes of quantification. Sorting through such analyses of tourism impacts, one generally finds that economic changes are imputed to be positive and sociocultural to be negative, thereby widening the gap between economic and the cultural.

This leads to absurdities, whereby the damage caused by economic activities is balanced by economic benefits! It is as though social costs can be compensated by monetary gains in order to produce a unified cost-benefit analysis. Thus sociocultural effects external to the economic, often judged as negative (i.e., as costs), are, by being neutralized, internalized into the calculations.

This distorts the sociocultural data to accord with the norms of International Tourism, as though admitting that culture, society, and identity are not associated with the context that gave rise to them. This dichotomy is illuminated if we consider that the same economic activity of tourism could be evaluated either as a benefit (+) for the development and preservation it brings or as a cost (-) for the degradation and misappropriation of meanings it entails.

This approach was generally considered an analytical advance, even though it is reductionist in weighing sociocultural data in terms of profit, wherein heritage and everything unique about a society is mummified and exploited as a resource.

The problematics of the alternative stems in part from this operation: the decision maker must catalogue the impacts, clearly defining the positive and the negative, in order to assess tourism. Measures are thus taken which appear to lead to this result, so that one can build a model for "discerning tourism." Even here the method is still contained within the economic framework.

THE PRECONCEPTIONS OF THE IMPACT STUDIES

This question dominates the study of the effects of international tourism and is made real within the system of action where the local society — nation, region, community or ethnic group — is "targeted" by a more powerful external organization. From this point of view the impact is the target! (The word impact comes from the Latin *impingere,* "to hit a target.")

This conceptual scheme is not limited to economics; many other studies tackle tourism as an intrusion or benefit, an external variable on the one side through its side effects on the local society on the other. This type of theory leads to a reductionist concept of the host society:

- It treats the host society as a place without specific sociological and historical characteristics, undifferentiated for the purpose of a foreign rationality.
- In its relations with tourism, "the target" is seen as limited to reacting by submitting to foreign penetration, by resisting conflicts with tourists, or by the kind of violence sometimes reported in the press.

As it is opening to International Tourism, a time when tourism breeds dissent in the social order, the host society is seen as deceptively unanimous.

The problematics of the impact and the underlying system of concepts prevent us from thinking about the *processes* by which local societies are integrated into the larger political field.

Such "impact studies," therefore, never understand the nature of the changes in the economic and political systems or in social relations and attitudes brought about by International Tourism policy worldwide.

Tourism management focuses on tourism alone but actually affects the whole society and its social structure, collective memory, and perspectives in an unfolding world.

But a long term change in thinking has recently surfaced. Economists have recognized that the immediate returns from tourism may not do much for the development of the whole region. Methods of measurement and statistical data are viewed with suspicion. Growth models are discredited and the relevance of economics is challenged.

Anthropologists and sociologists are undertaking studies with a radically different awareness. As a result of local field research, in the 1980s there has been a shift from the problematics of the impact to the problematics of the alternative. Is this a real change in the problematics of international tourism?

During the 1970s, planners were forced to see the limitations of their general development model and to take into account the interests of local people. The first reaction was to grant to the host society its own personality, recognizing its viability. One heard more of local dominance, participation and development.

Some have called this "the return of the local," not only in scientific research but in conceptions about planning. In a coincidence of concerns, this has become the solution to all ills. From "an area to be promoted in the marketplace," the local society has been granted its own importance, its own potentials, with its own capacity for initiative and decision making.

RETURN TO THE LOCAL/RETURN OF THE LOCAL

The "return *to* the local" as an important factor in planning has been matched by the "return *of* the local" in the form of a network of grass roots movements, much as wished by the ECTWT. The local society is no longer taken as passive but as capable of accepting or rejecting the dominant model or of coming up with its own.

"Local society" is no longer an advertising image aimed at a distant clientele also being manipulated by advertising, but has become one pole at the heart of a system of action in relation to a centre.

The local society is no longer just an end-point in a movement from "above" but a generator of impulses which can climb back up the technological chain and modify the whole. It is no longer merely a reactionary form, but as a force in negotiation, intervention, and creativity is capable of its own initiatives, with all their paradoxes.

Some would redefine tourism from local points of view, surpassing the norms of International Tourism. The idea of tourism is transformed to the point of rejecting the dominant model; according to the proponents of Alternative Tourism, the local people must be helped to take over the tourist operation, rather than just having suitable conditions defined for them. Thus one can no longer judge tourism on the basis of specific "positive" or "negative" effects but must see the phenomenon intertwined as part of a total social fact.

The problematics of the alternative becomes complicated when it tries to rethink tourism or propose new strategies of global development from the local point of view. Is this a reversal of perspective? It is up to the social sciences to examine this turning point and its methodological and epistemological foundations.

We must keep in mind the difference between an "alternative ideology" which rethinks tourism from the local point of view or in terms of local development and the scientific approach which chooses the local society as the point of observation.

The latter is concerned with constructing its object of study from field research using the inductive approach, but its foremost objective is not to increase the standing of the local community as would the Alternative Tourism movement.

It is troubling to observe these efforts to "rehabilitate" the local setting after it has been flattened or evacuated by planning 112 and scientific thinking. In the Alternative Tourism problematic, the tourism production system, which carries on ever upward according to its own logic, seems to have been bypassed. In our opinion, one must work with the assumption that many parallel logics are being pushed without contradicting themselves.

After listening to the different debates and declarations, it seems that what is called Alternative Tourism while claiming to be the "good tourism" has not, in spite of its forceful declared opposition, broken radically with the "other tourism."

Alternative Tourism, still included within the promotion and expansion of international tourism, may just be another stage. Doesn't Alternative Tourism still spur the local people to preserve their customs and traditions, and then use them as tourist products to offer on the market?

At Zakopane in August 1989, the members of the Academy considered Alternative Tourism as a means to contribute to the "sustainable development" of a society, whereas by October at the WTO meeting in Tamanrasset, Alternative Tourism had become co-opted as a way to ensure the sustainable development of tourism itself. That should give us something to think about.

Chapter 3

Lessons from Development for Tourism

We don't want tourism. We don't want you. We don't want to be degraded as servants and dancers. That is cultural prostitution. I don't want to see a single one of you in Hawaii. There are no innocent tourists. A few years ago, in a short note published in *Annals of Tourism Research*, Georg Pfafflin approvingly quoted these sentiments of a native Hawaiian, expressed at a church-sponsored conference on tourism and the Third World.

In that note, Pfafflin not only repeated the view that the chances for genuine encounters between tourists and host populations are extremely poor, but also wrote that "the public" in Europe "now realizes that tourism to the Third World is always connected with such North-South problems as hunger, the debt crisis and its povertyproducing effects, and the destruction of the ecological system".

It is not obvious that Pfafflin is right about "the" public, nor is it easy to understand what mechanisms are involved in these very different connections. Yet however sweeping his view of the ill-effects of tourism and however much it ignores many years of patient work to distinguish different tourism situations from each other, this view nevertheless needs to be taken into account.

It is relevant to much that has been written about Alternative Tourism. The concept of Alternative Tourism has been used in so many ways as to make it meaningless.

Even so, many of the approaches share an undertone of moral indignation, of rejection of normal, mass or "mainstream" tourism in which political hostility to transnational capitalism mingles with cultural and ecological unease over modern massconsumption society.

This undertone has also been present in the concept of "Alternative," or "Another," Development. However, it is not used in so bewildering a variety of ways as is Alternative Tourism. Alternative Development is a broader concept, which in some senses encompasses that of Alternative Tourism.

The parallels and contrasts between these two "alternative" concepts and the evolution in both cases from a predominantly "moralistic" or normative approach to one which is more concerned with analysis and understanding are the focus of the present analysis.

ALTERNATIVE DEVELOPMENT

There have always been a variety of approaches to development, and no one paradigm or theory has ever attained absolute dominance. Most discussions would recognize at least three contenders in the field: the neo-classical, the Marxist, and the structuralist "schools". During the 1980s, the recognition has spread that all three theories have failed to give satisfactory overall explanations of the process of development, or of its "absence"; and practitioners — decision makers, planners, advisers — in both market and state run economies have been clamoring for new guidelines.

Many have blamed the problems of development on the negative effects of a large scale direct role for the state in the economy, and a more or less hefty dose of neoliberal ("Thatcherite") policies has been injected almost everywhere, even in many "socialist" economies.

This has resulted in a broad and widely shared development "mainstream," but we are, it seems, not far from yet another turning point, one likely to reincorporate the view that the untrammeled operation of the market does not provide the ultimate answer and itself creates new problems. We can expect to see a measure of rehabilitation of the state's role in forcefully regulating the market, though not perhaps in the direct production of goods and services.

The emergence into prominence, at least in Europe, of Green political parties (the political expression of one of the hitherto more remote "counterpoints" to that mainstream) is likely to push the issue of curbing the market higher up on the political agenda.

A few years ago, those with a "green" approach to our planet and development were seen as cranks, their organizations as marginal. Since then, partly as a result of the success of their efforts in putting their views across and partly because of the remarkable impact of the Brundtland Commission, itself a sign of the times, we have all been "greened" to a greater or lesser extent.

In recent years environment, ecology and even "sustainable development" have moved progressively closer to the centre of the stage of public concern and politics. It is no longer considered outlandish to speak of Alternative Development, or Sustainable Development.

There are many explicit and implicit definitions of Alternative Development. Their constituent elements have become rather more distinct over time, and some of the "evangelical" fervor has been lost. Concern with the environment has been there from the start.

Among the Greens there are still some extreme antagonists to mainstream development in "a vocal ecocentric wing (which) continues its rather shrill opposition to the destruction of almost anything", but the more moderate demand for "ecologically sound" development is now heard in wide circles of public and government opinion.

While environmental sensationalism and scientific amateurism still abound, there are also indications that among critics of mainstream development a more sobre assessment of global ecological problems is emerging, in which less reliance is placed on discredited doom-laden predictions from the 1970s and more allowance is made for technical change and the probability that it will modify the problems as well as their solutions.

In addition, the proponents of Alternative Development agree that scaling down the operations of production and government is both necessary and desirable. It is necessary if development is to become sustainable — defined by Brundtland as development that "meets the goals of the present without compromising the ability of future generations to meet their own needs".

It is desirable in order to achieve a development which is more "people-oriented," in contrast to the present style. Such development revolves around maintaining economic growth without concern for the effects of such growth in ecological and social ("who benefits?") terms, especially with regard to the "essential needs of the world's poor".

Such scaling down involves encouraging smaller enterprises at the local level — paying attention to what has been called the "informal economy" — as well as promoting devolution of power from central political systems to local, self-reliant communities.

The resemblance of the political prescriptions to those of the nineteenth-century anarchists is striking, and they can be criticized on similar grounds; some of the purer ideas on community production also smack of nineteenth-century utopianism.

It is no wonder that these now dominant Alternative Development views are attacked from a more radical "red" perspective for disregarding the structural causes of ecological and other problems and for being naive about the political action required to change these structures.

Yet the basic traits of Alternative Development are clear: ecological soundness, small-scale production, recognition of needs other than those of material consumption, equal consideration of the needs of all (including future generations), and political involvement from below. These are also, broadly, seen as the traits of development that is sustainable.

As a concept, Alternative Tourism lacks even the tentative Gestalt which can be recognized in Alternative Development. While Alternative Development always refers to the developing economy or society, Alternative Tourism can have as its prime reference the host economy or society, the tourist, or the national or transnational tourism industry.

In fact, Alternative Tourism means all things to all people: "nowadays all travellers who do not undertake a normal type of vacation are lumped together under the general heading of 'alternative tourism'". Some writers appear to suggest that anything other than mass tourism should be graced with the "alternative" label: the collection put together by the Ecumenical Coalition on Third World Tourism leaves such an impression.

Various recent studies, such as the article by Pearce in this volume, have attempted to put some order into this confusion, mainly by distinguishing the different people or situations to which the concept refers.

Nevertheless, there are a number of themes that recur in many discussions on Alternative Tourism which echo the central issues of Alternative Development. First, Alternative Tourism is applied to tourism which does not damage the environment, is ecologically sound, and avoids the negative impacts of many large-scale tourism developments undertaken in areas which have not previously been developed.

Second, Alternative Tourism is thought to consist of smaller developments, or attractions for tourists which are set in and organized by villages or communities. These are seen as having fewer negative effects, social or cultural, and a better chance of being acceptable to the local people than mass tourism.

Third, and following from this, there is the question of "who benefits." Certain kinds of tourism are called alternative because they are not "exploitative" of local people, because the benefits flow to local residents or in general to poorer communities. Conventional tourism demands large-scale organization and resources not usually available locally or even in the country; as a result its rewards flow away to distant townsfolk or abroad. Finally, a shared perspective with Alternative Development is an emphasis on cultural sustainability.

Tourism which does not damage the culture of the host community is often called alternative; more than that, Alternative Tourism may actively try to encourage a respect for the cultural realities experienced by the tourists through education and organized "encounters."

These last two characteristics dominate in the approach of churchoriented groups active in the promotion of Alternative Tourism. Holden's definition fairly captures this:

Alternative Tourism is a process which promotes a just form of travel between members of different communities. It seeks to achieve mutual understanding, solidarity and equality amongst participants.

While the symmetry of this approach may seem attractive, it is not the line followed in this analysis. Here we shall focus predominantly on tourism as seen from the perspective of the host country and its inhabitants, rather than concern with the motivations, attitudes, or behaviour patterns of the tourists, let alone their ethos.

AUTHENTICITY IN TOURISM AND MEANING IN DEVELOPMENT

The idea of Alternative Tourism as centering on the search for authenticity would appear not to have an equivalent in Alternative Development. Authenticity as a characteristic of Alternative Tourism is wholly focused on the tourist; it concerns his or her perceptions of the reality encountered in the tourist experience.

Cohen's recent paper deals with this issue brilliantly and in detail, his main point being that authenticity does not have an "objective quality," but is attributed by moderns to the world "out there" and thus is a socially constructed concept with a connotation that is not given but "negotiable".

In spite of all the nuances brought to the discussion, authenticity remains an issue of importance only to the tourists, or to the hosts insofar as they want to please the tourists; the questions it raises lie outside the realm where Alternative Development provides the pointers for comparison.

Nevertheless, there is an area of overlap, because authenticity deals with meaning, and meaning — for the subjects of development — is an important issue in Alternative Development also. As Dudley Seers noted more than twenty years ago, the question of meaning in development addresses the issue of values often disregarded in the development discourse.

"The starting-point is that we cannot avoid what the positivists disparagingly refer to as 'value judgements.'...Development is inevitably a normative concept, almost a synonym for improvement". And however crucial it remains to the poor to have greater access to material goods, this does not define exhaustively what people regard as "improvement" nor what meaning they can discover in development.

Mainstream development is a child of Western civilization. With the growth of science and technology over the past four centuries, the manipulation and mastering of nature has become the driving force of material "progress." "Development," as it is now understood in mainstream Western thinking, translates this instrumental rationalism into action, constantly "transforming" and "improving" the world. Beyond science and technology, economics dominates the social and human sciences. The mainstream theories of development focus mostly on the economic processes in that material transformation (economics as the science of the management of scarce resources) and devote less attention to the ecological, cultural, and sociopolitical context within which the economy operates.

This has contributed to the dominance of economic policies in the political arena, with governments often paying scant attention to the impact of such policies on culture or nature or to issues arising in these spheres in the first place. Innovation in production and the stimulation of an everchanging demand for the latest in consumption became the final hallmarks of Western "consumer society"; these have provided the meaning of development for "Westerners" and those influenced by them.

Nature, culture, and community have been at the forefront of people's concerns in many non-Western societies. It is clear that in modern society these have moved backstage; they no longer provide the prime motivations for people's actions.

Proponents of Alternative Development want to change that and thereby give a new meaning to development. For even when their language is that of analysis and interpretation, the underlying thrust is political, ideological, and moral. "People-centredness" or "humancentredness" implies small scale institutions, a relocation of decision making, and a rearrangement of the locus of power.

Yet Alternative Development enjoins people to relinquish the meaning they have given to everyday life through the products of the consumer society.

They are called to reorient their *Weltanschauung* to the fulfillment of basic human needs, not only for themselves — the simplest life — but for all their fellow human beings (distributive justice) and their posterity (intergenerational justice). Included therein is a concern to achieve harmony with nature and its creatures. This ideological or moral streak in Alternative Development — and Alternative Tourism — has been prominent.

THE SENSE OF OUTRAGE

There are three areas in which this ideological concern has focused in regard to both Alternative Tourism and Alternative Development: nature, materialism, and culture.

As long ago as 1971 the Founex Report, prepared for the Stockholm Conference, characterized environmental problems as the "effluence of affluence" and the "pollution of poverty"; this evocative terminology encapsulated a battle cry for action.

From the same decade came the predictions of doom from the Club of Rome with *The Limits to Growth*. In spite of the torrent of scientific criticism unleashed, these are still being used in ecological arguments to portray economic growth as a cancer eating away at the earth's resources. Bandyopadhyay and Shiva accuse transnational companies, operating in the global market economy which has no built-in mechanisms to ensure ecological rehabilitation, of being in the forefront of this misuse of nature; once a mining company has exhausted the mine, or agribusiness has destroyed the grazing lands and forests, it will move elsewhere to maintain its profits.

They argue that mainstream development, in encouraging the use of hitherto unexploited resources, fails to take account of the ecological interrelatedness of the world and the way in which scarce natural resources have competing uses; often damage is done not only to nature as such and to the future productive base, but directly to people. Protests may occur against the disregard for these basic interests, as in India with the so-called ecological movements.

Movements by those directly affected are spreading in other countries, too, as are more generalized protest groups to highlight the costs of present day attitudes to the environment (Greenpeace, Friends of the Earth, etc.).

The alleged disregard for the environment by conventional tourism development also yields expressions of outrage. Hong expresses that mood:

Having ruined their own environment, having either used up or destroyed all that is natural, people from the advanced consumer societies are compelled to look for natural wildlife, cleaner air, lush greenery and golden beaches elsewhere. In other words, they look for other environments to consume. Thus armed with their bags, tourists proceed to consume the environment in the countries of the Third World — that last "unspoiled corner of earth."

Protest movements also arise around tourism development, witnessed by the recent impassioned call for international support by the Federation of Ecological Societies of the Dominican Republic to deal with the "extremely delicate situation" that has arisen as a result of ecologically destructive tourism development, involving massive damage to such elements as forests, mangroves, marine life. Such protests have helped place these matters on the agenda of analysts and policy makers.

Materialism has also brought its own hegemony. The emergence of "modernity" and consumer society as the twin pillars of mainstream development has already been commented upon. Neo-liberals believe that the market should provide the basic organizing principles of economic activity and that the role of the state in this area should be drastically reduced.

The market as it operates in reality, however, is far from "perfect." On the one hand, small numbers of powerful producers can influence market choice in their favour; on the other, large numbers of consumers are left with decreasing areas of choice and often with insufficient resources to operate in the market to their advantage. Individual acquisitiveness is at a premium; intervention by the state, notably to promote distributive justice, is limited domestically and virtually absent internationally.

This kind of development is seen as being narrowly focused on economic growth and expansion of the market; it leads to the growth of consumerism and is founded on short term commercial criteria. Many have applied similar arguments to tourism. A recently published Swiss doctoral dissertation can speak for them all:

> The thesis is put forward that the chief beneficiaries of tourism development in the Third World are foreign capitalists and, secondly, the local economic and political elite. Tourists from abroad benefit from comparatively low

prices in Third World tourist destinations, while the local population is left with modest employment opportunities, the loss of economic and political decision-making, and predominantly negative socio-cultural effects from institutionalized tourism.

This, as Krippendorf puts it, is because in "industrial *society*, values of being have been crowded out by values of having; possession, property, wealth, consumption, egoism are ranked above community, tolerance, contentment, modesty, meaning, honesty." The economy dominates and "man and the environment are at the service of the economy".

Krippendorf and Bachmann also extend their censure to the sociocultural effects of tourism and the "loss of culture," and in this they echo the more general anguish about the effects of modernity and industrialism as cultural homogenizers. The keynote address of the Jordanian Crown Prince to a conference in Morocco picks up many of the doubts about development as modernization and Westernization.

"Progress" has come to be identified with improvement in quantitative indicators; these concern mainly economic processes, seldom social, hardly ever cultural — and if they do, then it is simply to "measure" such matters as the number of museums operating or books published. As Prince Hassan pointed out, however, culture is more: a system of values and norms which give order and meaning to a society. Planners, however, simply cannot deal with what people want out of "development" and even less with why they want it (the meaning of development, again).

And as the planners treat "our peoples as simple numbers, they respond as numbers, multiply like numbers, increase their consumption like numbers" (author's translation). Others have examined this cultural impact of mainstream development on Less Developed Countries through the lens of dependency theory.

Erisman, for example, argues in a discussion of the West Indies that cultural dependency exists when those values, norms, and rules are conditioned by or reflect those in an external culture, leading to a relationship of domination and subordination between the cultural centre and the cultural periphery.

Cultural dependency results in the "incorporation of exogenous norms and values into a nation's socialization process, which can then be said to be penetrated," so that eventually the main stimuli for cultural development come from the outside and people lose their desire to maintain a cultural identity separate from that of the dominant nation.

In a more ideological and outraged vein Nyoni writes that ideas coming from outside the community are expressions of "imposed universalism" which "destroy local initiatives and self-reliance" through "self-colonization and elitism" of local elites, which "are heavily influenced and dominated by foreign and unworkable ideas".

Loss of culture is also explored with respect to the commoditization of relationships, when things and activities that were hitherto outside it are brought into the sphere of market transactions through exchange values. This is often said to be the result of tourism, but in fact it usually arises primarily out of those broader processes promoted by mainstream development.

The already mentioned debates over authenticity are also relevant. Though these have been pursued above all in relation to tourism development, those opposing mainstream development may also allude to these questions.

Thus we read in an already quoted article in IFDA Dossier, one of the main outlets for *engagé* discussions of Alternative Development is that the market economy defines people as poor who do not participate very much in the market and do not consume the products of consumer society — that is, if they eat "self-grown nutritious millets" instead of junk food or if they wear "indigenously designed handmade garments of natural fibre" rather than clothes made of manmade fibers. "The culturally conceived poverty based on non-western modes of consumption is often mistaken to be misery".

This quote represents the polar opposite to the often thoughtless sense of social and cultural superiority of those who stand for mainstream development because in its anger with cultural domination it appears to play down the very real poverty of hundreds of millions in the Third World. These neither eat their insufficient diet of "selfgrown nutritious millets" nor own just one set of simple "indigenously designed [?!] handmade garments of natural fibre" out of their own volition, and they would gladly exchange these for basic needs of the modern variety if they were available. There are, however, signs that more balanced approaches are winning adherents both in the scientific community and in the political arena.

SUSTAINABILITY AS AN ORGANIZING CONCEPT FOR POLICY

We have already seen how the Brundtland Commission's report has helped to place the issue of sustainability closer to the centre of the political agenda. This has drawn renewed attention to three areas in which the approaches, and reproaches, of Alternative Development can help to modify analysis and action without a "revolution" in social and economic organization: resource use and renewability, the issue of scale, and the equitable distribution of benefits (including to future generations).

The following discussion also suggests that making sustainability the focus of Alternative Tourism may possibly be the most productive way forward. It would not, of course, address the more tourist-oriented and normative issues often raised, but it would narrow the discussion to some of the central issues for the host economy, society, and culture.

In policy terms, making tourism sustainable would involve not just encouraging the development of "an alternative to" conventional tourism (though this could be part of it), but above all would force conventional tourism development to take greater notice of the three areas mentioned above.

First, we turn to the issue of resource use and renewability. The notion of sustainable development has been promoted largely from the rich countries of the North. Reducing pollution, carbon dioxide emissions, or the destruction of forests for the sake of "Our Common Future" is all very well for those whose unsustainable actions over decades have underpinned their high standard of living. But what about the poor countries?

Their need is continuing economic growth, for which they require many of the natural and environmental resources that are under stress. Where continued exploitation of these without concern for sustainability has occurred, as in Amazonia, it has brought out the Northern television crews and galvanized the North's politicians.

For Less Developed Countries, then, a crucial aspect of sustainability is the maintenance of the productivity of resources. One relatively easy means would be to seek a sustained increase in recovery and recycling.

The use and further development of new technologies, in which the materials of production or its polluting effects are decreased, can also help achieve this. Because the latter is an option that can be pursued without greatly affecting existing vested interests, it is attractive to some of the more advanced Less Developed Countries such as Brazil; this concept was also promoted by the Brundtland Commission.

More generally, environmental degradation can result from many small increases in environmental neglect, none of which is catastrophic in itself. Conversely, sustainability can be safeguarded by the avoidance of such cumulative negative threshold effects.

Tourism development again raises similar questions to development in general. Pigram sees Alternative Tourism as an exercise in sustainable resource management, where "safe minimum standards" would ensure that the threshold of irreversibility would not be crossed. Wilkinson (1989) discusses the possible negative environmental impacts of tourism development on small island environments.

Each such development raises different and specific issues, for example, the dangers of damaging coral reefs, beach sand loss, or the contamination of coastal waters. Sometimes, especially in self-contained and very small natural environments, it is clearly essential for the maintenance of the value of the "asset" to protect its ecological *raison d'être*, and so the enterprise itself has strong reasons to do so. But often these costs will not be "calculated" by the users unless an external authority forces them to do so, usually by means of taxation or other incentives and disincentives. What is clear, however, is that such issues are now being more widely discussed and that the analytical tools for moving in this direction are becoming available.

One such analytical tool is the concept of carrying capacity, which has been available to tourism planners for many years. Tourist carrying capacity is the number of tourists that can be accommodated without creating negative environmental effects. It links questions of resource use and renewability to the issue of scale, to which we now turn.

The proponents of Alternative Development, as has been discussed, are anxious to see a scaling down in virtually all areas of economic, social, and political activity — in production, distribution, consumption, government, and administration.

Brundtland, who addresses United Nation agencies, governments, and multinationals rather than "the people" as such, says virtually nothing on this issue. In discussions of tourism development, however, the question of scale has been an issue for many years, and recent writings have kept it in the limelight.

Four issues may be mentioned. First, how to deal with tourist carrying capacity in general. While there are obvious ecological advantages to keeping the number of tourists down, attention is also being paid to measures that can both increase tourist carrying capacity and improve the capacity to protect the environment. Second, there is the matter of the promotion of tourism in less massive form.

This can involve, as has been done in Bhutan, concentrating tourism development efforts on facilities for a small number of rich tourists. This option, however, raises questions of the environmental impact (e.g., energy and water) generated by facilities for the wealthy: "luxury tourism tends to require more imports, to be more capital-intensive, to be more dependent on outside control of capital, to encourage more of a sense of conspicuous consumption, and to result in a greater sense of relative deprivation than more modest facilities".

Conversely, of course, smaller operations not aimed solely at wealthy outsiders may be more within the reach of the local middle classes -also for non-resident use.

Scale can also be dealt with by dispersion, fostering the development of tourism in a larger number of smaller places. While this will incorporate development areas hitherto unaffected by tourism, the effects can be more easily monitored and controlled, especially from an ecological point of view. An example is the plan of the Indian Government envisaging the creation of a number of regional travel circuits.

These were to cover a total of 441 small centers to cater for budget and low income tourists interested in traveling "off the beaten track". More spontaneous developments can also follow this lead. A notable example is that of farm tourism in Europe, to which Pearce refers with much insight elsewhere in this volume.

Third, there is the question of organizing for smaller scale operations. Multinationals are successful precisely because they reap economies of scale and "aggregation" through massive integrated operations, as discussed below. If scaling down is to be effective, new institutions and organizations will be required (also true in the wider areas of Alternative Development). In tourism development the questions relate especially to the setting up of cooperative arrangements between small scale enterprises and the strengthening of local planning and regulatory capacities; this also is discussed later.

Finally, a word should be said about socialist systems and the question of scale. Command economies, where investment decisions are made centrally and where all significant productive resources are owned by the state, typically promote large scale tourism development. Hotels, built by state building enterprises or foreign contractors, are large and relatively standardized and usually owned and run by the government tourism para-statal.

Moreover, in such economies the legal system prohibits capitalist accumulation and only permits the employment of a very small number of workers by private concerns. Prior to 1989, this was the pattern over most of Eastern Europe, and continues to be in Third World socialist states such as China, Cuba, and Mozambique.

Yet even before recent changes which have resulted from economic and political reforms, this was never the whole picture. The earliest of the "reformers," Yugoslavia, has shown the way in this respect at least over the last 25 years. While statistics are unlikely to be wholly accurate, in 1987 private establishments such as boarding houses and restaurants made up almost 60 per cent of all such establishments and employed, in addition to the owners, 10 per cent of the employees in this sector.

The private boarding houses provided 34 per cent of all beds available, which accounted for almost one-fifth of the bed-nights. These are impressive figures. Hungary and Poland are now also following this road.

The general point to note is that anti-capitalist provisions in economic legislation have often left room for limited family enterprise. As political and economic conditions became more favorable to the latter, or more unfavorable to the public sector, more workers or farmers became small scale entrepreneurs and ventured into the tourism sector.

Nevertheless, economic legislation has continued to constrain essential aspects of these enterprises, for example, the number of workers that may legally be employed. Consequently, growth occurred in breadth (the number of establishments) but not in depth (their size). The result was a large, or growing, sector of very small establishments side by side with the large hotels and restaurants run by the state, and very little in between.

Another ongoing area of concern is the equitable distribution of benefits. Alternative Development has always emphasized the necessity to focus on basic human needs, but its frame of reference has often been the advanced consumer societies.

The implications of its nogrowth or low-growth prescriptions for the poor in Less Developed Countries have been given rather less attention. Most people in the Third World are still struggling to meet the minimum material conditions of a "decent" human existence. Distributive justice in many Less Developed Countries cannot be achieved by development policies which ignore that fact; if there is no cake, there is nothing to distribute.

The poor, wrenched out of their isolation by the transistor radio and the bicycle, do not want to be told to discard their aspirations as consumers — nor, incidentally, do the elites, who wish to emulate the life styles of their counterparts in the rich North.

The Brundtland Commission, with strong representation from the South, has corrected that bias. Brundtland has been accused of not facing up to some of the conflicts its proposals are likely to engender and of having a rather "bland" view of sustainable development.

But the Commission has not fallen into the basic-needs-via-no-growth trap. "We see...the possibility for a new era of economic growth.... And we believe such growth to be absolutely essential to relieve the great poverty that is deepening in much of the developing world".

So the Commission takes a position that is "reformist" of the present productive, socioeconomic, political, and international systems; and it raises the issue of equity wherever this seems relevant. Distributive justice is thus deemed henceforth to include consideration of the needs of future generations.

In the critique of conventional tourism development, the issue of equity also plays a role. For example, in a recent overview article on the sociocultural impacts of tourism, Dogan argues that tourism has aggravated income inequalities.

He stresses the need to differentiate between various host population groups (notably between those who are better off, who get more out of tourism) and the poor, whose lifestyle and culture are less like those of tourists and who stand to gain fewer benefits from tourism. He also draws attention to another distinction, that between those who are younger, who tend to be more susceptible to modern consumerism and the older people, who are more traditional in their way of life.

The impacts of tourism development differ between such different groups, and policy makers have to take account of likely outcomes in this respect. The lessons of European farm tourism have some relevance to this issue, too, as Pearce notes in this volume.

MODIFYING THE ANALYTICAL TOOLS

The congruence of mainstream economic (development) theory and conventional economic development policies has been referred to a number of times. The emergence of Alternative Development has led to a critique of the standard tools used in (economic) analysis and the development of new concepts and approaches more appropriate to a policy concerned with sustainability.

This is also visible in tourism studies. Two aspects will be examined: the refinement of certain tools of conventional economic analysis, and the beginnings of the formulation of different methodologies and theories.

Cost-benefit analysis and associated methodologies are the main targets of those who would refashion the tools of economics rather than "start from scratch." Cost-benefit and cost-effectiveness analysis are micro-analytical tools which set out to give guidance on investment choices, often as between different types of (investment) projects.

These methods deal with what happens within projects, or productive units; outside positive or negative impacts, commonly referred to as externalities, are not considered. Projects or enterprises can "externalize" costs; this means "the shifting of costs to third parties, or onto society, future generations, and nature".

In general, the weakness of many economic and business calculations has been that they do not take ecological issues sufficiently into account, that there are neither enough built-in "signals" nor institutionalized incentives and disincentives to warn decision makers away from environmentally damaging courses of action.

The same is true of the distributive effects of economic activity, and when industry damages nature it often also damages the livelihoods of poor people who, especially in Less Developed Countries, are particularly dependent on nature.

Productive enterprises cannot be expected to take account of such externalities when they calculate their costs. On the contrary, normal business practice motivated by profit maximization will attempt to "externalize" the relevant costs, thereby, for example, causing pollution. Governments, however, can force them to internalize such externalities and can shift the costs back to the problem-causing economic units through regulation or taxation.

By that means the state alters the price and cost signals on waste prevention, energy conservation, and the like taken into account by firms in their costings. Changing the legal and cost balance (the principle that the polluter, or even better the likely polluter, pays) could also help bring about a shift from ex-post to ex-ante solutions, from emphasizing cure to emphasizing prevention.

Exactly the same considerations apply to the tourism

industry. In tourism development, too, the cost of protecting the environment needs to be treated as an "internality," that is, as a cost of doing business. And, of course, the longer the time perspective of the developer, the easier it is to absorb such costs, as in the construction of a sewage treatment plant instead of using a sea outfall.

Government agencies themselves, however, can and should incorporate ecological effects in their broader cost-benefit calculations. They should modify the methodology itself so that it will take into account, as a matter of course, the costs and benefits of proposed actions for the environment.

Impact assessments do try to achieve this, at best also for other non-material (e.g., cultural) effects; and the Brundtland Commission discusses a whole array of institutional changes, as well as some new tools for analysis, that are relevant in this respect. This approach also needs to be followed by tourism planners.

Can changes in emphasis and perspective such as these direct us toward a new economics? The proponents of Alternative Development and Alternative Tourism continue to devote most of their time and writing to policy issues and to the advocacy needed to place these at the centre of attention.

Yet more interest is now also being shown in the theoretical underpinning of sustainable policies, and hence in the reformulation of economics itself. It is argued that the "nature" component in sustainability is neglected by economics; environmental questions are not taken into account in models or measurement.

The question of measurement has considerable importance. This is graphically captured in a quote which Brookfield lifted from a paper written by Repetto for the World Bank's Sustainability Issues in Agricultural Development: "a country could exhaust its aquifers, cut down its forests, erode its soils, and hunt its wildlife and fisheries to extinction, but measured income would rise steadily as these assets disappeared".

Traditional economic accounting, which produces that standard international "comparator" of GNP, omits essential elements. National accounting is incomplete on flows (notably non-marketed, directly consumed environmental services), while stocks (such as the surface area under forests) are left out of the picture altogether.

So "measured GNP can increase as a new industry starts production, but if associated air and water pollution are serious, the total welfare derived...may actually decrease." The tools of economic measurement need to take account of the fact that sustainable development "is essentially an asset management problem".

The economics of enterprise, particularly under a capitalist system of production, is oriented to profitability and the expansion of markets; hence growth is a favored outcome, monitored in terms of measurable output, physical quantities, or money equivalents. In nature, however, growth is not the driving force. Rather, nature appears to strive for stability (equilibrium, homeostasis), and it can be argued that ecological stability is the main precondition for sustainability.

Economic policy would take account of this basic fact by moving from the simple maximization of flows (growth) to paying more attention to increasing efficiency and maintaining substance. This would require a redefinition of the concept of GNP by including ecological measures, so that account could be taken of the different effects (positive, neutral, or negative) on the environment of different components of growth as measured by output.

The incorporation of environmental measures in standard national accounting would not solve the problem of "valuing" irreplaceable resources, as in the case of a wilderness region lost because of a hydroelectric development. But at least it would draw attention to the issues and force those responsible to make their value judgments explicit.

That would also be relevant to weighing the immediate consumption needs of the poor in Less Developed Countries against the long term demands of future generations, which is itself an extremely difficult issue.

Finally, there are those such as Bandyopadhyay and Shiva (1989) who would give economics an even more fundamental reorientation. Conventional economics deals, they argue, with market economics (or, one might add, command economies). Its models and theories, however, have no relevance to the operation of two quite separate and equally important "economies": the economy of survival, and the economy of natural processes (i.e., what happens in nature) to which the economy of survival is linked.

The market economy and the dominant form of economics employed in its analysis have been concerned with the use of resources for commodity production and capital accumulation. The resource needs of the people outside the commodity economy, the subsistence farmers and pastoralists who make up the majority in so many of the poorer Less Developed Countries, are quite different. In their survival economy, satisfaction of basic needs is the organizing principle for natural resource use.

In such economies there are normally built-in checks on overexploitation unless crisis, such as has been seen in Sub-Saharan Africa over the last decade, sweeps traditional safeguards away, leading to deforestation and similar phenomena.

Herein lies the link to the economy of natural processes, the third type, the economics of which analyzes the processes by which resources are regenerated in nature, as in the production of humus by forests, the regeneration of water resources, or the evolution of genetic products.

Bandyopadhyay and Shiva deepen the basic Alternative Development charge laid at the door of conventional economics — that it externalizes costs. They point out that the market economy has neither substantive nor analytical links with the natural nor survival economies.

Therefore it is not perceived that resource-intensive development, seen as positive within the market economy based on profits and accumulation, actually damages both nature and poor people. Unfortunately, they neither tell us what the economics of nature and survival would look like nor what tools need to be developed.

One may suspect that professional economists would have many good reasons for being skeptical of their approach, and that the approach would be particularly vulnerable to the criticism of neither understanding nor taking sufficient account of the findings of science. Nevertheless, it does provide food for thought and a starting point for others, concerning both Alternative Development and the development of more sustainable forms of tourism.

Thus, we have attempted to document the emergence of more analytical approaches to Alternative Development and Alternative Tourism. To end this part of the discussion a few words will be said about related changes in the political discourse of Alternative Development:

The world view of Another Development is likely to remain that of a minority, in part because most of its adherents adopt an uncompromising all-or-nothing stand which tends to alienate even those who could afford to adopt its back-tonature lifestyle.... The ideas of Another Development are likely to remain on the fringe, crushed between its somewhat dogmatic puritanism and the wish or need of most people (especially the poor in the Third World) to partake of the "fleshpots of Egypt."

These lines written only a few years ago, would no longer be accurate. The rather cranky image of the "alternative movement" is slowly dissolving, and its approach is no longer based solely on moral indignation and utopic blueprints.

Moreover, Green political parties have begun to make an impact in Europe. Of course their programs are not yet fully worked out and many differences of view persist in their ranks, notably between the "greener" and the "redder" Greens. The latter accuse the former of too much reliance on trying to change people's views.

As Marxists, they believe views change through action;

they generally accuse the non-Marxist Greens of a lack of realism, particularly as to what would be needed to bring off their bold and essentially revolutionary challenge to the mainstream capitalist system. They hence argue for a "vigorous dialectic" between the new ideas and the creation of new economic and social structures "by practical — even revolutionary — collective political action".

Yet the Greens have had a major influence on the Brundtland Commission and have jolted many of the established political parties into paying at least lip service to the issues of the environment and sustainability.

In addition, as they can begin to aspire at least to participation in practical power, their self-image is no longer quite that of a group doomed to continue crying in the wilderness. Some serious thinking about realistic courses of action is being done by their political leaders as well as by intellectuals identified with them. Mats Friberg, for example, recognizes that the Greens will not be able to achieve their full set of goals and that some goals will have to be given up, especially those that would "threaten corporate actors."

But he does believe that a "counter-cultural strategy of building a new society from the bottom up" could be put into practice. This would take much time to have an effect. (Friberg has studied earlier social movements in Europe, and the "distance" gained from such historical work gives him a sense of perspective.) Given perhaps fifty years to grow, the result could be a dual economy with the continuation of large scale bureaucracy and industry on the one hand and the growth of self-governing local communities and informal sector enterprises on the other.

There is no way of knowing whether, or when, this prediction will come true. We do know two things, however. First, that the future never quite follows any predicted course. Second, that the road toward more sustainable development policies, globally or nationally, will not be easy or smooth. Because of the widespread ramifications of sustainable development policies there will be many obstacles to their implementation. But, as the next section attempts to show, there are opportunities, too.

WORRYING ABOUT POLICY IMPLEMENTATION -CONSTRAINTS

The difficulties of policy implementation are greatly underestimated. Too often policy is made, but the instruments for its management have not been put in place. If moves toward a more sustainable tourism development pattern are to be successful, attention will need to be paid to institution building in the spheres of policy management and implementation.

Various constraints and opportunities are discussed in some detail in the balance of this analysis, but attention should first be drawn to the fact that not all policies have identical implications for implementation. Certain policies that operate at the macro-level, even though they may encounter resistance before adoption, "can be accomplished with minimal development of new institutional capabilities to support implementation".

Examples include adjusting exchange rates, removing subsidies, raising interest rates, or freeing trade restrictions. In contrast, micro-policy reforms depend on complex institutional changes that are difficult to implement. While there may be much less initial opposition to the new ideas than with macro changes, implementation is very hard.

In a similar vein Harvey, who deals with problems of structural adjustment in Africa, notes the difficulties of "sacking civil servants and marketing board employees, removing the power and patronage of those who appointed them, and cutting the costs and raising the prices of other forms of parastatal".

Comparable considerations apply to policies for sustainability. For example, once accepted, an increase in the tax on fossil fuels to raise the cost of contributing to the greenhouse effect (internalizing the externalities) can be implemented relatively easily, while monitoring polluting emissions by industry or hotels is more difficult.

Creating viable organizations to help smaller national or local enterprises make an economic success of Alternative Tourism is a difficult task. Changing the ingrained habits of the consumer society's consumers on the one hand, and the "instincts" of any private enterprise to "get around" obstacles to the promotion of its particular products on the other, are likely to be very hard indeed.

The following paragraphs examine some of the specific difficulties likely to be encountered when attempting to implement policies for sustainability.

Those who benefit from existing arrangements prefer to see them continued; and social, political, and economic institutions reflect such "vested interests." Sociologists examine social classes, political scientists study interest groups and parties, and economists look at the strain toward monopoly (which is the concentration of control over resources, and decisions relating to them, in the hands of minorities).

Recent work has emphasized that the state itself can be the instrument of private interests. This is also the case in tourism, as James Elliott has shown for Thailand. While the balance of power between different parts of the state apparatus allows the private sector room to manoeuvre, as discussed below, Elliott also points to the importance and power of the bureaucracy: its permanence, stability, internal cohesion, and knowledge of the administrative system.

The bureaucracy does not take initiatives but uses its power negatively, defending the status quo. It protects its own position, the "main aim being self survival and departmental growth, including more jobs". As the Thai bureaucracy needs resources for survival, it has been opposed to the abolition of the high taxes on hotel (16.5%) and restaurant (8.25%) bills, a step considered desirable for the further promotion of tourism.

So it comes as something of a surprise to read Richter's

early views of the policy process in tourism development. She may be right in her assertion that little conflict is apparent in the initial stages, but to suggest that in tourism policy there are "substantial rewards and few interests to placate or offend" is surely incorrect for most situations.

Those interests are especially apparent with respect to the transnational system, but a move to greater sustainability would also hurt many national and local established interests.

Tourism also responds to the demands of people for what Hirsch has called "positional goods," goods and services that give status because they are inherently scarce.

Ironically, long distance budget travelers (those paragons of Alternative Tourism) seek such exclusivity, which tends to be destroyed by its very success as wider groups learn of the new destinations and small scale local businesses expand or are displaced by conventional tourism enterprises. Where a tourism destination has become an exclusive status symbol for the very rich, recreating their favored environment at considerable cost, strong vested interests in the status quo within the industry are reinforced by those of their customers.

Among those organizations with vested interests in the status quo, transnational enterprises are particularly powerful. Their resources are often greater than those of the governments in the countries where they operate; they employ high-powered experts to advise them on the most profitable operating arrangements within existing legal and regulatory frameworks.

During the late 1960s and 1970s they were widely criticized for their role in the international economy; the scandals over the use of unsafe drugs, over the promotion of artificial baby milk, and over transfer pricing (subsidiaries charging their head office enormous prices for goods or services in order to repatriate profits) represented the low water mark.

More recently the controversies have died down. The political climate everywhere has moved back toward market forces and private enterprise; the worst practices of transnationals appear to have been eliminated, while Less Developed Countries' governments have become rather more adept at framing the necessary laws or regulations and at imposing relevant and collectable taxes.

Even so, forcing more sustainable policies onto transnational corporations will demand considerable skill as well as collaboration among governments of Less Developed Countries.

Many researchers have emphasized the power of transnationals in the tourism industry. Erisman, writing about mass tourism in the West Indies, shows how the industry there is primarily run by and serves the interests of American corporations and their customers, through marketing networks in the United States.

Already in the early 1980s, these networks were becoming increasingly vertically integrated, formally or informally, with the airlines standing at the centre. The three most lucrative components of tourism are handled by these networks: marketing and the procurement of customers; international transportation; and food and lodging.

More recently, Wilkinson has argued that micro-states which become involved in tourism find themselves enmeshed in a global system over which they cannot exercise control. They become the targets for "exogenous decision-making," as "many decisions governing their lives, even those dealing with local matters, are made elsewhere by other countries, multinational companies, or airlines".

Richter draws virtually the same conclusion and writes that in Less Developed Countries with few material and human resources "almost the entire infrastructure for tourism will be built with foreign goods, controlled by foreigners, and used by foreigners and...all too often profits will not remain in the country".

The decisions of the large international airlines are particularly crucial for small states in the realm of conventional tourism. Only by being on a regular flight route can a destination's associated services, notably accommodation, be included in the computerized networks now virtually indispensable for bookings through travel agents and tour operators. So the effective start-up decision often rests with an airline, or with the foreign donor who helps finance the building of an international airport.

The importance of those computerized networks and the power they give to those at their centre has also recently been stressed by Auliana Poon. She notes that computerized reservation systems, run by the largest airlines or by consortia of a few of these, are now used by about 90 per cent of the travel agents in the United States and the United Kingdom.

They constitute a total information system offering, in addition to hotel reservations, such services as car rentals, champagne and flowers, information about destinations, or bus and train connections. Experience in the Caribbean has shown that "without links to [these] international marketing and distribution networks, hotel bed-nights cannot be sold".

The momentum of this system is enormous, the interests involved truly global. As to the extent that Alternative Tourism is regarded as no more than the tourism of "alternative tourists," being bypassed by these systems may not matter so much. But this is not a tenable position if, in contrast, encouraging Alternative Tourism is seen as a wider move toward tourism with "sustainable characteristics."

It should be selfevident that any such policy must come to terms with the reality of transnational electronic power. The development of sophisticated electronic sub-networks that join together a limited number of smaller facilities may be a more viable proposition than attempting to "buck the trend."

Implementation is also confounded by fragmentation of government responsibilities. The idea of sustainable policies is likely to have a growing influence on international organizations and United Nations agencies, as well as on the declared policies of many Northern governments. Brundtland will be heard.

Yet as her Commission's Report emphasized, a few well-sounding declarations are but the first step on the road to sustainable development. Implementing the fine phrases demands enforcement. The responsibility for the different aspects of environmental and distributive policies is, however, dispersed throughout the government machine.

Sectoral organizations tend to pursue sectoral objectives and to treat their impacts on other sectors as side effects, taken into account only if compelled to do so. Hence impacts on forests rarely worry those involved in public policy or business activities in the fields of energy, industrial development, crop husbandry, or foreign trade.

Many of the environmental problems that confront us have their roots in this sectoral fragmentation of responsibility. Sustainable development requires that such fragmentation be overcome.

The complexity of modern government and administration, where authority must be delegated in order to be exercised effectively, is one cause of this problem. But there are others. Because those working in sectoral agencies, such as ministries and other official organizations, get few rewards for working with outsiders, intersectoral collaboration is at a discount.

In each sector one particular professional and disciplinary group tends to be dominant. Cooperation between such professional groups is limited because the different nature of their original training leads to different perceptions of what problems are important in the world. This is true even in contiguous sectors such as health, nutrition, and agriculture, where intersectoral collaboration has encountered many obstacles for such reasons.

This sectoral fragmentation in the public administration is reinforced by compartmentalized working links between civil servants and enterprises in the sectors their departments are supposed to regulate.

Ministries of agriculture deal with farmers, ministries of industry with industrialists, tourism departments with businesses in the tourism sector, and so on. Farmers, industrialists, and hoteliers soon form specialized lobbies; their viewpoints and interests come to influence the thinking of the bureaucrats in "their" sector. Sociocultural factors, such as "soft states," patron-client networks, clan politics, and "endemic corruption," may make this worse.

These sectoral dynamics of government and administration provide the backdrop to any effort at implementing more sustainable development and tourism development policies. While different from country to country and from culture to culture, they are deeply entrenched everywhere.

They are reinforced by the specialized multilateral agencies which usually have links with one ministry alone, such as the World Health Organization in the health sector, United Nations Industrial Development Organization for industry, FAO in agriculture.

Advice on tourism development comes from the World Tourism Organization, which is "concerned quite naturally with developing tourism and not with using tourism as a vehicle for development". Superministries, or highly centralized forms of government, may mitigate these problems but cannot overcome them completely. Constraints which need to be bypassed as much as possible are likely to remain.

ACHIEVING POLICY IMPLEMENTATION – OPPORTUNITIES

While it is compelling to recognize constraints for what they are, it is important not to exaggerate them and to be aware of opportunities and room for maneuvering. For example, certain aspects of the functioning of state and public administration have been revealed as obstacles to the achievement of more sustainable development policies. But in other respects it is only the state which can provide the conditions for movement toward greater sustainability.

In most countries tourism development will always centre

on private enterprise. While current conventional wisdom stresses the benefits of the market, the pendulum shows signs of beginning to swing back from recent extreme positions.

As Butler argues in this volume, in the absence of control and external responsibility the free play of the market will almost inevitably lead to overreaching capacity limits, and hence a lack of sustainability. It is likely that in general more attention will again be paid to the imperfections of the market and to those specific interventions which can correct the tendencies to disequilibrium and monopoly power, both in the private and the state sectors.

Interventions by the state are also essential with regard to the problem of externalities discussed earlier. By disregarding the costs of negative effects they may have on others or on nature, productive units in and out of the tourist industry are better able to maximize their profits.

So the state, or rather development policy makers and planners, must force productive units to take account of such effects. They do this by building appropriate cost and price signals into the framework within which productive units operate, by creating incentives and disincentives, and by straightforward regulation. Insofar as maintaining ecological stability is essential to sustainability, this institutional framework also needs to safeguard the reproduction of natural resources.

In the sphere of tourism, governments have long exercised controls in a number of areas, most fundamentally, of course, in the conditions on which tourists are admitted to a country and on the rate at which their currencies will be exchanged.

Governments have leverage to influence the development of tourism in specific areas or particular ways: they set the conditions of investment and access, determine what concessions will be given to foreign enterprises, and they can legislate about access to land, such as, for example, by not allowing straight purchase, but only long term leases.

In general, they can and do include tourism in their development plans, and they often play a major role in providing infrastructure for tourism development.

This general capacity can also be focused on creating the conditions for sustainability. It helps if sustainability, as a general issue, is high on the agenda of government policy as this can draw attention to sensitive issues such as restrictions on physical development or the effects on local populations. As they can for conventional tourism, governments can create an appropriate incentive structure for sustainable tourism.

Transnationals, if left to operate according to their own agendas, will prefer large scale developments and accommodations provided in mega-hotels; they will usually not be sensitive to ecological or local issues and will not be concerned that their projects yield benefits for the host country's development in general and for the poor in particular.

Such issues are more likely to be addressed by the state if tourism planning is integrated with development planning in general. This is, of course, more difficult in small countries with a slender government apparatus and a scarcity of professional staff.

Wilkinson also suggests that Alternative Tourism development, insofar as it comprises small scale facilities which are likely to be low rise, cottage style, and energy efficient, may require rather less government involvement than the conventional variety. Infrastructure demands should be less extensive, and with respect to regulation and incentive structures a more "passive" attitude toward this sort of development may be warranted.

However, Alternative Tourism development will require substantial institutional innovation (and hence certain kinds of state involvement) if it is to be successful. Some of this innovation may have to be aimed at methods of increasing participation and decentralization.

From the historical perspective which Mats Friberg brings

to bear on his analysis of the emergence of Green political movements in Europe, he sees the next phase as a deepening of earlier achievements (citizenship, democracy, social justice, and equity) by means of a further transformation of the state and the extension of participation through civic organizations. Participation has, indeed, become one of the rallying cries of development ideology of the 1980s.

It is heard in sundry contexts, from discussions of the informal sector in production to generalized blueprints for better health services. Non-governmental organizations (NGOs) have benefited from this new interest, attracting government development grants for carrying out small scale projects together with people at the grass roots.

The role of NGOs in development has shot into prominence, and they are seen as possible agents of "empowerment" of local communities vis-à-vis those who do, or may in future, dominate.

Similar views are expressed with respect to tourism. Wilkinson's paper, which focuses on the factors influencing the chances of tourism development with "alternative" characteristics in micro-states, ends with a clarion call for community participation in the development of local tourism.

Earlier he quotes Murphy, who holds the view that tourism development can be positive if the needs of the local community are placed before the goals of the tourism industry. Tourism should be seen as a local resource, and its management "for the common good and future generations should become the goal and criterion by which the industry is judged".

Yet such calls for community participation gloss over the well-known tendency for local elites to "appropriate" the organs of participation for their own benefit. Many studies have demonstrated that those who are locally influential and wealthy, will become the spokespersons for communities unless specific measures are taken to counter this pattern; this is so whether one examines local political structures or such less formal arrangements as community organizations and NGO-sponsored associations. As regards participation in decision making on tourism development, there is a further problem. Communities have coped with problems in areas such as agriculture or health from time immemorial and, therefore, have a store of traditional experience and knowledge which can be the starting point of their participation in such areas.

But local experience with tourism is wholly lacking, and people are largely at the mercy of the opinions of those who are presented to them, or who present themselves, as "experts." As Richter points out in her discussion of tourism development in the United States, this places the "developers" at an advantage; yet their expertise may well be that of an interested party.

In Less Developed Countries, too, advice is often provided by the "wrong" people. Perhaps specialized tourism related NGOs from the North, or international NGOs involved in tourism such as the already mentioned Ecumenical Coalition on Third World Tourism, could help in this respect and fulfill the "monitoring" function suggested by Richter.

A similar situation of unfamiliarity with relevant issues prevails within the public administration, where awareness of tourism issues is limited, even in so highly developed a country as the United States. In view of the shortage of public servants knowledgeable on tourism issues, public administrations in the U.S. all too often turn to the hardly disinterested travel industry for advice.

Such problems are exacerbated by the fact that many decisions about tourism development are made at lower levels of government and administration, where the range of expertise is usually more limited and the competence of senior public servants less solid, especially with respect to the broader questions of ecological and social sustainability. Hence there is a need to consider seriously what institutional and organizational changes are required if policies for more sustainable tourism development are to be put into place.

Perhaps the most formidable task on the road to

sustainable development, and tourism development, is that of building the institutions needed for policy implementation. Earlier we saw how the Brundtland Commission, too, regards this as the greatest challenge.

There are no quick fixes in this domain. Public administrations do not respond easily or quickly to new situations. And devising workable organizations that interface between the public and private sectors is also fraught with problems.

The variety of marketing, advisory, and support services available to European farm tourism enterprises, to which Pearce refers in this volume, emerged gradually over a fairly long period of "natural growth," itself helped by the large domestic markets for this kind of Alternative Tourism.

When these conditions do not prevail, devising such institutions is far from easy. We are then in the sphere of micro-policy; for this to be effectively implemented, knowledge of processes of learning and change is required and a real understanding of the interests involved is needed. This refers not only to those "vested interests" who might oppose the policy shift but also to those who are the potential beneficiaries of the changes, and hence potential allies in the process.

Recent developments in the organization of industrial production provide some useful pointers to the kind of innovations that might help achieve institutional support for Alternative Development and Alternative Tourism. Much has been written on "flexible specialization," the system pioneered in Japan and made famous in Europe through the fashion business of Bennetton, which enables enterprises to respond with much greater agility to changes in the market. Poon refers to that literature in her interesting paper on the relevance of these new forms of organization to Caribbean tourism.

Some of the characteristics which have been identified in earlier sections as coherent with sustainable tourism development, notably that of smaller scale, also figure in the discussion of flexible specialization. If more tourists were to take their holidays in "sustainable tourism environments," their handling in smaller batches would become a major organizational issue.

Poon shows that smallness by itself would not promise success for tourism enterprises under these conditions, notably because of the inexorable march of computerization discussed above. She emphasizes, however, the very great importance of networks: "For small firms, networks and systems have become their fundamental survival route".

Best, Murray, and Pezzini have made the same point, showing how the small manufacturers of Italy innovating with flexible specialization, in clothing, furniture, and so on, have been successful thanks to the creation of networks of mutual support. Particularly important have been the cooperative organizations which provide services — in design, or marketing — for all, which no one enterprise could have afforded by itself.

Sometimes simple institutional innovations are worth exploring, such as producing a serious local "Good Food Guide," as in the United Kingdom where there is a highly respected and widely used guide produced by the Consumers' Association. This approach, which is also being tried in Cyprus, helps tourists find good traditional eating places — a bit of Alternative Tourism in the face of much standardized international catering — while at the same time strengthening the local economy.

Developments such as these have often also involved innovative interface organizations between local industry and local or regional government; this contains further lessons for institution building for sustainability.

We have come to the end of a long road. We have seen how the somewhat strident advocacy of Alternative Development and Alternative Tourism, by movements on the political fringe and more often based on moral indignation than on sound scientific arguments, has made way for a broader concern for sustainability underpinned by a growing body of scientific and analytical work. Of course, in many ways conventional and alternative development paths not only diverge but go in opposite directions. Yet this analysis has tried to demonstrate that in many respects it is better to regard those opposites as continua; policies can push countries along those continua in either direction. This suggests that policy makers can, indeed, promote sustainability by constantly striving to make the conventional more sustainable.

This is also true for tourism. Most Less Developed Countries cannot hope to create acceptable living conditions for the majority of their people without continued economic growth and for many of them, especially the large number of smaller tropical mini- and micro-states, tourism represents one of the few apparently viable routes for such growth.

Policy makers can only proceed from what already exists in this respect, and that is a powerful and still growing, highly integrated, international tourism industry.

"Alternative" forms will presumably continue to evolve spontaneously, as Valene Smith notes in this volume, almost inevitably "riding piggy-back" on the more cost-effective forms of the conventional, integrated international tourism industry. How to coax that behemoth into less destructive behaviour is surely the main task ahead.

Chapter 4

A New Class: Trendies on the Trail

As Crick argues, 'human beings', the tourists themselves, are only infrequently the object of consideration in much tourism research. And yet it is upon tourists that the industry is founded. In part this has resulted from academic prejudices of analysing production rather than consumption and the tendency to focus upon the impacts (economic, environmental, cultural) of tourism where tourists are at best a homogeneous and undifferentiated group and at worst are deemed immaterial.

It has been suggested at various points in earlier that tourists need to be taken more seriously, and recent campaigns on the ethical forms of travel and tourism from development agencies (such as VSO and the Tear Fund) seem to suggest that they are. To this point in the book, a number of key factors have been stressed.

First, sought to demonstrate the significant economic changes that have resulted in post-Fordist modes of both producing and consuming goods and services. In part, these changes can be traced through to the emergence of new and varied forms of tourism in the Third World.

It was also argued that these changes have tended to invest more power in us, the consumers, or the tourists: we have more choice. Second, it has been suggested that the influence of the new middle classes can be linked to the emergence of what may be referred to as postmodern cultural forms.

The importance of these social groups in both producing

new forms of tourism in the Third World and forming a significant role in taking such holidays was highlighted.

Both points stress the increasing significance of tourists, with the second factor highlighting the importance of social class. Of course this is not to say that class is the only factor in studying tourism; far from it. But it is a significant factor and is especially important in the analysis of new forms of tourism, in that the 'world of tourism is rife with the class distinction in our everyday world'.

Yet an analysis of the significance of class and tourism is only weakly developed. It was argued that analysis of tourists has centred around either classifying tourists or carrying out motivation and attitude surveys. Although such approaches are of interest, they have tended to limit the scope of tourism analysis.

This chapter explores what use an analysis of class offers in developing a critique of Third World tourism. As elsewhere in the book, this is not a definitive statement of how tourists should be analysed and understood, but an attempt to broaden our thinking and approach to the field of tourism.

Initially, the chapter discusses the importance of social class as a concept and how it is reflected in travel and tourism. In particular, the relationships of contemporary global change to the way classes are formed will be considered.

The second half of the chapter identifies a number of crucial factors evident in the formation of new middle-class tourism, and it is argued that travel and tourism have an increasingly important symbolic role to play as social classes seek to define and distinguish themselves from other social classes. The final sections of the chapter indicate why social class analysis is of importance in considering the impacts of Third World tourism.

CLASS, CAPITAL AND TRAVEL

Of all social science concepts, arguably, it is class that has been subjected to the most thoroughgoing marginalisation since the 1980s. Politicians began to talk in terms of classless societies, academics became preoccupied with the fragmentation of traditional class lines (working class/middle class/upper class) and more and more people have begun to think in terms of their individual, as opposed to class, status. This is a lure of individualism that led Crompton to conclude that the 'retreat from class ... is becoming the sociological equivalent of the new individualism'.

However, a recognition of the role of social class in contemporary capitalism has begun to re-emerge. A number of authors have begun to illustrate the relationships between cultural changes and the development of new middle classes. In common, these authors agree that these significant and numerically expanding class fractions have an instrumental part to play in new cultural forms.

Indeed, Lash and Urry refer to postmodernism as a 'hegemonising mission' for the new middle classes, and elsewhere they are considered as both producers and consumers of postmodernism - *par excellence*. We identified a number of key characteristics of postmodernism and highlighted their relevance to the analysis of Third World tourism.

Briefly these involved: the emergence of specialist agents and tour operators (and its adjunct, more individually centred and flexible holidays); the de-differentiation of tourism as it becomes associated with other activities, and the growth of interest in *Other* cultures, environments and their association with the emergence of new social movements.

Nevertheless, the different ways in which different social classes consume tourism is vastly under-researched. This is significant in that we have argued above that much new tourism is based on the notion of individual travel.

A culture of travel (as opposed to tourism) that is shamelessly hedonistic has emerged: chill out, the world's a breeze, so experience it. But most of the existing commentary amounts to little more than the rhetorical and polemical ranting of middle-class writers bemoaning the scale, effects and popularity of mass tourism.

The analogy of tourism to pollution is commonplace and is often expressed in socio-cultural terms where it is the swarms or tidal waves of tourists that constitute a problem that must be contained. It is a view that appears to be prevalent across the arts, academia, the media and the industry.

The renowned French photographer, Henri Cartier Bresson, contends: 'I'm an adventurer ... The Africa I experienced was literally that of the "Voyage au Bout de la Nuit". It was a time when people were travellers, not tourists ... I travelled on a shoestring. Regimented tourism is a contagious form of pollution'.

Rosenthal admits that perhaps it is timely to 'accept that some areas will remain "sacrificial resorts" which continue to attract tourists who do not seek an experience of "deeper" quality'. And as an operator contends: 'With the days of the package holiday ... drawing to a close, we are about to discover very special holidays for very special people: like you'.

Equally limiting is the fact that the role of geography, the spatial dimension, is all but ignored, despite its fundamental role both to understanding tourism as a process and how social classes are constituted as part of that process. As Thurot and Thurot note, the ability of the middle classes to maintain their 'social distance' from others has become more difficult because 'great distance no longer offers substitutable destinations'.

The circulation of tourist areas has tended to focus either on the deterministic cyclical nature of tourist development or the cyclical character of tourists themselves. In the former approach, tourist areas are modelled as moving from discovery to overcrowding. In the latter approach, a taxonomy of visitor characteristics are noted. Although this approach offers greater scope for thinking about the relationships between social class and tourism, the links remain weakly developed.

By acknowledging the importance of cultural

consumption in the study of social classes, the French sociologist, Pierre Bourdieu (1984), has provided a productive way for thinking about the relationships of class and tourism. A number of authors have noted the applicability of his influential work to tourism.

Briefly, Bourdieu (1984) argues that social classes wage 'classificatory struggles' seeking to distinguish themselves from each other by education, occupation, residence and so on, and, of course, through commodities, which is taken to include both objects (cars, furniture and so on) and experiences, such as holidays.

They achieve this, Bourdieu suggests, by constructing 'lifestyles'. We have already alluded to this notion of lifestyle as a useful way of considering the individuals' uses of a range of objects, experiences, hobbies and beliefs to, sociologically speaking, 'mark their territories'.

These lifestyles, Bourdieu concludes, are the products of what he terms *habitus*, and it is worth spending a few moments considering the significance of this concept. Habitus represents the ability and disposition of individuals and social classes to appropriate objects and practices, to act in certain ways, that differentiate them from others.

A knowledge of 'foreign' food, good wine, classic literature or Latin American film, for example, may all assist in differentiating from others without such knowledge or appreciation. Habitus is, therefore, a 'cognitive structure' which 'gives people a sense of their place in the world'.

Or as Painter suggests, 'Habitus gives individuals a sense of how to act in specific situations, without continually having to make fully conscious decisions. It is this "practical sense", often described as a "feel for the game", that Bourdieu's theory of practice seeks to understand'. And for Bourdieu it is the necessary starting point for a theory of *strategies* that 'aims to account for the logic according to which groups, or classes, form and break up'.

Two important points emerge from Bourdieu's work. First, social classes are in constant struggle to ensure that differentiation from class fractions above and below are maintained. Travel has always had an important role to play in this process of differentiation, and as tourism has become more widespread the struggle has intensified.

It is difficult to deny that Marbella, Kos, Phuket and 18-30 provide a very different set of meanings and representations from Tikal, Chiang Mai, Kilimanjaro and Explore. So different places, the different experiences to be had, and even different operators, add up to what we could describe as a 'symbolic system'; it is the way in which we represent objects and experiences and then communicate this to others. And we can also argue that these different components 'each embody particular class "tastes"'.

Habitus, therefore, represents a certain 'class culture and milieu' and provides the basis for class reproduction and differentiation. The traveller/tourist distinction, although highly stereotyped, is reflective of a wider debate over social class differentiation.

These battles are an example of everyday hegemony in practice. Of course, this also suggests that social classes are themselves constantly formed and hence the term class fractions to distinguish from the 'once-and-for-all' idea of *the* working class, or *the* middle class.

Social class formation is, therefore, a dynamic process, 'a flame whose edges are in constant movement, oscillating around a line or surface', and of conceptual importance in helping to understand the dynamic nature of tourist consumption: today's cool spot is tomorrow's classificatory dinosaur.

Second, a discussion of class also suggests the importance that exploitation (of one class by another) should play in the analysis; in 'order for a social collectivity to be regarded as a social class it has to have its roots in a process of exploitation'.

Moreover, an exploitation-centred analysis of class provides for a more coherent strategy for considering the characteristics of the middle classes in contemporary capitalism; hence, the straightforward observation 'one person's welfare is obtained at the expense of another' (1985:65). Traditionally, class analysis has been undertaken with a production-side bias with the focus of the exploitation of the workforce by capitalists, and a principal focus on economic measures (occupation, income, and so on) as indicators of class position.

The critical part of Bourdieu's work is that 'domination remains, but it must be reconceptualised in a world of consumption. Domination is now mediated by taste'. Reflecting this power, Eagleton refers to habitus as a 'practical ideology', or what we might call an 'everyday hegemony', whereby the need to dominate is translated into routine social behaviour.

The importance for our discussion of tourism is that the struggles inherent in social classes have both a social element (ecotourism is better than package tourism) and spatial element (the Brazilian rainforest has more kudos than a Gambian beach). In other words, tourism can be used to differentiate and exploit both socially and spatially.

So exactly how are these struggles waged and differentiation achieved? An important part of the answer lies in the accumulation of capital. But in this case it is not the finance capital necessary to sustain profits or individual financial assets, but cultural and symbolic capital linked to certain kinds of tourism.

CULTURAL AND SYMBOLIC CAPITAL

As a number of authors have contended, consumption has become more skilful in recent years. Not only do consumers ask more questions of the commodities they buy (the least polluting car to buy or holiday to take?), they are also more sensitive to the symbols they are consuming.

The consumption of holidays has assumed an increasingly significant role in the cultural differentiation characteristic of other forms of consumption and the Third World has an important role within this and represents a sizeable cultural asset. It is a way of investing in and accumulating what Bourdieu refers to as cultural capital.

Unlike economic capital, cultural capital is not something that can be strictly bought, but instead relies on the ability of individuals to join the game of being able to 'know' and 'appreciate' what to eat, drink, wear, watch and what types of holiday to take. In other words, it requires the skill of reading the cultural significance of certain types of consumption; for example, the significance of 'original features' in the process of gentrification or the cultural significance of certain types of holidays, whether ecotourism in Kenya or backpacking in South-East Asia.

In the former case, 'it is not simply that a desire to see ecological attractions in far-off destinations conveys a sense of superior status; rather it is the actual ability to appreciate ecology which indicates cultural competence'. In the latter case, it will be argued that cultural capital is also accumulated through journeys to remote and hazardous regions.

It is these young travellers who often emerge as 'figures of admiration'. As Bob Samuel, information manager at Trailfinders, observes: 'There is a lot of kudos in coming back and telling your friends you have travelled overland in Cambodia. It gives you a certain cachet' .

If tourism has increasingly taken on a symbolic meaning (in part due to the dramatic increase in tourism), it has also meant that tourism as a commodity embodies 'sign-value', an important means of stocking up on cultural capital. It is symbolic in the way in which travel and tourism embody certain attributes: personal qualities in the individual, such as strength of character, adaptability, resourcefulness, sensitivity or even 'worldliness'. In a somewhat traditional sense, travel is widely regarded as 'character building'.

In this way tourism is not only something to be enjoyed but represents a strategy for building a reputation that can be converted into economic capital. In other words, it transforms travel into a commodity with exchange-value and can be traded in, so to speak, for material benefits; and hence the phrase 'curriculum vitae builders'. Trailfinders' 'long haul travel consultants' must be aged 22-30 and 'have travelled extensively'. But of course it is not only the travel industry that recognises the 'benefits' of travelling and there is a number of occupations where overseas travel is an increasingly significant component or, indeed, pre-requisite.

Curriculum vitae building starts young, as Sansom contends, with universities and employers agreeing 'that a constructive year out embellishes your CV', and myriad agencies offering opportunities for a 'year out' - in the UK, this includes Raleigh International, Group Activity Projects, Frontier, The Year Out Group and VSO's Youth Volunteering.

How are the sign and exchange values of these travel commodities maintained or enhanced? Before we try to answer this question, consideration will be given to how class fractions may be conceived in relation to tourism. This is not to suggest that class fractions are fixed and immutable as described below; rather, it suggests a heuristic approach - a style of analysis - that may help our understanding of tourism and class.

ECOTOURISTS

The first principal grouping Bourdieu terms the new bourgeoisie. They are located firmly within the service sector with jobs involving finance, marketing and purchasing, for example. They are also class fractions that earn a lot and are correspondingly high in terms of economic capital (finance). They can afford expensive holidays that are exclusive in terms of price affordability and the numbers of tourists permitted: private game reserves with luxury accommodation and limited capacity, for example.

They are class fractions, therefore, which can take holidays in environments which, by virtue of price, are exclusive. For shorthand, we shall refer to this group as ecotourists, older and professionally successful tourists or as Wood refers to them, the 'cream of Manhattan and the City'. 'Ecotourist' has a double meaning, however, for not only does it signal an interest and focus of this type of tourist on the 'environment' (*eco*logy), it also indicates the ability to pay the high prices that such holidays command (*eco*nomic capital).

It is not a coincidence that the 'taste' of which Bourdieu speaks is actually translated into culinary metaphors for the holidays aimed at this social class, for luxurious eating is another of this fraction's cultural characteristics. Thomson Holidays' 'Travel à la Carte' urges you to 'choose from the menu or dream up a dish of your own' and Barrett (1989) refers to 'delicatessen' travel agents. It embraces the delicate, discriminating and generally luxurious holidays to an off-the-beaten-track, out-of-the-way place.

And there are apparently no expenses spared on the level of service and culinary provision. As Africa Exclusive, a tour company specialising in East African safaris, put it, 'gastronomy is taken as seriously as zoology'. It carries a level of cultural capital as well.

It is a way of buying into a shared meaning that the environment has an acknowledged value: 'ECO-TOURISM ... It's not in any dictionary yet, but if you want to impress at your next dinner party, it's a dead cert'. So, not only are the new bourgeoisie high on economic capital, they are also high in terms of their ability to accumulate cultural capital.

EGO-TOURISTS

The second important class fraction that Bourdieu identifies, and one that is potentially more important, is the 'new petit bourgeoisie'. This social class is characterised by the increasing numbers working in employment involving 'presentation and representation' such as media and advertising, but it also encompasses a wide range of service jobs (such as the guides working for small tour operators) and the growth in the number of people working for charities, for example.

You may recall that some commentators have emphasised the significance of this social class in interpretation and representation. This not only includes opinion-forming in terms of the latest film to see, clothes to wear or designer alcohol to drink, but also how we should perceive issues such as homelessness or overseas development: in other words, a guide to the things we should be 'into'.

Made reference to this group variously as taste-makers, trend-setters, new cultural intermediaries or cultural brokers, labels which seek to capture the structural significance of such groups in postmodern culture.

Unlike the new bourgeoisie who are high on both economic and cultural capital, however, the new petit bourgeoisie are not so economically well endowed and must seek out cultural capital in order to establish their social class identity. In this way the burden of class differentiation weighs most heavily on this social class who must differentiate themselves from the working classes below (mass packaged tourists) and the high spending bourgeois middle classes above (ecotourists).

Part of the reaction has been for the new petit bourgeoisie to deem themselves unclassifiable, 'excluded', 'dropped out' or perhaps, in popular tourism discourse, 'alternative'; anything other than categorisation and assignment to a class.

And yet, as Bourdieu concludes, the A to Z of their practices, from 'aikido' to 'Zen' (or from alternative tourism to wildlife tourism) exudes classification, being nothing other than, 'An inventory of thinly disguised expressions of a sort of dream of social flying, a desperate effort to defy the gravity of the social field'.

This slide into individualism is an expression of what Smith (1987) refers to as a new ideology founded upon the 'pursuit of difference, diversity and distinction'. Indeed, the pursuit of difference is of critical significance in understanding the expansion of tourism in the Third World. Contradictorily, while the assertion of individualism becomes a frame of action of the new middle classes, it also reaffirms their class status and position. And, as already argued, the struggle and, by inference, exploitation, are 'quasi-inevitable'.

The idea of 'classlessness' or 'individualism' is an indelible mark among these class fractions, resulting, some argue, in the arrival of ego-tourists suggests, 'curriculum vitae builders'. Ego-tourism is more characteristic of less formalised forms of travel, such as backpacking, overland trucking (Truck Africa refer to their customers as 'would be backpackers') or small group travel, which often involve longer holidays overseas, especially in Third World regions.

'Going-round-the-world' or 'taking a year off to travel' has become a latter-day equivalent of the Grand Tour and an important component of the culture of travel. Ego-tourists must search for a style of travel which is both reflective of an 'alternative' lifestyle and which is capable of maintaining and enhancing their cultural capital.

Furthermore, it is a class fraction that attempts to compensate for insufficient economic capital, with an obsessional quest for the authentication of experience.

MacCannell (1976) portrayed the middle classes as systematically scavenging the Earth in search of new experiences and Errington and Gewertz note, 'For travellers, the encounter with what was seen as "primitive" - the exotic, the whole, the fundamentally human - contributed to their own individuality, integration and authenticity' (1989:42).

Stressing the link of ego-tourists to environmental issues, Gordon (1990) associates tourists he observed in Namibia to 'an emergent, urban-based, alienated petit bourgeoisie'.

Ultimately it is a competition for uniqueness with which ego-tourists engage. This is bound with the knowledge, difference and distinction that certain forms of tourism imply - a struggle, so to speak, to stamp the hallmark of individualism in the traveller's passport.

While individualism has always been a key characteristic of bourgeois culture, which regards travel as an 'activity for the stimulation and development of character', the rate at which individualism is sought now has significant consequences and impacts for places, especially in the Third World.

Individualism also underscores why ego-tourists feel they are exempt from the criticism levelled at much Third World tourism. First, as Sherpa Expeditions contends of its customers, 'They are involved and interested in the world around them, and in their turn are interesting people.' And, second, individualism provides the foundation for claiming the moral high ground in the battle over 'what kind of tourism?'

These are people travelling on a shoestring, and as individuals their practices are not harmful to environment or society. Ego-tourists conveniently disaggregate their actions - they are individuals and their actions therefore have no significant impact. In other words, they refuse to acknowledge their part in a larger entity or mass. By contrast, some argue their travels are actually beneficial, supporting local, indigenous businesses, or forging new cultural understandings with Third World communities.

Hutnyk's study of travellers working in Kolkata refers to the 'hegemonic understandings of how those mostly middle-class children of privilege who are able to travel - even, or especially, as "alternative travellers" giving "aid" as people who "care" - see their relation to the ... "Third World"'.

As we shall see below, however, moral claims are by no means sufficient to secure victory in this battle. The new middle classes have adopted strategies to remedy this by, for example, creating jobs and professionalising not just occupations, but consumption practices as well.

In effect, the boundaries between these new middle classes - between ecotourists and ego-tourists - are blurred: they share their ability to make relatively expensive journeys overseas and their willingness to wage hegemonic struggles to define and differentiate their forms of tourism. In this way, tourism has become part of that critical assemblage of goods, practices and experiences that are taken up as social 'bridges and doors', so important in bonding some and excluding others.

A new class of tourist? Tourism cannot be understood as just a means of having some enjoyment and a break from the routine of everyday, an entirely innocent affair where there are some unfortunate, incidental impacts or some fortunate incremental benefits to 'host' communities. To recap, so far we have argued that we need a deeper understanding of tourism to appreciate fully its content and expression and, of course, its potential impact.

There are two principal components to this argument. First, tourism must be understood as a commodity with both a symbolic or sign value and an exchange value. Second, much so-called new tourism is an expression of the new middle classes' hegemonic struggle for cultural and class superiority.

Travel, of course, has always been an expression of taste and a way of establishing class status. But, with the rapid growth in the numbers of people taking holidays, it has never been so widely used as at present. Put simply, the democratisation of tourism has created a social headache when it comes to classes attempting to differentiate themselves from one another.

Two fundamental questions arise from the discussion. How are the sign and exchange values of these travel commodities maintained and enhanced? And how do social classes pursue differentiation and to what effect? In answering the first question, we shall concentrate on three key methods that are used to define and legitimise contemporary tourism: the appeal to intellectualism and professionalism, together with the discourse that has arisen to describe travel today.

In addressing the second question we will identify what we have labelled 'hegemonic spatial struggles' pursued by the new middle classes. Underlying this discussion is the acknowledgement that much new tourism focuses on the Third World.

THE NEW INTELLECTUALS

It has been argued that the new petit bourgeoisie have

sought to intellectualise new areas of activity and expertise (Bourdieu, 1984; Featherstone, 1987). These 'new intellectuals' attempt to ape and popularise intellectual lifestyles and transmit intellectuals' ideas to a wider audience - arguably the ultimate in a cultivated, even scholastic and 'romantic flight from the social world'. Tourism is a particularly important component in this respect.

The 'de-differentiated' characteristic of much contemporary Third World tourism was noted, in which academic prefixes are increasingly apparent. Holidays have moved beyond sheer relaxation towards the opportunity to study and learn, to experience the world through a pseudo-intellectual frame.

With the acknowledgement of tourism as an environmentally, socially and culturally problematic activity among certain fractions of the new middle classes, tourism and tour companies catering for the intellectual demands of these class fractions are of increasing importance in the legitimation of travel.

Thus we find companies such as Academic Travel (part of STA, an ostensibly student-oriented travel agency), Adult Education Study tours (established in 1982), who offer 'special interest travel for thinking people', and Temple World, offering 'exclusive journeys into wildlife, archaeology, natural history and ecology', whose guest leaders are academics such as the geographer, Andrew Goudie.

Moreover, the intellectualisation of travel has been enhanced by interlinkage between academia and tour companies. It is convenient for companies such as Himalayan Kingdoms (1992-3) to prioritise places on their Bhutan visit (a country that has imposed severe restrictions on the number of tourists admitted each year) to Fellows of the Royal Geographical Society, and for Temple World to run a series of 'Royal Geographical Society African Tours'.

At the height of what we might term 'intellectual mimicry', the travel operator Voyages Jules Verne offers tour leaflets (or information sheets) that are indistinguishable from weekend broadsheet newspaper supplements and are appropriately entitled *Travel Reviews*. Intellectual legitimation is sought in this instance by interspersing descriptions of holidays and itineraries with other considered features: 'Islam', 'The Turkish Inner Man' and the 'Shepherds of Shanghai', for example.

Among the younger new petit bourgeois tourists, with less economic capital, intellectualisation is sought in other ways. Most frequently this involves the claim of cultural superiority, of true and real contact with indigenous peoples, pursued through organised tours, such as 'overlanding', or 'individual' travel informed by travel guides such as the *Rough Guide* or *Lonely Planet Guide* series.

As Guerba put it, this means more than 'scratch[ing] the surface', it requires getting participants 'personally involved in the country, its people and its wildlife'. In addition, as noted earlier, longer periods of travel overseas have in themselves evoked the spirit of intellectualism and are increasingly referred to as sabbaticals among the new middle classes. But intellectualising is insufficient in itself, and has necessitated the use of other forms of classification and legitimation.

TRAVEL PROFESSIONALS

In the context of socio-economic and cultural change discussed earlier coupled with the associated growth of the new middle classes, there have been two notable processes at work. First, professions have become relatively more open following the educational 'revolution' of the 1960s, and the aura (medicine, law, the City and so on) with which they had been traditionally conceived has, at least in part, been dismantled.

Second, however, with still relatively limited access to the established professions, the new middle classes have been busy legitimising new licences and certificates: a classic process of establishing new professions (with professional education and qualification periods, codes of ethics and accrediting bodies or institutes), or professionalisation as Bourdieu notes (1984).

This dual process may indicate that the infallibility of professional distinction is beginning to falter and surprisingly little analytical consideration appears to have been focused on a logical extension (or migration) of the struggle for distinction through professionalisation, into consumption practices.

Professionalism is a key characteristic assigned to company tour leaders, who in many cases are introduced personally: 'dedicated professionalism' as one brochure says indicating that a tour manager not only has a 'deep love of and insight into the areas visited', but also has 'academic credentials and expertise in a specialised field'.

This citation of 'experience' and academic qualifications is commonplace. The following pages cite and quote many tour company brochures dating from 1992 to 2000. In many cases the quoted passages are repeated from year to year.

In tour companies specialising in overland trucking and travelling for ego-tourists, this also means that tour leaders are 'experienced international travellers in their own right'. At Journey Latin America even the reservation staff are 'South American experts' and have 'travelled extensively in Latin America'; the tour leaders are all graduates (some in Latin American Studies), a portfolio similar to Trailfinders. Tour leaders in these companies also embody, and are ambassadors of, new middle-class lifestyles, testify.

In addition, the spirit of professional dedication is also widely cited, where work in this part of the tourism industry is more akin to a vocation. Encounter Overland refer to their trips as 'projects' and talk of their leaders in glowing terms: 'ordinary men and women - often previous trip members - who have elected to put promising careers on hold and devote half a dozen years or more to what they like doing best'.

And, of course, with greater flexibility in the service sector a higher proportion of new middle-class employees are able to take longer periods off between jobs or contracts, or are able to negotiate relatively long periods of absence. All in all a more dedicated, professional, and avaricious tourist class has emerged.

The point we anticipated earlier is that 'travelling' has emerged as an important informal qualification, with the number and range of stamps in a passport acting, so to speak, as a professional certificate; a record of achievement and experience. Not only is travel a professional pre-requisite for employment in parts of the tourism industry, but it is an important attribute in many new professions, such as overseas development work; it has become a rite of passage into certain occupations.

There are also indications that professionals working in other disciplines have begun to diversify into travel. Many of the occasional tour leaders, for instance, are professionals in other fields.

For example, the two directors of Papyrus Tours, a company established in 1984 with an aim to provide tours to East Africa, who were supportive of conservation efforts are also a senior officer in a large local authority and a self-employed professional landscape architect, respectively.

Of course, we should also note that Third World tourism has created a huge range of job opportunities for the new middle classes in the First World. It is not just operators in the industry but consultants, journalists, tourism commentators, academics and charities focusing on tourism issues; take The International Ecotourism Society (TIES), for example, whose founder and president, Megan Epler Wood, explains that: 'It was decided that The Ecotourism Society should be an organisation for professionals.

It was clear in 1991 that a broad array of professionals from a variety of disciplines was needed to make ecotourism a genuine tool for conservation and sustainable development'. And more recently, TIES website describes the organisation as 'Representing a worldwide network of 1,700 members from 55 professions and 65 countries ... We'd like to invite you to the growing ranks of ecotourism professionals who are working with TIES'.

It is these professionals who are the opinion formers, the teachers, the advisers, even the ones who take decisions, and a number of publications have sought to prescribe 'technical information on how to do ecotourism "right"'. But the degree to which these 'benevolent' organisations are somehow value free is questionable. It is clear who these professionals are: in the TIES's case, middle-class Americans, many of whom represent other powerful NGO interests (WWF, Conservation International, IUCN and so on - see listing of board of directors and advisers). We must ask what vision of the world they are pursuing and the degree to which such visions are imposed from the First World on the Third World, a question considered in the context of the activities of these organisations.

The commencement of professionalisation processes in consumption is also detectable. As noted earlier, consumption has become more skilled. First, there are clear signals that the distinctions between occupational professionalism, and consumption and leisure, are beginning to blur. Illustrative of this is the growth of outdoor management and 'team' building exercises, especially popular among the new middle classes.

High Places, for example, which offer mountain holidays in a number of Third World countries, also offer 'another type of HOLIDAY! ... training programmes for people at work in industry, commerce and the public sector'. This is an operation appropriately called 'HIGH PROFILE', an experience for people like 'YOU, the sort of people who come on our holidays', described elsewhere as 'intelligent and discerning people who wish to retain a taste of independent travel'.

Second, and more significant, tourists themselves are attempting to professionalise travel, a process encouraged, it would appear, by tour operators and environmental organisations. While the emergence of a formal travel qualification, such as the need to support an application for a Himalayan Kingdom expedition 'with your climbing CV', remains the exception rather than the rule for the time being, the number of tourist codes addressing the ethics and conduct of travel have exploded.

A tourist 'Code of Conduct' established by the ECTWT, has been reproduced in many places, especially by the network of organisations concerned with the effects of tourism, but also, for example, among travel agency associations and tour operators who have formulated their own versions. Area-specific codes with emphasis on ecological and cultural issues such as the 'Himalayan Tourist Code' formulated by Tourism Concern (in the UK) have also appeared.

Organisations such as these have attracted increasing support from members of the new middle classes and from new independent tour operators like High Places, which reproduces the Himalayan Code in full and which claims to strive to 'adhere to the ethics' of Tourism Concern. It is the emergence of an ethical, if not professional, approach to tourism reminiscent of Kutay's observed 'Peace Corps-type travellers looking for a more meaningful vacation'.

These codes of ethics form the backbone of a hegemony of travel (or ecotravel as it is now known in North America), which is advanced by the new middle classes, the small independent tour operators and the vanguard of this hegemony, tourism organisations.

Together they begin to represent a new tourism social movement with organisations such as Tourism Concern, the Campaign for Environmentally Responsible Tourism (CERT) and the US-based International Ecotourism Society, emerging as symbolic 'institutes of travel'.

These institutes now provide ethical yardsticks against which the activities of operators and tourists can be measured and classified. With an overwhelming concern for environmental ethics (such as the US National Audubon Society's 'Travel Ethic for Environmentally Responsible

Travel'), it is in the ecological and indigenous heartlands of the Third World that these hegemonic struggles are most readily detected and played out.

THE DISCOURSE OF 'NEW WAVE TOURISM'

'Out goes the "'ere we go, 'ere we go" Spanish Costa-style, in comes a more thoughtful middle class approach'. This was how Frank Barrett of the *Independent* newspaper, the UK's champion of new middle-class values, describes the shift to 'new wave tourism'. There can be little disputing that the attributes and qualities of the supposedly more alternative, individualised and sensitive forms of travel are generally unspoken but appear to be deep within the new middle-class psyche.

As The Travel Alternative, a specialist company offering craft and textile holidays, comments: 'On a recent tour a passenger said "You can either be a tourist or a traveller." We would like to think that our tours allow everyone the opportunity to be travellers'.

Of course, it is not only through the classificatory distinction between tourist and traveller that differentiation is pursued via discourse. But it is illustrative of the battle being waged to put into words exactly what kind of holidaymaker we are and what we stand for; and, conversely, state exactly what we are not for; as Barrett argues, 'tourist' is the 'worst kind of insult'.

Some observers have momentarily reflected on the highbrow nature of traveller and the intellectual snobbishness within which the whole debate is framed, and have attempted to rescue 'tourist' from middle-class derision. Tourist has become prefixed by benevolent adjectives such as the 'The Good Tourist' or 'The Reluctant Tourist', title to a series run by the UK broadsheet *Independent* which culminated in *The Reluctant Tourist's Handbook*. There are also references to ethical tourists, alternative tourists and so on.

Arguably though, this is further confirmation that contemporary tourism is charged with the classificatory struggles in and between class fractions. As Culler observes: 'Once one recognises that wanting to be less touristy than other tourists is part of being a tourist, one can recognise the superficiality of most discussions of tourism, especially those that stress the superficiality of tourists'.

By contrast, the term 'traveller' assumes that it is no longer a process of tourism with which the individual is engaged, but a considerably more de-differentiated, esoteric and individualised form of activity; travel is to tourism, as individual is to class. It is a strategy for seeking differentiation or a 'paper-chase aimed at ensuring constant distinctive gaps'.

Most importantly, the discourse adopted by these class fractions is a further reminder that consideration of the way in which power is expressed and imposed must lie at the heart of the analysis of tourism.

Many small tour companies and individual travellers have attempted to maximise the distinction. As already argued, the practices of travellers are perhaps best conceived as part of the 'cult of individualism', though it is deeply ironic that they are largely indistinguishable from each other by virtue of their discourse, dress codes and the informal 'packages' they follow through travel guides.

Whole regions have become travel circuits (in popular travel discourse 'doing' South-East Asia, Central America and so on). Errington and Gewertz (1989) reproduce excerpts from a Papua New Guinea guest house visitor book to illustrate the fundamental traveller distinction, with two US travellers advising: 'Explain difference between tourist and traveller ... Be a traveller, not a tourist. It makes a big difference'. Travellers, therefore, attempt to create their own aura, while attempting to prevent the encroachment of 'tourists' in their quest for authentication:

Momentarily alone in one of the wildest places on earth, you feel exhilarated, exhausted and scared. Unfortunately the feeling is unlikely to last more than a few moments. If you are lucky, all that will happen is another traveller will appear on the ridge to exchange pleasantries and wonderment. If you are unlucky ... your reverie will be interrupted by half a dozen Londoners swearing and shouting.

Mass tourism and tourists have also become the target of independent tour operators. Intellectualism oozes through, with package tourists 'invading' backpackers' discoveries and the celebration of areas where the invasion has been forestalled: at the height of aestheticisation, Cambodia is lucky for its 'fascinating culture bruised by war' and even luckier with a culture 'unscathed by tourism'. Companies refer to the 'anonymity and inflexibility' (J. & C. Voyageurs), of 'run of the mill', 'conventional' (Explore) and 'impersonalised' (Africa Exclusive) mass packaged tours, and celebrate their demise (Magic of the Orient). Ultimately, it is an appeal to the idea that travel is 'individual enough to be a sustainable alternative to the juggernaut of mass tourism' (Explore).

In its place, and by contrast, we have the emergence of Zimbabwe, where 'nothing is packaged' (Africa Exclusive), and the 'Unpackaged Caribbean' (Kestours). For luxury tour operators and their new bourgeois clientele (ecotourists) exclusiveness is sufficient enough a distinction, with Cox and Kings taking 'a select few to Africa', and operators speaking of 'a small and select clientele' (Abercrombie & Kent) and 'limited edition holidays' (EcoSafari).

For tour operators catering more for the young and adventurous ego-tourists where economic capital is clearly insufficient to confer taste, it is the invidious distinction of participant travellers from tourists that has become critical. It advances the distinctions beyond a mere reference (or 'charge') to packaging and instead focuses on the qualities and practices of travel and contrasts these to tourism.

This is particularly notable of overlanding operators such as Dragoman specialising in trucking for young travellers, a world 'shunned by the masses who prefer the resorts and beaches', or, as Explore put it, travel for 'people who want more out of their holiday than buckets of cheap wine and a suntan', a stereotype also used by Exodus Adventure. In similar vein Journey Latin America contrast their ('Small Group Escorted Tours') participants to those who prefer 'two weeks in Torremolinos' and where preference is for a 'cold beer after a three hour walk in the jungle, not nightly booze-ups'. As Tours to Remember warn, if you are looking for 'two weeks in the eastern equivalent of Benidorm', look elsewhere.

Logically, tour companies also promise 'tourist-free' zones (Naturetrek), 'few lager and litter louts' (Cara Spencer) and avoidance of 'Tourist haunts' (High Places). In a more positive sense, Encounter Overland celebrates the traveller-cum-wayfarer: 'today's custodian of the ancient relationship between traveller and native which throughout the world has been the historic basis of peaceful contact'.

So what of the qualities and practices that are claimed to constitute the distinction and embody the traveller? The simple listing of adjectives applied to travellers in travel brochures begins to map the key coordinates. By implication, if not explicitly as noted above, the counter-distinctions constitute tourists. If, for any reason, the citation of these *qualities* proves insufficient, however, there are other pre-requisites which help define travellers.

High Places tours of India, for example, demand 'patience, stamina, humour and adaptability', and Journey Latin America cite 'essential qualifications for all trips' as 'emotional balance, maturity, a spirit of adventure, and a desire for good companionship'.

There are two other notable features of travelling and travellers. First, with an overwhelming emphasis on a mixture of often physical activities, especially among ego-tourists, bodily fitness is important.

High Places offers the symbolically new middle-class holiday: mountain biking. Second, and most important, there is need for the fellowship of other like-minded travellers, whether it be small intimate group tours (with generally between six and twenty participants) or individual backpackers meeting at predestined travel guide-recommended hotels, restaurants or sites. In both cases, albeit in rather different ways, the emphasis is on participation, on 'action and involvement' (High Places) and, ultimately, on accomplishment (a recurrent theme in tour brochures).

It is not that travellers are unreflective; just the opposite, as Hutnyk observes of back-packers in Kolkata (India) where a 'popular alternative critique of travel' emerges from their reflections, and manifests itself in:

- The search for 'authentic' experiences; b) dismay at the effect of tourism; and c) condemnation of other tourists and sometimes themselves. The correlates of these three moments are a) claims to the 'once-in-a-lifetime' experience; b) nostalgia for the days when such and such-a-place was not so well known; and c) 'of course I'm doing it differently' stories.

As Hutnyk (1996) concludes, not only is there an intense struggle in classifying and legitimising this notional traveller-tourist distinction, but ego-tourists vie among themselves over what actually constitutes a traveller in the first place. Borzello considers that 'Truck travellers are not travellers but a very peculiar sort of tourist.' And it is an intense classificatory struggle that has pronounced spatial reflections, a point to which we turn below.

TALES OF THE UNEXPECTED

Both explorers and dragomen journeyed through far-flung lands in search of long-forgotten civilisations and empires. They explored hostile deserts to find nomadic tribes and ancient cities. They went in search of legendary mountains deep in the heart of jungles and brought back stories of fabulous wildlife.

These fabulous stories or 'travellers' tales' have a deep history. There are noted discussions and a resurgence of interest in ethnographic travelogues and travel writings. But debates around the contemporary nature of tales, myths, or rumour-mongering and 'traveller lore', have remained sketchy. This is of particular significance for, as Massey argues, tales are a culmination of the ongoing process of travel which fill out our geographical imaginations, and that story-telling is the archetypal 'traveller's medium'; 'rumour-mongering is the architect. Rumour is the stuff of the social'. Travellers' tales are a modern (or perhaps postmodern) continuation of the stories of colonial encounters.

They are a useful way of demonstrating how discourse is used to represent or recreate a reality and impose meaning, in much the same way as the fantastic tales retold by colonialists in the nineteenth century. As Hutnyk shows, 'word of mouth, the say-so of a friend of a friend, and rumour and gossip, operate to orientate and produce experience for travellers. This discourse must be read as a text'. In this way discourse can be conceived as part of that everyday hegemony.

Latter-day travellers' tales are a powerful way of sustaining the aura and mystique of the Third World (reminiscent of Said's *Orientalism*) and in turn sustaining the value of travel as a commodity. Their construction is often complex and draws upon a range of images and representations, including film, travel writing and colonial explorations.

Tales also have an important part to play in the reproduction of social class. It has already been suggested that tales have an important symbolic currency as a form of cultural capital; the example used suggested that travelling on a 'shoestring' simultaneously denies the existence and need for substantial lumps of economic capital and confers status, uniqueness, worldliness and resourcefulness.

As Calder records of travelling in rebel-held Nicaraguan territory, by the time you reached the 'safety' of neighbouring Costa Rica 'all that backpacking bravado returns and you have a couple of cracking stories with which to trump fellow travellers' tales'. Travel and the construction of tales, therefore, represent an informal credentialism.

The construction of tales is also intimately bound with

the quest for authenticity. It is a way of creating an aura in an effort to remove this experience from the tourist's world. These are feelings that cannot be 'snapped'. Take this example from High Places:

The trip begins with a short drive from Nairobi down into the Great Rift Valley, to our camp set among the trees, overlooking grassy plains where zebra and giraffe graze. The only sound is the breeze and a kettle boiling on the stove. Time to relax as the trip unfolds ... Walking through the Loita Hills, in Maasai territory, following little-used trails and using local warriors as guides ... watching a majestic herd of elephants cross the Mara plains, or a cheetah stalk its prey; sitting round the fire, swapping stories with Maasai warriors; relaxing, as the sunset turns the empty plains red.

Of all modes of travel, it is trekking in areas of solitude that most gives rise to a romantic gaze and the construction of tales almost spiritual in their content. The phenomenal growth of trekking in South-East Asia, Latin America and Africa underlines its importance in new middle-class travel. It is the authenticity of this form of alternative tourism that lies at the heart of trekking, and the accumulation of tales relies upon authenticity to verify its uniqueness and currency: as High Places promote, 'Our trips are unpretentious, authentic and adventurous', and Trailfinders contrast 'staged tourist "shows"' with the experience of 'untouched' and 'traditional' villages in the highlands of Thailand.

In this case authenticity is expressed in a somewhat different manner, conveyed through an emotional response that is either unique or intensely difficult to achieve. It is an exclusionary experience, that even if the struggle to dominate and control a spatially discrete area is lost, tourists are still unable to share the aura. Frank McCready (Sherpa Expeditions Managing Director) comments on the realisation of dreams: 'When the ordinary person reaches a place like Annapurna Base Camp it changes their whole view of life ... Some of the places we take people are so fantastic I've seen grown men entirely overcome with emotion.' It is this experience of exhilaration and exhaustion that culminates in the eulogising of trekking. Himalayan Kingdoms comments: 'The blend of grandeur and timelessness defeats all superlatives and such a place should be visited at least once every lifetime'.

To return briefly to the theme of aestheticisation: in order to legitimise and authenticate the travel experience, tales must be aestheticised in two important respects. In the first place, there is the dual requirement to make trips both purposeful and distinguishable from those of the average tourist or, indeed, traveller.

Travel is purposeful, tourism is not. For example, one travel writer notes of a visit to Nepal, 'We had tea and increasingly battered chocolate to deliver to a friend of a friend working in a health clinic there'. Sabbaticals, 'research' work, the presence of friends, colleagues and relatives, the emergence of work brigades and the visits promoted by overseas development charities - a range of work - and activity-centred holidays, are all used by the new middle classes to signal that *this is more than just a holiday*.

It must be sufficient in distancing itself from supposedly inactive or inert forms of tourism. Exodus ('Overland Newsletter', summer 1994, 'What the customers say' section) notes, 'I think that was the best trip I've ever done, partly because of, rather than despite the difficulties and challenges we faced.'

Second, there has always been a nagging inadequacy around the assertions that 'one cannot sell poverty, but one can sell paradise'. The quest for authenticity, like travel itself, has had to seek out new experiences. No longer can it rest upon the cultural preservation and discovery of highland tribes and deep forest natives.

It has migrated to the quest for danger and risk and the emergence of contemporary travelogues and diaries: '"I'm keeping a journal; maybe I can make it into a book," says one traveller to me as we sit in a bar in a small village'.

Tales legitimise travel by sensationalising it, making it

appear daring and risky, while at the same time peripheralising danger. Of Vang Tau (Vietnam) the *STA Travel Guide* notes: 'a two hour boat ride from Ho Chi Minh City and a million miles away from conflict'. Similarly, Encounter Overland's philosophy remains: 'With true adventure there is always an element of chance and of risk. This fact is not regrettable. It is often the fact upon which the best travel experiences are based.' Suffering can often enrich the travel experience, as extracts of Morrison's *Tales of the Unexpected* suggest:

A glass of fiery rice liquor was thrust into my hands, and I sat down with them and joined in their infectious laughter, without a single word of common language between us ... Seven years on I'm none the wiser about the purpose or origins of that strange harvest festival in northern Thailand ... As it was I could find no mention of the festival or town in anything I read, which probably accounted for the fact that I was the only westerner on the scene.

But it wasn't this smug one-upmanship that made it so special, but rather the very act of discovery. For one impetuous moment I dared to stray from the charted territory ... and it was bliss ... To me, surprise is the primary reason to travel. All those other time-worn clichés about broadening the mind and stimulating an appreciation of the world are merely justifications, not motivations ... Think about those special moments from your last few trips, the ones that you bore your friends rigid with at parties.

Are they accurate reports of the splendour of the temples or the excellent cuisine? I hope not. No, it's those unexpected events when your plans are interrupted by that out-of-the-blue experience ... To my mind, if there's one thing worse than a holiday that fails to meet your expectations it's one that *does* ... And let's be brutally honest here, if in the second week of your big adventure you haven't had at least one near-death experience you're going to want your money back. Right? ... do we really want a boil-in-the-bag cultural experience? No we bloody well don't - we want an unpolished, unbleached wholegrain adventure with bits of stone and finger-nail in the bottom!!!

Most invidious, however, is to utilise tales to aestheticise risk and boost the cultural capital accumulated in travel. As suggested earlier, while the hazards of travelling in particular regions may act as a warning, it simultaneously signals the degree of legitimacy or coolness to be attributed to particular destinations.

As Gordon-Walker notes of Peru, 'travellers who are disappointed not to have captured a Sendero Luminoso flag raise their spirits ... and swap stories about friends of friends who have been robbed'. Similar experiences were recounted by Warde and in 'Weekending in El Salvador'.

Travelling in potentially dangerous regions, being hoisted from a bus and frisked at midnight or braving certain urban areas are experiences to be enjoyed and admired by other travellers. Risk titillates, even eroticises, adventures in the Third World. And it is this genre of tale-telling that has come to the fore in discussion among fellow ego-tourists, in travel guides and reviews and within television coverage. In short, it is now widely adopted discourse focused toward social differentiation and the insurance, or hope, that certain places will stay unexplored by other groups of tourists.

THE SCRAMBLE FOR THIRD WORLD DESTINATIONS

We have argued that a pseudo-ethical and moral infrastructure underpins the growth of Third World tourism (Lea, 1993), with new middle-class tourists (or travellers) contrasting their morally justifiable means of travel with the morally reprehensible practices of tourists.

There is a temptation to conclude from this, as Gordon-Walker does, that you 'cannot help suspecting that the campaign for "sustainable tourism" is little more than a rationalised desire to keep the Third World a cheap place to visit' (1993:19).

But such a conclusion would result in underselling the

importance of how First World tourists impose their desires on Third World destinations.

If the new middle classes are forced to wage this hegemonic classificatory struggle founded on taste, then it might be reasonable to expect that such struggles will also be reflected spatially. So at the very heart of this campaign lies, not just the preservation of a nice cheap place to visit, but the playing out of the battle of social class differentiation.

The professionalisation and intellectualisation of travel, together with its associated discourse, have been insufficient in themselves to ensure social differentiation and, more importantly, the creation of physical distance between mass tourists and travellers.

The new middle-classes must adopt strategies of exclusion, to seek and protect the new travel commodities. Extracts from veteran correspondent Martha Gellhorn's piece, 'Too good for tourists', illustrate the process by which this is achieved. It is an attempt to persuade and to impose the idea that this First World view is correct:

The airport terminal at Belize City is very encouraging. It is an overgrown shack ... After each passport has been examined as if passports were new-fangled inventions, you enter a square, wooden room where the baggage has been dumped in the middle of the floor. A free-for-all follows ... My heart rose like a lark. This is how it used to be before the Caribbean was homogenised by tourism. Tourism, even ... minor, modest tourism, corrupts. I cannot exaggerate the pure physical pleasure of underpopulation and empty space ... Half a century ago I thought this ghastliness of packed humanity was the peculiar doom of China: now much of the world I knew and loved is ruined because there are too many of us and we move everywhere. For my taste, Belize is ideal.

A young American in the shortest possible frayed shorts was questioning the American Rum Point owners about the effects of tourism on the population and the environment, his thesis for the University of California at Berkeley. We agreed that tourism is a destroyer and Belize is far too good for it. None of the inn owners I had met, English, French, American, Belizean, Irish, want to expand, though, between them, they could take care of less than a hundred perceptive guests. They love the country as it is. How much better if oil is found in viable quantities in the north, and tourists go somewhere else. It is astonishing at my age to stumble on a new country. I feel astonished.

As some authors contend, the near-absence of other tourists to which Gellhorn alludes is most efficiently achieved by the consumption of 'positional' goods (Hirsch, 1976), with dominant class fractions attempting to impose scarcity (Featherstone, 1987; Leiss, 1983). At the simplest level this involves claiming certain areas 'receive very few tourists' (Detours, 1992), are 'tourist free' (such as national parks visited by Naturetrek), or that even whole countries are for the 'traveller rather than the tourist', as Meon describes Ecuador (1992).

But this amounts to little more than marketing, and alternative strategies and claims must be pursued, such as active searches for 'off-the-beaten-track' (or, as Asian Affairs claims 'even further off-the-beaten-track') and 'lesser visited areas', areas 'rarely visited' (Himalayan Kingdom) or just 'secrets' (Okavango Tours and Safaris). Exclusiveness, uniqueness, romanticism and relative solitude are central to the philosophy of these tour operators.

This philosophy both embodies the contradictions in contemporary travel to the Third World and reveals the protracted and increasing difficulties which companies and travellers have in spatially defining separated practices from other like-minded travellers.

As tourism spreads to more and more destinations in the Third World, the distinction of a mass packaged tourist from the individual character of travel is spurious. Ego-tourists crowd into cheap guesthouses, basic bus stations and out-of-the-way beach resorts, while ecotourists crowd into game reserves and national parks. So how far is travel little more than a figment of wishful middle-class thinking? It is worth considering the views of Budi (aged 28), an Indonesian guide from Bali, interviewed by Tourism Concern's Sue Wheat:

Q. Do you think there is a difference between a 'tourist' and a 'traveller?'

A. The traveller thinks they know everything about the local people and the country. But it's usually because some other traveller told them before. But they do whatever they like - some travellers are good, but 90 per cent are not, they can be very impolite. With the tourist, everything is organised, so they don't destroy as much.

The traveller wants to see something new, and wants it to be cheap and then tells others about it. I prefer tourists ... they go to specific places, it is more professional. But the traveller is uncontrolled - they won't go to the places already prepared for them; they want to go to other places and then they spoil it - and don't spend any money! Travellers always talk the same and say: 'Don't go to Kuta because it's spoiled.' Then they go to a new place.

The example of the island of Bali is taken further, which alludes to this blurring of tourist distinctions, and with an examination of the effects of tourism policy on the island.

It is a context, therefore, within which new tourism must not only do battle with mass tourism and tourists, but contend within itself both spatially and qualitatively for the most virtuous practice. This is particularly notable in safaris. For example, Papyrus Tours ensure that they spare you 'any involvement in safari bus "rat runs"', referred to by Africa Exclusive as the 'herds of landrovers that ... plague some other parts of Africa' (but which do not afflict, of course, this tour operator's safaris in Zimbabwe).

Even vehicles themselves are a point of differentiation among safari operators and overland trucking companies, with Into Africa claiming that 'landrovers do less damage' than larger trucks and are more sensitive to both wildlife and local people.

Similarly, trekkers face increasing difficulties in spatially legitimating their experiences, as Edwards's (1992) lamentations have already indicated. With the sharp increase of trekking in northern Thailand, for example, it is more difficult to find a trek which visits 'untouched' or 'traditional' villages, we are warned by Trail-finders, a company with which it is possible to visit 'more remote villages less exposed to western influences', where 'Groups are welcomed as a refreshing diversion to normal

Tourism is no recent phenomenon on the Indonesian island of Bali. Colonised by the Dutch, the Balinese held on to a unique blend of Hindu, Buddhist and animist religions that imbued their cultural and social life. Tales of this exotic society living in tune with art and nature attracted foreigners as long as a century ago, and since independence, Bali has been the jewel in the crown of government tourism policy, hosting ever larger numbers of visitors.

Contemporary tourists to Bali display a wide mixture of motivations. The island accommodates seriously wealthy hedonists and conventional package tourists (many on long-haul stopovers or multi-centre holidays), alongside large numbers of young Australians who arrive on charter flights and regard the island as a cheap and cheerful holiday spot and a surfing mecca. There is a huge pool of homestays and guesthouses, known locally as *losmens*, catering for this budget market.

Bali's enduring image as a cultural paradise still draws independent travellers who also patronise the *losmens*, and it features frequently in the brochures of companies appealing to the new tourist as a land where it is possible to get off the beaten track while never straying far from creature comforts: 'the industry has been controlled so that hotels are primarily located in the southern peninsula, leaving the rest of the island essentially unchanged and uniquely Balinese'.

The village of Kuta, close to Bali's international airport, has been a favourite haunt of budget tourists since the 1970s, when its residents woke up to the lucrative possibilities of turning their homes into *losmens* and offering other services from bike hire and restaurants to massages on the huge crescent-shaped beach, which soon became a haven for novice surfers.

Losmens began appearing in nearby Sanur, and on the north and west coasts too - for example at Lovina Beach patronised by the backpacking fraternity as a restful retreat from an overdose of culture or socialising in southern Bali: 'It's a good place to meet other travellers, and there's quite an active social scene' (Wheeler and Lyon, 1994).

The inland village of Ubud, renowned for its artists and lush beauty, has also grown rapidly. From a scattering of *losmens*, restaurants and artists' studios attracting backpackers and longstay visitors, Ubud has mushroomed into the alternative inland base for anyone not locked into a standard beach hotel package deal. Nowadays, new tourists wishing to escape the mass market experience still favour Ubud, but may well avoid the commercialised southern coastal resorts, opting instead for accommodation in less developed spots.

However, if the entrepreneurs of outposts such as Candidasa and Lovina Beach are counting on increased custom from this source, they may be disappointed. Like the first visitors to the island, new tourists are specifically interested in Bali's unique harmony of culture and landscape and they still tend to visit the prime sites on every tourist's itinerary.

As many commentators have remarked, Bali's cultural life has so far been remarkably resilient. But as tourist sites become increasingly crowded and as its distinctive art forms become increasingly commercialised, new tourists may well decide not to bother with Bali at all, taking up instead the Indonesian Tourist Board's invitation to explore the rest of the republic's giant archipelago and leaving this particular 'paradise' to the surfers and conventional package tourists.

This analysis of Bali's tourism industry was prepared

especially for this book by Alison Stancliffe before the October 2002 bombing of Kuta in Bali. We believe that the effects of the bombing will be felt largely in the short term and the long-term analysis made here will continue to be relevant.

village life.' At possibly its most advanced, spatial legitimation involves promises of carefully researched itineraries which avoid the 'overcrowded trek routes, often exploring untravelled or Restricted Areas, or visiting cultural festivals unknown to most westerners'. Ultimately, legitimation for this company is sought through the pages of the *Geographical Magazine* with the co-director writing of their trek to Mustang:

An understanding and appreciation of both cultural values and ecological balance is essential when visiting such remote and unspoilt regions. This expedition was the first in a series which it is hoped will help turn the tide of 'tourist pollution' to remote areas of the world.

This form of tourism therefore means the need to ensure the absence of other tourists. Some areas are considered especially attractive by virtue of the exclusionary nature of state policies which limit the number of tourists, and the political scientist, Linda Richter, identifies a key issue in tourism planning as *class versus mass tourism.*

The small, land-locked, Himalayan mountain kingdom of Bhutan, to the north of India, is undoubtedly the most unequivocal example of this phenomenon. Bhutan has chosen to concentrate its tourism on high-spending, 'classy' tourists. The country allowed entry to its first tourists in 1974, but only at the rate of 1,000 per year. The rate has increased in recent years so that up to 5,000 may now enter per year, although in 1988 the government closed some monasteries to foreigners because of 'growing materialism' among monks who accepted trinkets such as sweets and pencils together with money from visitors.

A glance through several of the trekking brochures shows that Bhutan is an expensive destination as a result of the weekly charge levied on all foreign tourists. This restrictive entry has been utilised by some 'alternative' travel companies to demonstrate the exclusivity of their holiday destinations (Naturetrek; Himalayan Kingdoms; Coromandel). In 1986, a study made by the WTO/OMT praised the Bhutanese system. WTO/OMT planner, Edward Inskeep, agreed that 'selection' can be achieved: 'the limited tourism approach can be applied, through selective marketing techniques, to attract tourists from any socio-economic groups who respect and do not abuse the local environment and culture' (Inskeep, 1987).

Trekking companies thus enter an intense competition for the most authentic locations, and that means destinations with the least tourists and, by implication, the most difficult to enter. Take the following sample of statements from the UK-based Himalayan Kingdoms, for example:

As yet undiscovered by mass tourism, our 'Hindu Kush Trail' provides an unspoilt route to the base of Tirich Mir.

Special permission is needed to enter Chitral ... so already there will be a noticeable lack of tourists. This is a trek with plenty of time to interact with local people ... The inhabitants have rarely seen Europeans and are friendly and hospitable. [We] will not see human habitation for two weeks.

In March 1992 the first trekkers were allowed access to the former Kingdom of Lo, and it is now the Government of Nepal's policy to restrict numbers ... Our first trek ... came back with wildly enthusiastic descriptions. Our own expedition to Ramdung ... was the first British group to gain entry for twelve years . [Tibet] has always been a difficult country to enter. This is little frequented by western trekkers. ... but few follow the routes we use ....

But it is with environmental conservation that tour companies and tourists have discovered perhaps the most effective method of exclusion, or 'inclusiveness'. Many tour companies are now supportive of conservation measures and cite membership of both global (WWF, CARE, FOE and so on) and the more localised (such as Elefriends and

Mountain Gorilla Project) environmental organisations. Such projects are essential to both ecotourists and ego-tourists in restricting the number of visitors to such areas and in so doing securing some form of exclusiveness, however circumscribed in practice.

Beyond this, some companies have actively pursued conservation policy. Examples are Papyrus Tours, where the director is a founding trustee of the Kenya Wildlife Trust (a UK-based trust seeking to support conservation initiatives in Kenya), or Worldwide Journeys and Expeditions (1992), which claims management involvement in the only formerly privately managed national park in Africa, Kasanka (Zambia). Similarly, the certificated purchase of an acre of rainforest has also been encouraged by multinational environmental organisations such as Programme for Belize and the Nature Conservancy; these areas are often reserved for the consumption of discerning First World ecotourists.

Sustainability has proved the perfect ally of the new middle classes, with the social construction and application of ecological concepts such as carrying capacity proving the ultimate justification for natural exclusiveness.

As already argued, notions of sustainability are hegemonic in their own right and are readily translated spatially. The inflated ranks of academia have been quick to seize upon this, using 'research holidays' to impose their own ethnocentric analysis and recommendations.

Of Thailand, Brockelman and Dearden (the latter a former President of TIES) argue that the number of trekkers be kept relatively low, concluding that 'nature trekking should ... be promoted for special tours and not among general tourists' (1990:146).

The social exclusiveness of their proposals, the class-laden nature of this debate, and the cultural capital that is to be accumulated and invested, are plain to see:

It should be designed for serious naturalists or Nature enthusiasts and others wishing to experience genuine local cultures. Most such persons are reasonably affluent and educated and read a variety of Nature, conservation, and botanical or zoological society publications ... Such clientele is likely to get the most out of the experience, and probably also leave behind the best impressions.

In this chapter we have attempted to show how the contemporary socio-cultural changes outlined are reflected through the growth and popularity of travel in many parts of the Third World.

While the discussion does not imply a determinism that social class lies at the heart of all tourism, it has sought to show that it is an important and frequently overlooked factor in attempts to explain why tourism spreads and seeks out new frontiers.

In this respect, it is a further demonstration of why the boom-to-bust cycles of tourism, which are most frequently used to demonstrate the circulation of destinations, amount to descriptions rather than explanations.

The chapter has argued that a sizeable proportion of new forms of tourism in the Third World can be related directly to the burgeoning new middle classes of the First World. This group is being joined increasingly by new middle-class tourists from the Third World, most particularly from South-East Asia.

This growth was also related to the increased interest in otherness, with a particular concern for ecology and ethnicity, both of which are found in plentiful quantities in the Third World.

In addition, it was argued that central to the swelling ranks of the new middle classes is the necessity to differentiate socially from other social classes. This is most readily achieved through the construction of lifestyles, of which holidays are undeniably an important part.

The chapter explored how both ecotourists and ego-tourists are able to accumulate what has been identified as cultural capital and the strategies - professional, intellectual and discursive - that are employed to ensure that the accumulation of such capital is sustained and enhanced. In particular, we have argued that this provides a rather different understanding of the current debate over sustainability.

This debate can be recast, in part, as the drive towards sustaining the opportunity and ability to consume authenticity and exciting experiences, which simultaneously necessitates the exclusion of other types of tourists. Ultimately, this represents a cultural and social reaction of the new middle classes to the crassness with which they perceive tourism and a craving for social and geographical distance from tourists.

Chapter 5

Selling Tourism

The central governments of nation states together with the global multilateral institutions are the last of the key players in this analysis of tourism. It is governments that have a pivotal role and possess the potential power to control, plan and direct the growth and development of tourism. And it is largely through governments that tourism-related international investments and loans and overseas aid is agreed and channelled. As such, it is widely agreed that for tourism to assist in development, a favourable national policy environment is required.

It has already been argued that tourism has come to represent a considerable attraction to many Third World governments. It has been widely promoted both within the Third World and by First World 'experts' as a means of economic diversification and an important mechanism in producing foreign exchange. There can be little surprise that in Third World countries characterised by indebtedness and by primary industries (such as agriculture and mining) adversely affected by world market prices, tourism has come to represent something of a panacea.

In this chapter we take global governance as a further way of exploring the politics of Third World tourism development. By governance, we mean the web of institutions and agencies that are central players in the political environment, and the focus of our discussion is on national governments, bilateral development agencies and the supranational institutions (such as the World Bank, IMF and United Nations). As already argued, the consideration of politics has been a poor partner in tourism analysis. The assessment of government activity has tended to focus on strategies, policies and programmes of national-level planning. While such analysis is an essential part of assessing the approaches of Third World governments to tourism, it tends to minimise broader consideration of the inherently political nature of tourism development.

In other words, the pressures that governments face from external influences such as lending policies, First World foreign policy or the activities of international NGOs tend to be bypassed; similarly internal forces may also be overlooked. In short, the politics of tourism is another way of exploring unequal and uneven development.

In the first half of this chapter, politics is established as a critical factor in Third World tourism analysis. Most importantly, the need to acknowledge that tourism is not a neutral factor that can be assessed as just another government economic activity is established. Tourism is used for a variety of political purposes and there is a wide range of external influences.

The structural adjusment policies of supranational institutions such as the World Bank and IMF, for instance, are considered along with the policies promoted by the World Trade Organisation (WTO/OMC), World Tourism Organisation (WTO/OMT) and the World Travel and Tourism Council. This provides the opportunity to reflect on the political globalisation outlined and in particular to consider the nature of sustainability promoted by such institutions.

The second half of the chapter uses a number of case studies to illustrate the development of new forms of tourism and the ways in which these are intimately related to sustainability. In particular, we analyse sustainability and sustainable tourism as part of a political discourse. Throughout this chapter, the ways in which politics is reflected through the power jigsaw are considered.

THE POLITICS OF TOURISM

We are constantly reminded by the media of the hazards of travel in the Third World and by implication the critical nature of the politics of tourism. At its most dramatic are the newsworthy events, the killing or kidnapping of western tourists often by political factions eager to further their causes. For these factions, tourism becomes a means to an end: access to the system of global communication.

To First World populations, such events provide a succession of countries - Algeria, Cambodia, Colombia, Egypt, Indonesia, India, Morocco, Peru - which, we are told, are plagued by fundamentalist groupings and where terrorism is rife. The most dramatic of these events was the September 11, 2001 terrorist attacks on the USA.

This event clearly had an immediate impact on the perception of travel security of First World tourists. The international airline and hotel industries were hit hard with the bankruptcies of airline companies of significant size and hotels all over the world reporting dramatic falls in visitors and revenue in September, October and November 2001 over the same period a year before. Lay-offs of workers involved in the tourism industry became commonplace in these same months.

Although this was an incomparable event, evidence from another traumatic event suggests that the effects on international tourism may not be long-lasting. In November 1997, 58 foreign tourists were killed by terrorists at the Temple of Hatshapsut at Luxor in Egypt. Tourism to this part of Egypt, and to most of the rest of the country, dried up overnight. The livelihoods of a majority of the population of the town of Luxor came to an abrupt end.

The effect was also generalised to some extent to other countries in the Middle East. In 1998, international tourist arrivals to Egypt fell by 14 per cent, and tourism receipts by 45 per cent. However, by 1999 international tourist arrivals were back to a level that might have been expected had the yearly rate of increase up to 1997 continued without the terrorist interruption. It is by no means certain that international tourism after September 11, 2001 will recover as rapidly and as thoroughly as it did in Egypt after the 1997 Luxor killings.

But ten months after the attack on the USA, signs of recovery in international flight bookings were already apparent and it seemed appropriate to conclude that perceptions of danger can change very quickly. Then in October 2002, the bombing in Bali occurred and once again it became easier to see the short-term effects of the politics of tourism than to analyse the long-term impacts of such events.

Western government presentations of supposedly dangerous countries have been one of the principal ways in which our geographical imaginations are filled out, and show how tourists and the tourism industry decide where, and where not, to visit and invest; for example, it was suggested that 'dangerous' regions may actually act as a bonus for some adventurous 'new tourists'.

As Richter (1994) demonstrates, the USA has dozens of countries for which *DON'T GO* warnings are provided, of which over 80 per cent are in the Third World. But such warnings, Richter continues, appear to be based as much on ideological reasons as on potential security risks to US tourists. Countries to which the USA is more kindly disposed, such as Israel, Brazil, Mexico and Egypt, appear to require much higher levels of danger to tourists before travel advisories are made against them.

For example, up to 1994, although tourists had been signalled as potential targets for attack by Islamic groups in Egypt, this large-scale receiver of US foreign aid had not been mentioned in State Department advisories. Similarly, despite the seeds of a civil war in southern Mexico, this country too has escaped travel advisories: a reflection, some would argue, of Mexico's 'integration' into NAFTA.

At the other extreme, countries to which the USA considers itself ideologically opposed, such as Cuba and

North Korea, remain off-limits to US tourists. The notion that *tourism is politics* is forcefully expressed by Conrad Hilton (of Hilton Hotels), who is reported as saying 'each of our hotels is a little America' and 'we are doing our bit to spread world peace, and to fight socialism'. Conversely, tourism is used by some Third World governments to gloss over glaring social inequalities and in some cases, as discussed later in this chapter, the systematic abuse of human rights.

Of course, for many Third World countries, political stability is one of the principal keys to securing steady stream of First World tourists. The case of The Gambia shows how profoundly political instability, or just the First World's judgement of such instability, can affect a country's tourism fortunes.

The Gambia experienced a period of economic restructuring with two major IMF-instructed economic reform programmes (1985 Economic Reform Programme and the 1990 Programme for Sustained Development) which attempted to diversify the economy. As Thompson *et al.* report, 'Both programmes emphasise the important role played by tourism in the development process'. Tourism made a substantial contribution to the Gambian economy, estimated to be 12 per cent of GDP by the end of the 1980s and became the principal source of foreign exchange.

In 1994, Captain Yahyah Jammeh seized power in a *coup d'état* and established the Armed Forces Provisional Ruling Council (AFPRC). A failed counter-coup in November 1994 resulted in the British Foreign Office issuing travel advice not to visit The Gambia.

As a result of this advice, air charter arrivals (December to March, the peak of high season) dropped from 45,733 in 1993/4 to 8,363 in 1994/5. There was an estimated 60 per cent reduction in the contribution of restaurants and hotels to the GDP and an estimated direct job loss of around 10,000. The indirect or knock-on effects are estimated at least double this impact. Overall, tourism contracted by 60 per cent and the economy shrank by 6.2 per cent. The Gambian tourism industry all but collapsed. Despite the lifting of the formal travel advice for the 1995/6 season, the Economist Intelligence Unit identified what appeared to be further pressure applied by the British Foreign Office: 'the UK appears determined to maintain pressure for an early return to full democracy and civil freedoms, and this position is likely to influence other trading and aid partners' (Economist Intelligence Unit, 1995:17). 'Tourism, accounting for around 12 per cent of GDP, has yet to pick up after the most recent season, ruined by European governments' advice to their nationals to stay away'.

Teye has argued that the perception of political instability arising from the liberation wars and frequency of *coups d'état* after decolonisation in sub-Saharan Africa has seriously stunted tourism development in some states. The perception of political instability is not the only likely deterrent to new tourists. After Hurricane Mitch hit Honduras, Nicaragua and El Salvador in October 1998, the tourist money on which many Central Americans depended dried up.

In Honduras the effects were so dramatic that in spring 1989 the Honduran Institute of Tourism, in concert with a number of US tour operators and tourism service providers on the country's Caribbean coast, promoted a type of 'disaster tourism', attempting to attract wealthy North Americans to witness the devastation caused by the natural disaster and to assist in the recovery programme.

Clearly, then, it is not only the actual occurrence of political and civil instability that is of critical importance, but rather the way that it is perceived, constructed and represented in the First World.

These are perhaps dramatic examples, but they help to emphasise the inherently political nature of tourism development and the way in which power is transmitted through tourism. Countries promoting tourism (both mass and new) can be influenced by a range of factors, from the decisions of First World institutions and tourists, to the way in which particular Third World destinations are perceived in the First World. Consequently, Third World governments are also eager to control the way in which their tourism image is projected. We must therefore ask whether the messages we receive reflect truly what is happening in reality.

ASSESSING THE POLITICS OF TOURISM

Although the size and scale of the global tourist industry would seem to suggest that tourism is a hot political issue, so far we have argued that the politics of tourism has remained relatively underexplored. In terms of assessing the activities of Third World governments, the majority of analyses have been policy studies focusing upon national tourism policies, including both individual case studies and comparative policy analyses between countries.

A good deal of this work is also focused upon the identification of relevant and appropriate methodologies for planning and implementing tourism policy. Clearly such discussion is of interest and use, and has a wide appeal to practitioners.

Its weaknesses, however, lie in both its often prescriptive nature and its formulation from within the First World and, in many cases, the failure to set policy and action in a broader and more critical framework which acknowledges that there are competing interests. It was argued that the political economy approach is one of the few attempts to illustrate the way in which control of tourism development is held firmly in the First World.

As Britton argues: 'The World Tourism Organisation, International Monetary Fund, United Nations, World Bank and UNESCO, among others, set the parameters of tourism planning, promotion, identification of tourism products, investment and infrastructure construction policies often in conjunction with metropolitan tourism companies'.

Of course, it is not just external influences that affect tourism policy and development, but internal factors as well. This includes the conflicts between governmental and non-governmental interests, and conflicting interests and priorities within governments themselves. The latter are particularly prevalent where responsibilities over tourism resources overlap more than one government department. In Uganda, for example, there are three separate government departments with responsibilities for national parks, the focus of Uganda's tourism. A similar problem of different outlooks adopted towards its national parks by different government departments in Guatemala. Clearly, it is necessary to avoid the crude suggestion that government policy and action is an undifferentiated whole.

A non-critical approach also tends to assume that there are rational policy decisions that will lead to the surmounting of potential problems. As Hall and Jenkins argue, while 'rationality' represents an influential approach to policy analysis, it is also 'extremely misleading as it fails to recognise the inherently political nature of public policy'.

Take, for example, the approach of Edward Inskeep, a tourism planner who has worked with the WTO/OMT, World Bank and UNDP in many Third World countries: '[the] planning of tourism is necessary not only for scientific purposes and to conserve the environment for the benefit of residents, but also for the protection of long-term investments in tourism infrastructure, attractions, facilities, services, and marketing programs'.

What is important here is to question who benefits from planning and policy formulation and who controls these decision-making processes. If anything the 'benefit to residents' is a poor partner of the need to protect 'long-term investments', but the latter is couched in terms of conserving the environment for local people.

The suspicion that environmental conservation is not really about a concern for local people is confirmed: 'Increasingly, tourists are demanding that their environments be high-quality and pollution-free as well as inherently interesting, and some tourists will change travel patterns if environmental quality expectations are not met'. The results and effects of the Tourism Master Plan for Bali, outlined in one of the case studies given later in this chapter, are also interesting to note in this regard.

Ultimately then, we must ask who controls government policy and planning and what forces drive the processes of its formulation and implementation. Sustainability is a critical consideration here, for Agenda 21 designates national governments as having the lead responsibility for the process.

The overall aim of developing a sustainable tourism programme has been set out by the WTTC, which defines Agenda 21 as the process 'to establish systems and procedures to incorporate sustainable development considerations at the core of the decision-making process and to identify actions necessary to bring sustainable tourism development into being'. We must also ask in whose interests such actions are undertaken and explore how the uneven and unequal nature of development is reflected through this.

The notion of 'interests' is a useful one in focusing attention on which groups, organisations and institutions have influence and power in decision-making. Such influences can vary from the structural adjustment policies of the World Bank and IMF to the campaigns against visiting certain countries.

The differences between the two were technically due, in the main, to INGUAT's inclusion of all the areas whose status as a protected area was only proposed rather than actual. But these differences also reflect the roles and outlooks of the two departments. INGUAT is in the business of enhancing the country's image, of making it look attractive to potential visitors; so it covered as much of the national area as possible with the status of a protected area, with the greenwash of pristine natural areas. CONAP, on the other hand, is more realistic; it was aware that it did not have the resources necessary to oversee those areas which were already designated as protected, still less all those which were proposed.

The infringement of human rights within that country. Our discussion of The Gambia helps to identify different ways in which power is expressed through political processes. It is illustrative of the typical problems faced by Third World countries in their efforts to develop tourism. In this case, the expansion of the sector has been encouraged by the internationally inspired structural reform programmes which have clearly pushed The Gambia along a particular development path. But First World countries also retain the potential to control the tourism industry (especially when much of the industry caters for mass packaged charters, as in this case).

Showed how political economy critiques have revealed the shortcomings of Third World tourism and how tourism is an additional element in uneven and unequal development. However, this has not prevented countries which pursue socialist strategies and ideologies from dabbling in tourism, and in some cases arguing for forms of tourism that are not subordinating and are responsive to the issues of power and control exercised by the First World so heavily criticised in the political economy framework.

As Crick (1989) argues, in some countries this has resulted in seemingly glaring contradictions to the anti-colonial ideologies adopted by newly independent countries. Indeed, some critics suggest that tourism may help to maintain systems of neo-colonial power and control.

Tanzania is a frequently cited example where an emphasis on tourism development in the 1970s ran contrary to the anti-colonial socialism adopted by Nyerere in the wake of independence and the policy of self-reliance pursued by the government.

The Tanzanian intellectual, Shivji, was critical of the separation of politics from economics: 'The justification for tourism in terms of it being "economically good" though it may have adverse social, cultural and political effects, completely fails to appreciate the integrated nature of the system of underdevelopment'.

Other independent countries pursuing socialist ideals have also explored the development of tourism. In Cuba, for example, as much effort has been put into widening the appeal of Cuba as radical chic, with solidarity and study tours, as has been devoted to stemming the foreign exchange leakage characteristic of other destinations in the region. In order to reduce the leakage of foreign exchange, Cuba has established a tourism industry that seeks, if uneasily, to separate tourism spending from the national economy, and forces tourists to buy goods and services in foreign currency (mainly US dollars).

Following a successful *coup d'état* in 1979 in Grenada, a regional neighbour of Cuba, Maurice Bishop, head of the People's Revolutionary Government (PRG), acknowledged the shortcomings of mass tourism as it existed in the Caribbean and started to identify the basis of an alternative type of tourism. Outlining the parallels of tourism with colonialism which we discussed earlier, the socialist Prime Minister argued:

In the early days and even now, most tourists are white. This clear association of 'whiteness' and 'privilege' is a major problem for Caribbean people just emerging out of a racist colonial history where we had been so carefully taught the superiority of things white and inferiority of things black.

Bishop elaborated his ideas further at a Caribbean regional conference on the impact of tourism, where he identified the need to replace 'old tourism' with what he termed 'new tourism'. Along with Jamaica under the socialist leadership of Prime Minister Michael Manley, Bishop attempted to chart the development of a tourism designed to escape the problems that had been associated with 'old' tourism, bound up with 'colonial and imperialist connotations'.

It was foreign-owned and controlled, unrelated to the needs and development of the Caribbean people, and it brought with it a number of distinct socio-cultural and environmental hazards such as the race question and undesirable social and economic patterns such as drug abuse and prostitution.

Bishop's vision was for a 'new' tourism to escape these characteristics. It was to involve all people (as both 'guests' and tourists); it would seek to create linkages between the different sectors of the economy; and above all it was conceived as a tool for development.

However, the construction of Grenada's airport, a key part of the country's attempt to attract tourism, encapsulates and symbolises the political nature of tourism development. Bishop was murdered in October 1983 and with him died this vision of new tourism. Of course, it is questionable whether such a vision was realisable given the context of uneven and unequal development in which Third World tourism operates.

A rather different aspect of the inherently political nature of tourism is the way in which the USA sought to destabilize both Grenada and Jamaica, under Bishop and Manley respectively, through negative publicity and foreign policy statements that were hostile to both countries (Thomas, 1988).

In the case of Grenada this is particularly poignant. Grenada quickly gained an extraordinary international reputation, with Fidel Castro assessing that in conjunction with Nicaragua and Cuba they were representative of 'three giants rising to defend their rights to independence, sovereignty and justice on the very threshold of imperialism' (Clark, 1983, quoted in Thomas, 1988).

As Thomas concludes from the radical agendas pursued in these countries and the reworking of tourism that they advocated, 'they confirmed that any attempt at radical social reorganisation in the region would be met by insistent efforts on the part of the US to destabilise the process (or worse), especially if the proposed reorganisation involved new options for foreign policy and external relations' (1988:246).

The absence of an international airport was a clear weakness in Grenada's tourism plans and a brake on its development, a shortcoming that Bishop readily acknowledged in describing the airport as 'the gateway to our future' (Marcus and Taber, 1983). The majority of capital

(US$60 million) and technical assistance for the airport's construction came from Grenada's ideological neighbour, Cuba.

President Reagan, however, claimed that the construction involved a new naval base, a new air base, storage bases and barracks for troops, and training grounds. 'And, of course, one can believe that they are all there to export nutmeg ... It is not nutmeg that is at stake in Central America and the Caribbean, it is the United States' national security' (President Reagan, March 1983, quoted in Ferguson, 1990).

As Ferguson points out, despite the US development agency's (USAID) hostility to the People's Revolutionary Government policies and projects, it was deeply ironic that USAID were financing and administering the completion of the international airport, especially given the initial announcement that the USA had no plans to assist a project that was never intended to promote the development of Grenada's tourism.

After the murder of Bishop and the US invasion of the island, post-revolutionary Grenada provided US technocrats an opportunity for a structurally adjusted blueprint - a 'USAID inspired restructuring and free market deregulation'. Grenada was subsequently a laboratory and showcase of US ideological superiority.

Much USAID/NNP [New National Party] policy and finance was targeted on environmental and infrastructural improvements designed to attract foreign investment and tourism. As Pattullo (1996) states of Grenada, 'mass tourism became entrenched by the 1980s'. Indeed tourism has been one of the principal factors in the US-approved development strategy for the Caribbean.

In many other places too, tourism is alluded to as a peace industry, and a way of allowing the expansion of capitalist economies in a stable and peaceful environment. 'The overwhelming majority of USAID funds have ... gone towards dismantling the state sector, encouraging private enterprise and wooing foreign capital - with negligible success'. As Ferguson argues, the failure of the model is all the more significant given the symbolic importance placed on Grenada's development by the US government.

SUPRANATIONAL INSTITUTIONS

Supranational institutions involve a degree of political integration between states but are not subject to the laws of national governments. Such organisations operate in a global sphere of activity and are able to influence, and in some cases determine, economic and political activities in the national sphere.

Supranational organisations exist in many fields of activity. Those described as socio-environmental organisations were discussed. While these may in certain instances influence the policies pursued by national governments, this section deals with those organisations dedicated to direct and deliberate involvement in the formulation of

The International Bank of Reconstruction and Development (the World Bank) and IMF were born at the Bretton Woods conference in the USA in 1944. Their purpose was to provide an order to the global economy to prevent the collapse of international trade and the development of isolationist economic policies, which it was believed had led to the Depression of the 1930s and the rise of fascism.

The conference rejected the proposals of John Maynard Keynes to establish a world reserve currency administered by a central bank. Instead, it 'opted for a system based on the free movement of capital and goods with the US dollar as the international currency'.

Initially, a more specific purpose was to provide funds to assist in the rebuilding of war-torn Europe. The European countries objected to the severe loan conditions, so the World Bank worked through the Marshall Plan which provided US finance to re-build Europe mainly through grants rather than loans. Third World countries did not receive the same treatment.

Instead, they were pressured to keep their economies

completely open to foreign goods and capital; and in exchange for financial assistance, countries were expected to adopt structural adjustment policies.

Partly as a result of the debt crisis of the 1970s and 1980s, both institutions now exercise enormous leverage over the policies pursued by most governments which require financial assistance. 'That influence is enhanced by donor insistence upon an IMF and World Bank seal of approval as a condition for aid and debt relief' (Oxfam, 1995:8).

As Duncan Green points out, the two organisations are not democratically run: 'decisions at the IMF and World Bank are taken on the basis of "one dollar, one vote", guaranteeing the dominance of both by the US government' (1995:34). In 1995, for instance, the USA had 17.18 per cent of the total vote at the World Bank while the total vote for 23 of the poorest African countries together amounted to 1.58 per cent of the total.

The three most powerful and dominant of these are the International Bank for Reconstruction and Development (known as the World Bank), the IMF and the World Trade Organisation (WTO/OMC), although regional finance and development organisations, such as the European Bank for Reconstruction and Development (EBRD), the Inter-American Development Bank (IDB), USAID and increasingly other bilateral aid programmes also wield very considerable power over the policies pursued by Third World countries. Given the significance of the World Bank and IMF, a brief background to their formation and role is given.

The economic system promoted by these institutions is based on the free movement of capital and goods with the US dollar as the international currency. In such a system, tourism can be seen as much the same as any other cash crop, and pressure exerted by the development banks upon the government of a country to increase its export earnings by boosting production of export crops is as applicable to tourism as it is to sugar, coffee, cotton, bauxite, or other products. Foreign exchange earnings can be boosted by attracting more international tourists and the foreign exchange which they bring with them.

The debt crisis of the 1980s and the First World's reaction to it increased the power of the IMF and the World Bank. Spurred on by the prevailing ideology of President Reagan and Prime Minister Thatcher, the two institutions of the World Bank and IMF embarked on a mission to structurally adjust Third World economies so that they could meet debt obligations and fall into line with the right-wing economic orthodoxy sweeping the globe.

The origins of the debt crisis can be traced back to the huge profit made by members of the Organisation of Petroleum Exporting Countries (OPEC) in the early 1970s. These profits were surplus to requirements within the OPEC countries and much of the money was therefore banked and invested in the commercial banks of the First World. Awash with petro-dollars, the banks sought to make the most profitable use of this money.

One of the ways in which they recycled it was by financing development projects in Third World countries, including tourist resort schemes.

In the rush for 'development', many of the projects financed were ill-considered and poorly planned. Some of the money was spirited away by Third World elites with access to power brokers and decision-makers, and more was paid direct to First World companies taking part in the projects. A proportion of it therefore found its way back into the same First World banks that lent it in the first place.

In the late 1970s and the first half of the 1980s, interest rates on these loans rose sharply, an event that had not been anticipated by the lenders or borrowers in the early 1970s. Many borrowing countries found themselves unable to pay back even the interest on the loans, quite apart from the principal loan itself. First World bankers and politicians became concerned 'that the sheer volume of unpayable loans would undermine the world financial system.

They turned to the World Bank and the IMF, who were

to restructure Third World economies so they could meet their debt obligations' (*New Internationalist*, 1994:15); hence, the rise of structural adjustment programmes (SAPs), which since 2000 have become known as poverty reduction strategy papers (PRSPs), and which are produced by national governments themselves.

It should be pointed out, however, that they are produced with substantial input from IMF and World Bank officials and the two organisations retain the power of veto over PRSPs. Critics such as the World Development Movement believe that PRSPs are merely SAPs containing language about poverty reduction.

From the point of view of our analysis, what is crucial here is that SAPs/PRSPs imposed by the IMF and World Bank on Third World governments effectively force those governments to pursue specific policies not of their own design, although it was precisely in anticipation of such criticism that their means of production and title were changed.

These policies make living conditions for the population harsher and more difficult while supposedly enabling the government to increase its foreign exchange earnings and thereby pay off its debt. The kind of policies associated with SAPs/PRSPs is listed. It is worth noting, however, that most Third World countries already had little effective control over the direction of their policies before the debt crisis began. Colonial powers of the First World and transnational corporations (TNCs) dictated the main thrust of economic policy throughout the Third World.

The IMF, World Bank and other supranational lending agencies along with the TNCs took over the mechanism of power from the former colonial powers. Moreover, proponents of SAPs/PRSPs point out that once the debt had become a reality, there were no policies other than those given which could realistically be imposed to support global capital accumulation.

The loans which form part of the SAPs/PRSPs are made

only on strict condition that the national economy is restructured according to these policies. And this conditionality has meant that the economic and fiscal policies of most African and Latin American countries are now dictated from Washington. In the words of Green:

In the aftermath of the debt crisis, the IMF and later World Bank's use of conditionality allowed the powerful industrialised nations to revamp one Third World

Policies and conditions associated with SAPs/PRSPs

A Increase earnings of foreign capital

- *Boost export production* One implication of this is that the production of goods for local and national needs is relegated in importance as a result of the drive for export production. Tourism is seen as an export product, attracting foreign currency into the country. Many Third World countries which used to be self-sufficient in foodstuffs now have to import basic grains and other foodstuffs. In 1996, for instance, Honduras began to import beans for the first time in its history.
- *Devalue the national currency* Devaluation makes the country more attractive to foreign investors seeking a cheap place to produce their goods. The cheapness of its currency against other currencies also increases its attraction to foreign tourists.
- *Reduce and/or abolish import tariffs* Import tariffs are designed to protect the price of the production of goods for home consumption against the entry of cheaper imported goods. In practice, removing them can have the effect of flooding the country with expensive luxury goods and durables with high value added in production from the First World - for purchase by tourists and the rich elite.

B Reduce state involvement in the economy

- *Privatise state-run enterprises* Tourism is a flagship of the private sector.
- *Cut public spending on activities which cannot be*

privatised For example, social services, health provision, education - although increasingly attempts are being made to privatise these services too.

- *Deregulation* Reduction of all forms of controls, especially economic regulations, which inhibit industry's ability to maximise profits.

C Fiscal measures

- *Reduce inflation* This increases security of investment, including investments in tourist developments.
- *Cut interest rates* This increases investment, including investment in the tourism industry.
- *Encourage investment rather than saving* economy after another along free-market lines. Critics believe that in the process, the IMF has systematically put the powerful nations' self-interest before the welfare of the Third World poor.

The initial hope that SAPs/PRSPs may be successful in delivering widespread prosperity through highly dubious mechanisms such as the 'trickle-down' effect and belief in the benefits of economic globalisation is confounded somewhat by the evidence. As Ayesha Imam states:

In most countries in Africa, SAPs have not led to increases in production or investment ... In fact, according to the UN Economic Commission for Africa, production has decreased over the decade since SAPs have been implemented. Investment as a proportion of GDP has fallen too.

Budget deficits have grown and a greater proportion of export-earned money is now used solely to service debts ... The general standard of living has fallen. There have been painfully deep cuts in the provision of health, education and other social services and in the subsidies on basic necessities.

In 2001, the UNDP's *Human Development Report* showed that in terms of control of total world income, the ratio between the richest 20 per cent to that of the poorest 20 per cent had increased from 34 to 1 in 1970 to 70 to 1 in 1997 (UNDP, 2001:16); in other words, in 1997 the richest 20 per cent of the world's population received an income 70 times greater than the poorest 20 per cent, which represents a widening of the gap since 1970.

Even within the World Bank, there is awareness of the effects of these policies. Herman Daly, a renowned and respected economist in the Bank's Environment Department, has identified some major conflicts between the ultimate goal of international free trade, at which the Bank's policies aim, and national policies pursued in the national interest (1993:124).

Joseph Stiglitz, a Nobel laureate in Economics and former chief economist at the World Bank, has suggested that 'the IMF was run by hard line "market bolsheviks"' (World Development Movement, 2000:6), and that:

The 'invisible hand' of the market is just nonsense. The liberalisation of capital markets has produced more instability but no more economic growth. We knew this fine, economic science did not recommend such a step, but the IMF has gone on promoting it ... the IMF's policies have little or nothing to do with concern for the poor.

In the world of tourism, as in many other industries, this process of structural adjustment effectively delivers control of development to the TNCs and consultancies, most of which are based in the First World.

This relegates the role of the national government to one of providing the necessary infrastructure. For this, it must seek more loans, leaving it yet more indebted than before. Some countries, such as Honduras and Panama for example, are now even offering free trade zones for tourism companies wishing to build and operate resorts. Gonsalves concludes that 'the economies of the so-called Third World are in effect mere extensions of the economic priorities of the First World' (1995:39).

The list of development disasters caused by these supranational organisations in funding such schemes as large-scale dams, roads through sensitive eco-systems, monocultivation practices, infrastructural developments for the promotion of tourism, and many others, is long and well documented. And they have not just been confined to the IMF and World Bank.

During the 1980s, the USAID also gained notoriety for its arrogant and callous disregard for the environments and people affected by its development projects. Organisations such as World Bank Watch, Survival International, the World Development Movement (WDM), FOEI and others have documented these effects, exerted heavy pressure against them, and publicised the events and examples to such an extent that the start of the 1990s saw a growing recognition by the supranational organisations themselves of the effects of their policies.

Both the IMF and World Bank increased their staff who examine the social and environmental impacts of their programmes. The USAID also made strong efforts to green its image and to promote, for instance, community-based tourism schemes rather than grandiose resort projects. A tourism-related example of the mis-direction and failure of their efforts was given on pp. 226-8.

That these efforts to foster a new environmentally friendly image for themselves have failed should come as no surprise, given that their *modus operandi* of forcing national governments to pursue a dictated development path has remained unchanged.

In the wake of the protests at the Seattle trade talks in 1999, arguably the gathering momentum of a global social movement has prompted further attempts at image improvement by the supranational organisations such as the metamorphosis of the structural adjustment programmes into poverty reduction strategies.

With this increasing awareness of the need to demonstrate that they are changing, even if they are not doing so in reality, the IMF and World Bank have acknowledged the role of NGOs and have made attempts to enlist their advice. Despite this, Pierre Galand, Oxfam-Belgium's general secretary, resigned from the NGO working group on the World Bank and its Steering Committee. In his letter of resignation he said to the World Bank:

You have stolen speeches from NGOs concerned with development, eco-development, poverty and popular participation ... The Bank has learned to do excellent analyses and is capable of saying what is important: popular participation - particularly of women - the popular struggle against poverty, and the necessity to protect the environment ... Why are so many beautiful speeches accompanied by such scandalous practices?

More recently, in 2000, Ravi Kanbur, lead author of the World Bank's *World Development Report 2000/2001* (World Bank, 2000), resigned in protest at the Bank's decision to expunge criticism of globalisation from his work (WDM, 2000:6).

In 1995, the Uruguay Round of the GATT gave birth to the World Trade Organisation (WTO/OMC), essentially set up to continue and further the process of international trade liberalisation. The organisation establishes international agreements on rules of trade that are binding on parties to the agreements and it adjudicates in trade-related disputes between member states and between a member state and the rules. It has powers to impose sanctions on member states which break its rules.

To support her claim that WTO/OMC is leading us into an era of 'corporate-led, corporate-driven globalisation' (George in Bircham and Charlton, 2001:14), Susan George cites David Hartridge, director of WTO/OMC Services Division as stating that: 'without the enormous pressure generated by the American financial services sector, ... there would have been no services agreement and therefore perhaps no Uruguay Round and no WTO' (2001:14).

Brookes and Harrison also refer to the WTO/OMC as 'heavily influenced by the interests of big business' (2000:32), and expose the large number of powerful industry associations which influence the WTO/OMC through their positions on consultative committees.

That the WTO/OMC is driven by the corporate lobby is rarely denied, but its proponents point to the need for agreed sets of rules to govern international trade, the need for a body to manage and adjudicate on such rules, and to the fact that: 'The WTO's consensus decision-making means that in theory even the smallest country can hold up a trade deal if it doesn't like what is on the table' (Denny, 2002b: 14).

On the other hand, the perception that the WTO/OMC works solely in the interests of corporations and their profits is the driving force behind the rapid growth and conspicuousness of the anti-globalisation movement. Essentially their arguments are that the WTO/OMC ignores the needs of the poor, the environment and the rights of workers and consumers, and 'locks countries into a system of rules that means it is effectively impossible for governments to change policy, or for voters to elect a new government that has different policies' (Coates in Bircham and Charlton, 2001:28).

The WTO/OMC affects the activities associated with tourism through the GATS. Service industries, of which tourism is a part, now make up the greater part of the world's economic activity and the GATS negotiations would give major new rights to TNCs and reduce the power of national governments to restrict their activities for reasons of environmental protection, labour rights, planning regulations, or similar considerations. It is to the GATS and its effects on tourism that we now turn.

TOURISM AND THE GENERAL AGREEMENT ON TRADE IN SERVICES (GATS)

The GATS is one of several trade agreements administered and controlled by the WTO/OMC. The principal motive for the recent round of economic globalisation, of which GATS is the newest agreement, is arguably to ensure the continued expansion of markets for goods and services produced in and provided from the industrialised nations.

In theory, the WTO/OMC works on a consensus principle to create a rules-based system for the conduct of multilateral trade, and GATS works on the same principle for the same aim. Under the agreement, any signatory country has to accord the same treatment to foreign companies as it does to domestic companies in specified sectors of trade to which they have committed themselves. As Kalisch explains, it

is designed to ensure that host governments, confronted with powerful transnational corporations who import both their own staff and the majority of goods needed for their tourism operation, cannot compel them to use local materials and products to enhance the 'multiplier effect', or to take special measures to secure a competitive base for their domestic businesses.

The GATS defines import tariffs, subsidies and other measures designed to assist domestic companies as 'trade-restrictive', and thereby effectively undermine the power of governments to legislate in the national interest. In practice, according to a report by the WDM, one of the major UK critics of GATS: 'WTO staff and negotiators openly acknowledge that GATS exists only because of pressure from service multinationals and that this influence has continued since GATS came into effect'. Moreover, the European Commission's website describes GATS as 'not just something that exists between governments. It is first and foremost an instrument for the benefit of business'.

The mechanism of reaching agreement by consensus appears to be given as a major justification for the GATS. But whether a genuine consensus was achieved at the Doha Ministerial meeting in Qatar in November 2001, called to discuss GATS, or at previous similar meetings, is highly debatable: for instance, the 481 delegates from the G7 nations present at the Doha meeting was almost double the 276 delegates from the 39 Least Developed countries, and it is difficult if not impossible to achieve consensus agreement in such unbalanced circumstances.

Indeed, the WDM also reports that widespread pressure

is exerted by industrialised countries on Third World country negotiators, including suggestions that aid would be withdrawn. In general, the GATS appears to reflect and reinforce rather than challenge the existing unevenness and inequality in the global economic system.

In GATS, tourism falls into the sector labelled *Tourism and Travel-Related Services* which has four categories: hotels and restaurants; travel agencies and tour operator services; tourist guide services; other (unspecified). Kalisch points out that under GATS:

it would be impossible for a government to impose on foreign companies practices to limit negative environmental, social and cultural impacts in their country, such as restricting the mushrooming of foreign owned development, (including all-inclusive hotel developments, which are highly controversial among local people because they contribute almost nothing to the local economy), and making the employment of local workers, the use of local products and materials a condition of their investment. It could also render a government powerless to stop tourism developments on indigenous land, including sacred sites, in response to community protests.

Kalisch's analysis also suggests that GATS is likely to place fair trade in tourism at a disadvantage since 'the beneficiaries of Fair Trade in Tourism are poor communities, for whom the informal sector (vendors, traders, guides) is an important source of income, as well as small entrepreneurs and workers employed in the tourism industry'.

Representing the UK NGO Tourism Concern, Kalisch (2001) identifies the following concerns about the role that GATS is likely to play in the emerging tourism industries in Third World countries: the manner in which GATS negotiations are carried out in the WTO/OMC disadvantages and marginalises Third World countries and civil society organisations; GATS fails to integrate sustainable development as identified in major international treaties and agreements, such as the Convention on Biological Diversity which includes decisions on tourism; GATS does not address the specific environmental, social, economic and cultural impacts of tourism in a destination; expanding global tourism increases the threat of biopiracy under the guise of ecotourism, when tour operators and clients collect rare medicinal plants from areas inhabited by tribal peoples but without consulting them; and GATS makes no provision for the monitoring and regulation of TNCs.

Of all these concerns of relevance to the activity of tourism, it is perhaps the fear that the GATS will further deepen the increasing poverty and inequities experienced in some Third World countries that prompts the greatest protest. In the last two decades of the twentieth century, structural adjustment was the major economic policy employed in up to ninety Third World countries under programmes imposed by the IMF and World Bank.

During this time, 'the people of sub-Saharan Africa have become 15 per cent poorer, and growth rates in South Asia and Latin America have stagnated while inequality has risen dramatically'. The possibility that the GATS will further deepen these effects is feared not just by anti-globalisation protestors but also by the protagonists of fairly traded tourism and propoor tourism. The last of these, pro-poor tourism, is a relatively recent extension of governmental activity into the field of tourism development, and one to which we turn next.

DONOR DEVELOPMENT ACTIVITY AND PRO-POOR TOURISM INITIATIVES

The supranational organisations have had difficulty coming to terms with and adapting their policies to the effects of increasing poverty and inequality beyond cosmetic alteration of names, titles and terms. The need to examine their *modus operandi* in order to reduce poverty and inequality significantly does not appear to have been recognised.

A number of developments in bilateral donor policies, however, have given cause for a little more optimism in this regard, among them the development of pro-poor tourism initiatives.

In one of the few analyses of the current approach of development agencies to tourism, the UK DFID *Sustainable Tourism and Poverty Elimination Study* (Deloitte and Touche, IIED and ODI, 1999) concludes that few agencies regard tourism as a key development sector and yet many agencies, such as the World Bank and European Union, do indeed provide considerable support to tourism related projects, ranging from economic development and employment generation to sector planning and product development. Nevertheless, no agency is regarded as developing and implementing a tourism and poverty elimination agenda.

Reviewing the approaches of the three key agency sectors, multilateral agencies, bilateral agencies and development banks, the DFID report concludes that in general tourism projects respectively involve infrastructure development, tourism master plans and private sector development, community and conservation based tourism, and infrastructure and resort development loans.

In terms of the approach of agencies to tourism as a poverty elimination strategy, the DFID reports two contrasting representations. The first, exemplified by the Danish (DANIDA) and Dutch (NEDA) government agencies is that tourism cannot and should not compete with traditional development sectors (such as education and primary health care).

The second, promoted by the Finnish development agency (FINNIDA) and some multilaterals such as the United Nations Development Programme and EuropeAid, is that as a result of the considerable impact of tourism on poor peoples' livelihoods, intervention is critical.

Such interventions at the local level include the support of small and micro-enterprises, support to rural tourism projects, the development of partnerships between communities and private sector operators, participatory pro-poor planning and a range of measures that have clear benefits for the poor, such as working condition improvements, training and staff development and protected area management.

With the emergence of development approaches focused on the poor, by the end of the 1990s development practitioners had begun to think about the possibility of applying poverty elimination goals to tourism. Tourism had traditionally been viewed as a commercial sector, and considered a 'frivolous or elitist industry' and not a 'serious' development related activity. The DFID has supported a number of studies (including case study research) that seek to elaborate a pro-poor tourism approach and promote tourism as a 'legitimate' development activity.

The emergence and development of pro-poor tourism must be understood and analysed within the global development orthodoxy that economic growth is fundamental to pro-poor development. Ultimately, it is an effort to see if tourism can become more pro-poor and if, in the much repeated sound-bite of its proponents, it can meet the need to 'tilt the tourism cake rather than expanding it'.

Pro-poor tourism is a direct intervention in the debate between the advocates and detractors of tourism. Advocates point to four potential advantages of tourism as an economic sector capable of facilitating pro-poor growth: the high potential of linkage, labour intensity, tourism's potential in poor countries and the ability to build tourism on natural and cultural assets. Detractors are critical of the level of leakage, negative impacts on the poor, displacement and socio-cultural disruption.

Pro-poor tourism is defined by its proponents as tourism 'that generates net benefits for the poor ... [it] is not a specific product or sector of tourism, but an overall approach. Rather than aiming to expand the size of the sector, pro-poor tourism strategies aim to unlock opportunities - for economic gain, other livelihood benefits, or engagement in decision-making - for the poor'.

Pro-poor tourism, it is argued, differs from other tourism

types that claim to have some 'developmental' value (principally ecotourism, sustainable tourism, community-based tourism, 'fair trade' tourism and other ethically based tourisms), in that it focuses directly on the needs of the 'poor'.

As such it is premised upon the sustainable livelihoods approach, of increasing significance in discourses of so-called 'people-centred' approaches to development that seek to build upon the capabilities, assets and activities of the poor. However, advocates also recognise that general support for and integration of pro-poor strategies with the mainstream tourism sector (for example, developing tourist boards or the provision of key infrastructure such as roads or water supplies) is essential to complement pro-poor tourism, and that 'interventions do not always need to be poverty-focused to benefit the poor'.

In this way there are clear similarities with other forms of new tourism, in that the success of pro-poor tourism relies on an appropriate policy environment that allows such forms of tourism to grow; and thus, pro-poor tourism initiatives may also include so-called 'top-down' government promoted approaches.

Like other forms of tourism, as an economic activity pro-poor tourism must compete effectively in the tourism marketplace, and access to the market and ability to compete will depend on a number of fundamental factors common to all forms of tourism: the geography of the place of tourism, the level of understanding and knowledge of the tourism function and level of disposable resources, and access to decision-making (much of which is done internationally).

Despite the acknowledged desire of pro-poor tourism advocates to overcome existing problems and encourage new approaches to development through tourism, two key problems arise: the first relates to an understanding of power relationships in tourism; the second to the ability of pro-poor tourism to reduce poverty.

Table. Pro-poor Tourism Strategies.

Issues	Strategies
Barriers to participation in the industry for small and micro-enterprises	• Credit training • Policy reform and planning mechanisms • Partnerships with the private sector
Apparent potential for linkages with other sectors rarely realised of local products	• Improved quality, reliability and competitiveness • Change incentives and attitudes in the business sector towards local products • Facilitate linkage process, reduce transaction costs
The number of tourism jobs available to the poor limited by their lack of skills, and quality of employment in the industry can be low standards	• Training in hospitality skills, targeted at poor • Development and implementation of labour people • Initiatives aiming to reverse the growth of sex tourism and child labour
Tourism can result in lost or reduced access to land and natural resources, or their degradation. Environmental mitigation measures sometimes conflict with, rather than enhance, livelihoods	• Development/reform of planning frameworks • Devolve tenure rights over land or wildlife to local people • Employ appropriate mitigation measures
Tourism can undermine basic services of poor communities by over-burdening water and sewage systems; can	• Combine investment in basic services for tourism with provision for local needs • Local codes of conduct and local

result in cultural intrusion and loss of privacy; and has led to a growth of the sex industry	tourism initiatives • Raise awareness of cultural issues among tourists
Institutions and decision -making processes often structured in such a way that interests of the poor are not taken into account	• Participatory planning processes • Local institutional capacity-building • Cross-sectoral coordination • Incentives and capacity for pro-poor tourism
Many governments see tourism as a means to generate foreign exchange rather than address poverty. Where commitment exists, it can be difficult to identify and implement the wide range of policy reforms needed	• Assess and build government commitment to pro-poor tourism • Build capacity to implement pro-poor commitments
The reasons for business to promote the pro-poor agenda are not clear	• Business partnerships promote pro-poor tourism on the business agenda
Pro-poor tourism not currently on the international agenda, yet many international activities have potential to influence pro-poor tourism	• International voluntary codes • Consumer education • Assessment of the impact of European Union tourism regulations on poor producers • Good practice' guidelines in pro-poor tourism • Promote pro-poor tourism on international agenda

First, the DFID Report is critical of the misrepresentation of tourism as an 'industry where foreign interests dominate', and which directly challenges critiques of tourism that have emphasised the significance of power relationships.

However, the authors of the Report themselves point out that 'Developing countries have only a minority share of the international tourism market', refer to the major players in tourism and their 'low level of commitment to any one destination' and point to the significance of 'customer requirements' - the fundamental needs and desires of tourists that must be met for tourism to be a going concern.

And as later pro-poor tourism analysis suggests, 'Most of the critical decisions that affect the sector are made outside of the country or by a few powerful local interests'.

All such elements seem to confirm, rather than question, the significance of the spatially uneven and unequal nature of tourism production, consumption and development. Indeed, this appears to be reflected in advocates' claims that many of the disadvantages that have been attributed to tourism are in fact 'characteristics of growth and globalisation' and that tourism is little different from other economic sectors in that 'negative impacts that arise as a result of tourism development would also occur with development in other sectors'.

While, for the arguments advanced we would stop short of claiming that tourism is no different from other economic sectors, some of the oft-quoted problems of tourism such as leakage or economic volatility or the structure of social relations and power that involve local elites as well as foreign interests, are indeed characteristic of other economic sectors too and that the 'difference between tourism and other sectors might be perceived rather than real'.

For these reasons we have argued that tourism must be understood primarily within an analysis of relationships of power (foreign or otherwise) and that tourism must be considered little different from other economic sectors when assessed within a development context; in this sense, it is a 'prism' for understanding broader global issues and relations.

Our challenge was to try and understand tourism within the context of power and how this affects local livelihoods, and to measure the veracity of the claims that have been made about the ability of new forms of tourism to assist development. A key question is, given the size and strength of growth in tourism, is new tourism capable of facilitating development?

Given the global 'consensus' on the need to dramatically reduce absolute poverty, the second fundamental question centres on the ability of pro-poor tourism to deliver poverty reduction. As might be expected at the initial stage in the development of a prospective approach that is 'relatively untried and untested' and where a blueprint for implementation does not exist, accounts of pro-poor tourism are replete with imponderables (the 'may', 'should', 'likely to') and with acknowledgement that impacts are not easy to measure objectively.

Equally, there has been justifiable caution in extracting too many conclusions from an initial case analysis. While this is certainly no good reason for not embarking on pro-poor tourism initiatives, it does perhaps call into question the confidence invested in pro-poor tourism approaches and the manner in which it has been preferenced and mainstreamed into bilateral development assistance.

Like any other form of activity or approach, pro-poor tourism has needed to capture its unique selling point and appeal to the emergent development policy agendas. In this case the UN poverty reduction targets and the consensus surrounding the needs of the poor as *the* focus for development activities has meant that pro-poor tourism advocates have been careful to define their approach in contrast to other types of tourism, even where the needs of the poor are already being addressed. Inevitably, this has meant trying to rationalise away potential inconsistencies.

So while the UN targets are unequivocally focused on

the reduction of the poor living in 'absolute poverty', on less than a dollar a day, pro-poor tourism advocates point to the problems of defining poverty and the 'poor'.

In terms of an intervention in poverty, the DFID report's initial conclusions were that 'tourism probably does not compare with more direct tools, such as investment in health, education and agriculture. But as a strategy for promoting *broad-based growth* (also essential for achieving poverty elimination), pro-poor tourism has good potential', and it is the so-called 'not-quite-so-poor' (55) that are in a better position to be involved in tourism.

On the basis of a review of supporting pro-poor tourism case studies from Ecuador, Namibia, Nepal, St Lucia, South Africa and Uganda, Ashley *et al.* conclude that a 'focus on "the poor" often translates in practice to a focus on local residents or the "community"' (2001:11).

Researchers have highlighted both positive and negative impacts on the livelihoods of the poor through their initial case studies which are all less than ten years old, but show uncertainty about the strength of positive impacts for it is 'difficult to tell how much this is because pro-poor initiatives have fewer negative consequences, or how much it reflects researchers' and respondents' quest for positive results'.

As advocates of pro-poor tourism concur, it is certainly not a panacea: 'it is probably true that the small size of ... initiatives has meant that tourism provides a *minor dent in the national poverty* even when multiplier effects are taken into account'. Pro-poor tourism is not, therefore, a tool for eliminating nor necessarily alleviating absolute poverty, but rather is principally a measure for making some sections of poorer communities 'better-off' and of reducing the vulnerability of poorer groups to shocks (such as hunger). As the DIFD commissioned research suggests:

Economic benefits generated by pro-poor tourism may not reach the poorest - workers and entrepreneurs are unlikely to be from the poorest quintile. Nevertheless, those with sufficient assets to make crafts, sell tea/food, service the accommodation sector, or work in infrastructure may still be poor by either the international definition or by national poverty lines (particularly where tourism occurs in places where the majority are 'poor').

Additionally, it is difficult to draw conclusions from national aggregate data and analysis that 'shows that in most countries with high levels of poverty, tourism is significant (contributing over 2 per cent of GDP or 5 per cent of exports) or growing (aggregate growth of over 50 per cent between 1990 and 1997)'. While this may well present opportunities for the poor, it must also recognise the geographically uneven and unequal nature of tourism development and activity.

Tourism, and its potential benefits, will not be distributed evenly and may well display sharp regional and social disparities - the Maoist insurrections in areas of Nepal, for example, emphasise the potential volatility of uneven regional growth. As a prerequisite therefore, there needs to be a 'large number of poor people, in areas with tourism assets' and the commitment of government to pro-poor approaches.

It could be argued that in absolute terms the main effort and resourcing should be deployed in addressing the impacts on the poor, reining back the negative impacts of the mainstream tourism industry and seeking to develop mainstream poor-focused initiatives. As tentative analysis suggests, and as conjectured in pro-poor tourism analysis, 'Even if tourism does not directly involve poor people, it may have pro-poor impact, *if* it improves government revenue and *if* that revenue is used in pro-poor ways'.

Equally, given that the implementation of most pro-poor tourism initiatives require subsidies (and this would especially be the case if such initiatives were 'scaled-up' and replicated on a broader basis), and in the light of the need to allocate funds where the impact on poverty reduction will be optimal, Ashley *et al.* (2001) conclude that donors, NGOs and indeed governments, must ultimately consider how cost effective pro-poor tourism is in reducing poverty in relation to other approaches. Of course, there are advantages to the growth of new tourism (and pro-poor tourism) and there is a number of case studies that appear to demonstrate the real advantages and benefits to the poor that arise from tourism.

As advocates of pro-poor tourism understandably maintain, while in absolute terms the scale of benefits may appear small, they can be relatively very significant when viewed from the perspective of the beneficiary groups.

Our tentative conclusions, however, remain the same: given the growth in global inequality and poverty, the benefits to the poor of poverty elimination (however real they may be where they occur) will be marginal within the overall context of tourism.

Finally, it is not unreasonable to consider the degree to which pro-poor tourism analysis and promotion is a repackaging of existing initiatives so that they fit within the prevailing development paradigm with an emphasis on poverty reduction, sustainable livelihoods and a focus on the poor and pro-poor growth.

The re-adjustment and representation of existing projects and the structure of new initiatives are a key feature of the development merry-go-round in the competition for limited development funds. In addition, it will prove necessary in the long run to consider the cumulative effect of supporting (through multilateral and bilateral aid programmes focused on economic growth) the expansion of capitalist relations and the manner in which this may undercut 'sustainable livelihoods' and exacerbate, rather than alleviate, poverty.

AGENDA 21 FOR THE TRAVEL AND TOURISM INDUSTRY

An examination of the global governance of tourism must include the activities and approach of tourism's supranational agencies such as the WTTC and the WTO/OMT. Together with the Earth Council, these organisations elaborated the role of different tourism interests and their responsibilities following the establishment of Agenda 21 which arose from the 1992 Earth Summit at Rio de Janeiro in a document entitled *Agenda 21 for the Travel and Tourism Industry: Towards Environmentally Sustainable Development* (1995).

Extracts the duties placed upon central and local governments (and national tourism authorities and representative trade organisations such as the WTTC and WTO/OMT) in facilitating 'sustainable' tourism development.

There is a number of observations that can be made about the priorities set out in this document. First, it is clearly set within a framework of environmental sustainability. This is indicated in both the report's rubric, *Towards Environmentally Sustainable Development*, and in the respective forewords of the collaborating bodies:

A key conclusion of the Earth Summit was the importance of harnessing the entrepreneurial drive of the private sector in the cause of environmentally compatible development ... The environment is our core asset, the key component of product quality, and an increasing priority for our consumers.

(Geoffrey Lipman, President, WTTC)

Table. Agenda 21: Responsibilities of Governments.

Priority area	Priorities and objectives	Responses and examples of success
I	Assessing the capacity of existing regulatory, economic and voluntary framework to bring about sustainable tourism, and developing policies to facilitate sustainable tourism	Charge negative externalities to producer; provide cost incentives to companies minimising waste; encourage responsible entrepreneurship through codes of practice. More than 100 codes now exist
II	Assessing the economic, energy, social, cultural and environmental implications of an	Ranges from a more efficient use of water to encouraging staff to use environmentally benign transport and

	organisation's own operations	ensuring the destination's character is truly represented in marketing. Green Globe was established
III	To train and educate all stakeholders in travel and tourism about the need to develop more sustainable forms of tourism	Organisations should work with government departments. The WTO/OMT has establishe a worldwide Network of Education and Training Centres to promote tourism education and training
IV	Develop and implement effective land use planning to maximise the environmental and economic benefits of travel and tourism and minimise environmental and cultural damage	Includes working with government planning authorities on sustainable tourism planning, i.e., transport planning and coastal zone management. Bermuda - one of the world's most affluent countries because of planning regulations?
V	Facilitate information exchange between 'developed' and 'developing' countries	Includes developing partnerships with 'less developed' countries, advising them on sustainable tourism
VI	Provide opportunities for all sectors of society to participate in sustainable tourism	Promote and ensure the participation of women, indigenous people, etc. Develop appropriate training courses. A key example would be the CAMPFIRE project in Zimbabwe

VII	Design new tourism products that are sustainable: socially, culturally, economically and environmentally	Ranges from defining what makes resorts sustainable to using local materials in construction and ensuring government departmentsrealise the benefits of tourism in include conservation. Examplesthe game parks of Kenya and South Africa
VIII	Measure progress in sustainable development by setting realistic indicators at national and local level	Ranges from assessing which data are appropriate to exchanging experiences with other organisations
IX	Develop partnerships to facilitate sustainable tourism development and responsible entrepreneurship	Includes government departments providing a coordinating mechanism for those responsible for sustain able tourism development and ensuring the necessary infrastructure (e.g., sewage treatment, recycling facilities, etc.) is in place

A good deal of our Travel & Tourism activity relies on ... fragile natural or cultural resources, so it is in our interests to protect them for the future ... Travel & Tourism will inevitably continue to increase. Meeting this growth in a responsible, sustainable way, that preserves and enhances the beauty of the attraction, is the challenge we all face.

The overriding concern for the industry must be to seek out ways to enhance rather than degrade its core product, the environment. Reflecting for a moment on some of the words used here to describe the environment: 'core asset', 'core product', 'product quality', 'resources', 'preserve' - the treatment of the environment as a marketable product is clear. It is also clear that the drive 'towards environmentally sustainable development' is a commercial necessity, in order to maintain the marketability and attractiveness of this commodity.

More noticeable is the way in which much, if not all, the discussion bypasses the interests of local people. Where social considerations do appear they are an adjunct. Social development, it is assumed, will be achieved at the same time as improving the environment; the benefits will magically 'trickle down' to local people in the same way as the World Bank and IMF suggest. The ability for local people to choose whether they wish to engage with tourism is not on offer. Rather, it appears to be an agenda for removing the 'growing resentment of residents in some destinations' and allowing for the expansion of the industry.

As the quotations above imply, the report fails to reflect the inherent inequality expressed through global tourism. It is written from a thoroughly First World perspective, where the majority of the tourism industry, tourists and tourism interests are located. The forewords talk of 'our Travel and Tourism activity', 'our consumers', 'our interests'.

The supporting statement for priority (vi), for example, extols the participation of all sectors of society in sustainable tourism and identifies the promotion of the participation of women and indigenous people in 'appropriate forms of tourism development'. But, of course, these remain the receivers of tourism and the report is silent on the gross inequality of who is, and who is not, able to travel. The Third World, so it would appear, is there for our entertainment.

It exists to serve us and see to our needs. As the report states, the 'challenge ... is to ensure that tourists don't "love nature to death"'; in other words, to ensure that the tourism product is retained.

Even 'peace' is invoked as an essential prerequisite to successful sustainable tourism development, further reflecting the overall intention of protecting the tourism product while allowing for overall global expansion. Priority (vii) supporting statement urges the use of 'the potential of the tourism industry to promote peace between nations and people', acknowledging that 'Peace is a pre-requisite for a sustainable Travel & Tourism industry and, by facilitating contact and understanding between cultures, well-designed tourism products can make a significant contribution to world peace.'

While peace is of course a noble goal, once again there is an insipid suggestion that we need to move towards one happy global community, 'In recognition of economic and social cohesion among the peoples of the world as a fundamental principle of sustainable development' with implicit suggestions about the need for global security, a concern that has been greatly enhanced since the early 1990s.

Not only are Third World populations the receivers of visitors; according to this report they are also receivers of (First World) information. Priority area (v), for example, involving the facilitation of information exchange, more accurately involves advising Third World countries on how to make tourism sustainable.

Rather than exchange, this appears to be information delivery and represents a First World perspective on how certain goals are to be achieved. Similarly, priority (viii) supporting statement encourages the 'exchange' of indicators with other organisations 'especially those in developing countries'. Cynically, many of the priorities and objectives advocating 'training' courses are a further indication of the cycles of dependency and development aid-giving - a 'jobs for the boys' syndrome - that such frameworks maintain.

Participation, so the report suggests, is to be undertaken after key initial decisions have been made. In the wake of the discovery of Mayan ruins near the city of Tekax (in south-east Mexico), and the realisation that this had significant tourism potential, it was agreed that the 'people of the area should participate in the development in order to maximise economic benefits'. The critical point here is that the decision to develop the site and to maximise its economic benefits had already been taken.

Finally, the report offers a Framework for Action, although on the subject of the means of implementation the report is baffling and also reflects the First World perspective. It is difficult to conceive of the processes and procedures set out in the report - that is, securing the commitment of top management to the concept of sustainability, communicating this to all staff, establishing realistic and achievable targets, implementing action programmes, monitoring progress and so on - working in practice.

In short, it amounts to top-draw management-speak: many windy words within a highly ambiguous and inappropriate framework. It is difficult to believe that many grossly under-resourced and under-staffed government departments would be in a position to undertake such a grand scheme. How the report's recommendations are to be implemented in practice represents a serious failing.

The report and its Framework for Action are in effect just one more in a pile of conventions, codes of conduct, declarations and the like weighing down on the governments of Third World countries in respect of tourism development. All these pressures are full of fine words and lofty principles, but few if any of them offer the resources required to enable Third World governments to consider sustainability in the development of their tourism industries.

THE UNITED NATIONS INTERNATIONAL YEAR OF ECOTOURISM, 2002

In November 1998, the United Nations' General Assembly declared the year 2002 as the International Year of Ecotourism (IYE) and invited UN states, members of specialised agencies and pertinent intergovernmental and governmental organisations to participate in the programme, especially regarding ecotourism in developing countries. The UNEP and the WTO/OMT were mandated by the UN to organise events around the IYE. Along with UNEP and the

WTO/OMT, TIES was given the role of coordinating the organisation of a series of six regional preparatory conferences in partnership with local organisations, 'to focus on fostering a genuine dialogue among all stakeholders involved, especially local communities and ecotourism practitioners'. These were held in Belize, India, Peru, Thailand, Kenya and Sweden from November 2001 to April 2002, and each preparatory conference presented reports to the World Ecotourism Summit in Quebec, Canada in May 2002, in which TIES was also an active organisational participant.

The IYE was met with enthusiasm by many tourist boards and tour operators, but with varying degrees of scepticism by many NGOs, especially some in the Third World. Most prominent among these was the Tourism Investigation and Monitoring Team (usually referred to as the TIM-Team) of Bangkok, Thailand, with support from the Third World Network based in Malaysia.

Soon after the declaration of the IYE, the TIM-Team called for a fundamental reassessment of ecotourism and for a change of the name to the International Year of Reviewing Ecotourism. In an October 2000 letter to Oliver Hillel, UNEP's tourism programme coordinator, the TIM-Team and a coalition of other groups from Asia and beyond stated:

> We, the undersigned NGOs from the South and the North, feel compelled to warn all concerned parties not to skirt the critical issues of ecotourism and the fact that a mountain of money will be spent and a flood of projects initiated around the IYE in order to boost the ecotourism industry. In contrast to advocates who tend to portray ecotourism development as a 'win-win' approach, a means to protect biodiversity and enhance the well-being of local people, we are gravely concerned that this IYE will result in a 'lose-lose' situation for communities and the environment in destination countries.

Citing work conducted on projects including Taman Negara, a national park in western Malaysia, a number of development projects in Thailand and the Greater Mekong sub-region covering six countries, the organisation argued that:

Tourism provides the physical infrastrucure and logistics for freer movement of people and goods within countries and across borders in general and, thus, it naturally has knock-on effects on other sectors. Accordingly, ecotourism development has opened opportunities for•a whole range of investors to gain access to remote rural, forest, coastal and marine areas.

There is the observation that the more transportation systems are established into remote areas, the more encroachments, illegal logging, mining and plundering of biological resources occur, including biopiracy by unscrupulous individual and corporate collectors.

Three months later the same coalition of groups sent the same letter to Kofi Annan, UN Secretary General, along with an urgent appeal that the name and focus of the year should be changed. The substance of their appeal and the contrast in the different approaches to the year were reflected in one sentence: 'The new name will convey an unmistakeable message to the international community that the year 2002 is not the time for celebrating the ecotourism industry, but is primarily meant as a period of reflection, stock taking, learning and intensive search for solutions to the various problems associated with ecotourism' (TIM-Team letter to Kofi Annan, 18 January 2001).

The TIM-Team continued to produce regular articles and letters critical of the IYE, culminating in a January 2002 article entitled *UN 'International Year of Ecotourism 2002' in a Deep Muddle - Scrap it!* (TIM-Team, 2002). The UK-based Tourism Concern also expressed its misgivings thus:

How can ecotourism to the Ecuadorian rainforest be taken seriously given the resources consumed to take tourists to the product in the first place? The IYE also seems to be failing to address many critical issues: the fact that people are still displaced from their homes because of tourism, including 'ecotourism', denied access to local resources and losing their livelihoods because of so-called ecotourism; that ecotourism rarely takes on board issues of core labour standards, or gender; or that large environmental NGOs managing 'ecotours' too often behave like large corporations, employing 'top down' methods that rarely support local decision making. Perhaps most crucially of all, Tourism Concern believes that promoting ecotourism means promoting a niche market that does nothing to change the industry as a whole.

A statement presented by a range of indigenous peoples' representatives and NGOs to the Convention on Biological Diversity in Nairobi, Kenya, in May 2000 went further still, naming several of the 'large environmental NGOs managing ecotours':

In our experience, large nature conservation and development organisations do not respect (local peoples') rights. ... several activities undertaken by the [International] Ecotourism Society, Conservation International and IUCN do not respect the rights and interests of Indigenous Peoples and local communities, particularly in regard to the Year of Ecotourism activities, and often threaten cultural and biological diversity.

Many of the criticisms and dangers of ecotourism raised in the run-up to the IYE have been acknowledged by its organisers. And although the title of the year was not altered, some efforts were made to improve the inclusivity of the events by spreading invitations to participate far and wide. The TIES IYE website is peppered with terms such as 'critical evaluation of ecotourism', 'share the benefits of ecotourism equitably', 'multi- stakeholder consultation', 'active networks of regional stakeholders', 'foster dialogue', and makes repeated references to 'local communities and indigenous groups'.

Nevertheless, as Vivanco points out, 'Since its inception, the IYE has been aggressively marketed as a celebration of ecotourism's role in facilitating sustainable development'.

Despite acknowledgement of the criticisms of ecotourism, this celebratory tone is unlikely to be reconciled with the views of those who consider it inappropriate and who would have preferred a more critical approach.

SUSTAINABLE TOURISM AS POLITICAL DISCOURSE

'Beautiful, multi-faceted jewel' (*Financial Times*, 22 September 1992); 'To sea is to Belize'; 'Mounts, mountains and Mayans'; and 'Too good for tourists' - this is how four UK broadsheet newspapers referred to the small Central American country of Belize. Virtually all tourist sources on Belize cite large tracts of 'pristine' rainforest, numerous Mayan archaeological sites, and the second-longest barrier reef (after Australia) in the world. Writers point to a number of successful community-based and conservation projects, including the Community Baboon Sanctuary, Sandy Beach Lodge (Women's Cooperative), the Toledo Ecotourism Association, the Hol Chan Marine

Reserve, the Cockscomb Basin Wildlife Sanctuary (Jaguar Reserve), and Crooked Tree Wildlife Sanctuary. On paper, much of the surface area of the country enjoys some form of designated protection from development.

Up to the late 1980s few would have heard of the former British Colony of British Honduras, which gained independence in 1981. In the post-independence period, tourism has become an attractive strategy for diversifying the economy away from the export of agricultural produce. Belize is an excellent example of how a country uses the notion of sustainability to promote the development of new types of tourism and how a government's use of the language of sustainable tourism is often sufficient to win international accolade, even among academics and environmentalists. In the early 1990s it seemed as if Belize had emerged as the ecotourism capital of the world, hosting a number of international conferences. The experience of Belize provides an example of sustainability as a political discourse.

Unlike its Caribbean Community and Common Market (CARICOM) partners, Belize recognised the need to avoid the negative externalities, foreign exchange leakages and the foreign control of the mass tourism industry developed throughout much of the Caribbean. It also acknowledged the potentially disastrous impact that large-scale tourism development would have on the relatively fragile sub-tropical environment.

In their first term of office, the United Democratic Party (UDP), a right-of-centre and pro-US free market economics party, was the first Belizean administration to focus upon tourism. It approved an *Integrated Tourism Policy and Strategy Statement* in its last year in office, acknowledging the significance of tourism to the government, which had made it the second economic priority next to agriculture. In this way, significant emphasis was placed on the overall potential of tourism, 'its economic stimulus and linkage with other subsectors of the economy' (1989:1), and the guiding objectives stressed the maximisation of economic benefits. This included a particular emphasis on 'long stay and upper income travellers'.

In the 1989 general election the victorious People's United Party (PUP - a nationalist party and like its increasingly indistinguishable rival, a pro-US and free market oriented party) had spelled out clearly the advantages of ecotourism in the party's manifesto in what it also termed *Tourism with Dignity*:

> Belize has in abundance what few countries in the world still have left - nature. Ours, for the most part, is still intact. And nature is rapidly becoming tourism's Holy Grail. Belize has so far escaped the most brutal blows of man's destructive hand ... But, we must ask, for how long? The answer is, forever if we safeguard them. The protection of our national environment and development of eco-tourism are compatible goals which will be given high priority. The new PUP Government will place the portfolios of Environment and Tourism in one Ministry.

In the wake of its election victory, the PUP did indeed combine these portfolios and Belize has subsequently enjoyed popular international support and praise for its stand on the environment and promotion of sustainable tourism development and has hosted a number of conferences on ecotourism.

As we argued earlier, however, these conferences hint at the serious deficiencies and contradictions in ecotourism, not least that the conference fees, half the average monthly Belizean wage, ensured that the only local representation was from professionals representing and paid for by government departments and non-governmental organisations. Higinio and Munt (1993) describe two particular conferences held in Belize thus:

Hosted in a new luxury hotel - the construction of which necessitated stripping the protective mangrove cover - on the ecologically fragile outskirts of Belize City, two recent major international conferences on ecotourism highlighted the conflict between environmentally conscious activists and entrepreneurs who have seized upon ecotourism as a convenient marketing tool.

The keynote speaker at the First Caribbean Ecotourism Conference in 1991, Voit Gilmore from the American Society of Travel Agents, promised 'millions of Americans just waiting to come'. Howard Hills, a US investor speaking at the 1992 First World Congress on Tourism and the Environment, promised money. Ecotourism, Hills argued, is just like any other business. He boasted that the Overseas Private Investment Corporation would lend up to $50 million to any 'environmentally sound' tourism development, conditional upon a 25 per cent US stake in the project.

Environmentalists consider such sentiments anathema to the very ethos of ecotourism. They argue that a small-scale, locally controlled and ecologically sensitive industry can neither sustain many visitors, nor be a big money-maker. In contrast to the Belizean government's view of ecotourism as a way to develop economically and to earn foreign exchange, environmental activitists see ecotourism as justification for ecological and cultural conservation. An incredulous anthropologist from Scotland's Edinburgh University could only express dismay at Hill's remarks: 'The whole idea of ecotourism,' he said, 'is that it is like *no* other business.'

In the wake of these conferences, commentators began to express concern over the nature of the business of ecotourism and what it had to offer Belize. Despite these concerns, the Belizean government has used its commitment to sustainable tourism to full effect.

At an ecology and tourism symposium in Costa Rica for example, the then Tourism and Environment Minister, Glenn Godfrey, emphasised the relationships between environment, conservation and ecotourism and the fundamental requirement of local control: 'Conservation and therefore ecotourism thrives best where the sunlight penetrates to the lowest levels of autonomous local and community government.' It was a stance he later reiterated at the 1992 Rio Summit, assuring the audience that the Belizean government was committed to 'community-based ecotourism'. But the government's statements have not always matched their actions and a succession of examples from Belize provides a rather less optimistic picture of the use of sustainable tourism.

In 1992 the popular Belizean weekly *Amandala* carried the headline 'Eco-terrorism at Hatchet Caye', following a US resort owner's attempt to blow up part of the ecologically fragile coral reef in order to make his resort more accessible to visiting boats. The developer, Donald McKenzie, was subsequently arrested, fined US$2,000 (for 'dynamiting without a permit') and fled the country.

Of course similar incidents have been reported elsewhere in the world where government rhetoric extolling the virtues of the controlled growth of tourism has been contradicted in practice. In some cases this is a direct result of weak and ineffectual legislation controlling environmental impacts, particularly the inability to enforce legislation. In other cases it reflects the complete absence of necessary controls or the government's willingness to turn a blind eye.

More than environmental damage, however, the Hatchet Caye incident further underlined the unease with the degree and growth of foreign ownership of tourism resources in Belize. *Amandala* reflects these concerns in statements that clearly resonate the political economy of tourism.

> As Belize struggles to find the balance between the development and conservation of our natural resources, more and more we will run into the Hatchet Caye syndrome: foreign nationals and corporations who do not believe that they are answerable to us ... Belize and Belizeans are beginning to be trampled in the rush by those who regard our laws and traditions as inconvenient at best, and our sovereignty as theirs, bought and paid by their money.
>
> They wheedle, bribe and connive to extract their fortunes. And when all the above fail, they will resort to terrorism; covert campaigns, destabilisation and destruction, to have their way.

The concerns of Belizeans, especially the government's interpretation of what is and what is not ecotourism, were heightened by the announcement of a joint venture with a Mississippi-based company for a US$1 billion development to cover two-thirds of Ambergris Caye, the biggest of Belize's offshore islands.

The Ambergris Caye controversy raised serious doubts about the scale and nature of tourist development. Presented as a major contribution to re-investing in the Belizean people (a reflection of the PUP's 1989 Election spin 'Belizeans First'), the government bought back the northern two-thirds of the 20,000 acre Ambergris Caye from its US owner. It was expected that a newly established Ambergris Caye Planning Authority (ACPA), would have its jurisdiction and planning powers extended over this area of land, known as the Pinkerton Estate.

Without the knowledge of ACPA, however, the

government set up a semi-autonomous development corporation, appointed by and answerable to the then Tourism and Environment Minister, Glenn Godfrey (who was also the attorney general). It was planned to earmark approximately half the 20,000 acres for conservation and 2,500 acres for Belizeans. But it was on the remaining 7,500 acres that the corporation proposed a US$50 million 'sustainable development'.

In the relatively fragile ecology of Ambergris Caye, it is difficult to reconcile Minister Godfrey's statement that 'in Belize we must keep tourist developments small' (address to First World Congress on Tourism and the Environment, April 1992) with the claim that the proposed development represents 'an integrated and ecologically sound resort development' when the development was to comprise at least one international hotel, two 'all-inclusive spa hotels', three to five upscale lodges, two golf courses, town houses and villas, a thousand luxury homes, polo fields and stables.

Although the scheme did not progress, it is illustrative of the 'seductions of mass tourism' as Godfrey referred to it, and the manner in which local control is compromised, if it is not entirely absent. Just two days before the contract was to be signed between the developer and the Belizean government, Godfrey presented the document to ACPA for the first time in spite of discussions having proceeded over the two previous years.

A furious member of the ACPA encapsulated the mood of local people arguing that if the proposed agreement of North Ambergris Caye was as good as claimed, why had the minister not let the people know: 'When the government acquired the Pinkerton Estate, we were told in no uncertain terms that we were getting back control of the land and meaningful participation.

To me, 75 per cent to foreigners and 25 per cent to Belizeans is not fulfilling the promise.' As Otis reported in *The Nation* newspaper, one Belize-based diplomat commented,

'There is a latent resentment of foreign ownership. But Belizeans made a devil's bargain. They sold the place' (1992).

A further case in point was the proposed multi-million dollar Belize City Tourism District Project, which would have involved large-scale foreign capital investment or large-scale multilateral borrowing. New Orleans-based architects completed a USAID-sponsored initial study for a waterfront-style regeneration project. The planners hoped to build an exclusive downtown area complete with new hotels and shopping facilities, a promenade with seafront restaurants and cafés, an ethnic crafts and food market and marina for small yachts cruising the Caribbean.

It was, in other words, a mini Miami - the consultants even used Baltimore's Haborplace as an example of good practice and an aim to strive for - designed to transform the seafront district into a vacation *pied-à-terre* for would-be ecotourists, who would presumably feel protected from the urban problems that have become legendary in guidebooks to Belize.

The scheme was also underpinned by the philosophy that the benefits would, somehow, trickle down to the rest of the city's population. This would-be gentrification and a facsimile approach to new developments of certain city quarters globally - aping the style of western water-front developments-is becoming a particularly notable trend.

Not only would ordinary Belizeans gain little from this upscale project, but local representatives were not consulted in the planning process. In a bizarre twist, the city's planning department first learnt of the scheme when a three-dimensional model appeared in the window of the city's supermarket.

In a city of 60,000 where the city council is severely strapped for money and poverty is on the increase, the consultants also lauded the scheme for allowing the authorities to 'concentrate its resources' (and by inference cutting back spending in other, poorer, neighbourhoods) in one area. In this way, it was argued, the district would be a showcase, with cleaning, street lighting and road maintenance, for example, maximised.

Much of this expressed concern over the control of tourism development in Belize is also reflected in the ownership of tourism resources and facilities (a point already emphasised by the *Amandala* quote above). Some commentators have observed that much of the tourism industry is already in the hands of the country's small, but powerful expatriate community. Cater, a delegate at the ecotourism conference in 1991, found that 25 per cent of the registered delegates were US citizens, and more significantly, that among the 43 per cent registered as Belizeans were many expatriate Americans.

This is a phenomenon witnessed in many countries with expatriates running bars, restaurants, tour operations, lodges and hotels. Similarly, at the 1992 First World Congress on Tourism and The Environment in Belize City, more than 40 per cent of the 300 delegates came from the USA and Canada, and again, many of the 29 per cent of delegates from Belize were expatriate Americans. And as Linda Baker (2001) has pointed out:

Two decades after it won independence from Britain, Belize finds itself yoked to another kind of colonial enterprise; the foreign-dominated ecotourism trade. ... although Belize is one of the most environmentally conscious countries in the world, a significant percentage of its ecological wealth is concentrated in the hands of expatriates and foreign investors ... In 1998, a Belize Department of Environment report found that foreign-owned resorts and hotels were flouting environmental laws, causing damage to coral reefs and fishing grounds.

In Belize the expatriate community is a resolute and well-represented lobby. Expatriate riverside lodge owners from the western district of Cayo, for example, demanded strict zoning laws to protect their interests from further tourist development. The depth of expatriate ownership is further reflected through the USAID-initiated Belize Tourism

Industry Association (BTIA), an umbrella group representing private interests. In 1992, BTIA was thrown into turmoil when during the annual election of officers, a dispute erupted over whether seats on the committee should be restricted to Belizeans, even though 65 per cent of the membership were expatriates.

It appears, therefore, that the Belizean government's stated commitment to community tourism development is becoming more elusive as foreign control of the industry takes over. It is not just the large multinational companies and developers singled out in political economy approaches, but small-scale, alternative tourism businesses as well.

As Everitt (1987) comments of the post-independence period in Belize, with foreign (mainly Canadian and US) interests in control of the country's most successful tourist facilities, tourism has emerged as a symptom or contributory factor in the creation and aura of neo-colonialism. And it is difficult to escape the impression that Belize is primarily a piece of real estate; an advertisement for Ambergris Caye's Club Caribbean in the US publication *Belize Currents* claims: 'own your own piece of paradise ... Prices start as low as $9,950 ... Values are starting to soar'.

With the importance of tourism growing in the national economy, and the lure of perceived gains from the growth and development of the industry increasing as one of the most positively cited laboratories of successful ecotourism, the Belizean experience must be critically assessed. The government's need for foreign exchange is often in direct conflict with the need to control the scale and content of tourism development.

Expensive new infrastructure projects such as airports, roads and ports require a return on investment. Locally based and controlled tourism projects, while worthy, do not provide the return necessary for foreign investors and multilateral lending institutions. Indeed, a government's aspirations and expectations of tourism development often stand in contradiction to the aspirations of local people.

Sloan concludes that 'Belize is fast becoming one of the most popular ecotourism destinations in the hemisphere. But there's a hitch: All those ecotourists are threatening to trample the place to death - literally'. For others, the problems are considerably more deep-rooted.

As Everitt concludes of tourism, it is 'clear that economic imperialism is rife in Belize despite independence, and ranges throughout the economy which also sells its produce to the United States' (1987:51). Like citrus fruit or bananas, tourism has emerged as another cash crop in the national economy, and one that is challenging the image of small-scale locally owned projects.

Belize is also a perfect example of the complex interaction between a range of interests and why it is problematic to examine individual interests in isolation. In this case the interests of local people, multinational environmental NGOs, aid agencies and the Belizean government are intimately intertwined.

The second and third case studies provide further examples of the relationships between government policy and the discourse of sustainable tourism development. The second case study is from another Central American country, Costa Rica, and the third is from Bali.

Since the 1970s Costa Rica has developed a system of national parks and other protected areas which now cover just over a quarter of the country's land area. Despite severe under-funding for the protection of these areas, this system has formed the base resource of a tourism industry that has relied heavily on the attraction of the country's natural diversity of flora, fauna and landscape.

Consequently, it has become renowned as a destination for ecotourists. Outside San José, the capital city, its tourism industry has been largely based on small-scale, locally owned lodges and hotels which form an integral part of both the communities and natural environments in which they are located. Even within San José, there is a good supply of small hotels and only a limited supply of large-scale, luxury hotels. Partly through the efforts of its ministers speaking at international conferences, Costa Rica also gained an international reputation as a leader in environmental conservation. Whether this was deserved or not is rather debatable given its high rate of deforestation, especially during the 1980s, outside its protected areas.

As the 1990s progressed, however, international admiration of the Costa Rican government's shunning of large-scale, mass tourism developments began to fade as numerous contracts were signed with international consortia to build tourist condominia offering the 'four Ss' of mass tourism but also claiming to be environmentally sensitive and offering nature as part of the attraction. A number of features of these schemes are briefly outlined in the following paragraphs.

In Tambor on the Pacific coast peninsula of Nicoya, a subsidiary of the Barceló Group, a Spanish holiday firm which owns 4-star and 5-star hotels in Tunisia, Mexico, Spain, the Dominican Republic, Costa Rica and the USA, built a 400-room hotel complex within 50 metres of the high water mark. In so doing they stripped a hillside, filled in a swamp, extracted sand from a nearby river, destroyed a hillside to quarry its stone and threatened local species, all without the necessary building permits from the ministries of Housing, Health, Public Works and Transport and Natural Resources.

Additionally, it was reported that white sand was removed from a nearby beach and used to cover the original black sand beach at the complex. The hotel opened in 1992 and has been accused of depositing its sewage in the Rio Pánica.

In 1996 just to the north of Jacó on the Pacific coast of Costa Rica, construction began on the Los Sueños resort hotel, condominiums and marina at the once tranquil village of Playa Herradura. Apart from its negative aesthetic effect on the village, the project altered the extent and ecosystem of a tidal estuary and a marsh that used to stretch along the entire beach. These wetlands were an essential habitat, food source and nursery for a wide range of wildlife. The new yachting marina at the Los Sueños Resort was formally opened by the then President of Costa Rica and the then Minister of Tourism in February 2001.

The massive Papagayo project included the construction of 1,144 homes, 6,270 condohotel units, 6,584 hotel rooms, a shopping centre and a golf course. It formed a large part of the Costa Rican Institute of Tourism's development of Culebra Bay, also on the Pacific coast. The scheme went under the title 'Papagayo Ecodevelopment', but despite the planning which obviously went into it, the 'eco' more appropriately referred to the economic wealth it was intended to generate for its investors rather than to the local ecology it was supposed to save. During the planning of the project, Jeff Marshall, a regular commentator on Costa Rican tourism, said:

The enormous scope of this project is entirely inconsistent with the concept of sustainable and socially responsible ecotourism, which forms the very foundation of the highly successful tourism industry in this country ... It is nothing more than a high-profit real estate scheme designed to make a bundle of money for a few Costa Rican insiders and their foreign corporate allies.

In the mid-1990s, after work on the project had begun, it ground to a halt and people in the region were unsure of its future. Smaller-scale development continued, however, 'with hotels with golf courses being the latest development craze - a seemingly mad idea in this semi-arid landscape' (McNeil, 1999).

Environmentalists expressed concern that the enormous amount of water needed to maintain the golf courses would be taken from wetlands, mangroves and other delicate habitats, while the locals were worried that their water supplies may be curtailed. While the original extravagant plans may not be realised in this case, it appears that the scale of development will still be grandiose and may outstrip the area's carrying capacity.

The Arenal Volcano National Park provides a further illustration of the differences between the Costa Rican government's stated policies and its practices. The Arenal Volcano has two craters which erupt 24 hours a day giving a spectacular exhibition of nature which attracts ecotourists and gave rise to the development and expansion of the Arenal Volcano National Park.

This process of park expansion led to the forcible eviction of some local communities and the formation of an unholy alliance between the park authorities and hotel and resort owners to market the natural environment in an expensive and socially exclusive manner. Isla reports on one example of this process in the Arenal Volcano National Park:

Communities also lost the Tabacon river's hot spring. This spring is highly regarded as medicinal; it has been privatised by Tabacon Resort, which is an international private consortium with the involvement of some 'national' capital.

Tabacon Resort has built 11 swimming pools, using the hot spring water, at the very foot of the Arenal Volcano ... Tourism increased deforestation to build cabins and resort centres ... Forest conversion into resort centres endangers wildlife habitat by provoking mudslides, biotic impoverishment, and species forced migration.

A Tabacon Resort worker, who wishes to remain anonymous, says, 'Before building the swimming pools, we carried hundreds of frogs out of the area. After five years of activity, the frogs disappeared and the toucanos do not stand in the trees any longer. Massive use of chemicals to clean the swimming pools, washrooms, etc. left chemical residuals that force the animals to leave the surrounding areas.'

The link between the burden of international debt and government capitulation to the pressure of transnational companies to develop large-scale tourism projects in order to gain much-needed foreign exchange may be denied in some quarters. But while it may be difficult to prove the direct existence of the link, it is also difficult to refute with any degree of credibility.

The examples outlined above illustrate the subversive power of the pressure exerted by international consortia - baying at the heels of the international lending agencies which stipulate the need for national governments to raise foreign exchange to service their debt. As Michael Kaye, president of Costa Rica Expeditions tour company, has stated: 'the short-term temptations of the fast and easy money from mass tourism development in the context of an economy the size of Costa Rica's should not be under-estimated' (1994).

Under such pressure, it should be no surprise that the government of Costa Rica has felt obliged to abandon its previously cautious support for a sensitive and responsible type of community-based tourism development from which it, the government, gained relatively little financial benefit as most of this was received directly by Costa Ricans.

In 1992, Deirdre Evans-Pritchard, an English academic who formerly ran the Eco Institute of Costa Rica, pointed out that the Costa Rican Chamber of Tourism (CANATUR) was under the same kind of pressure as the government: 'the 1992 CANATUR congress championed noble causes and concerns in the name of small scale sustainable tourism development and then, in the final ceremony, awarded prizes to the four largest, most resort-like hotels in the country' (1993:779).

In 1994, the Costa Rican government suffered from another loss of power over its tourism industry which may account, at least in part, for the 1995 reduction in tourist numbers. The then Minister of Environment, René Castro, increased the entry fees to most national parks for foreigners by a factor of ten, ostensibly to further the government's sustainable development programme

by limiting the number of tourists using the country's natural resources. In one sense, his policy 'worked' - between '94 and '96, the nation's parks recorded an overall 26.5 per cent decrease in visits. Castro may have been motivated by more than the principle of sustainable development. The majority of foreign visitors to Costa Rica are 'shoestring' travellers, low-budget backpackers from the US, Europe and Australia. Both Castro and Figueres [then president] ... may have hoped that the tourist industry could recover any losses incurred by the decrease in backpackers through its promotion of Costa Rica as a travel destination for affluent visitors.

In response to the widespread complaints arising from the price increase and the significant decline in tourism receipts, from 1 April 1996, the entry fees were lowered from $15 to $6. Additionally, hotel and car rental companies reduced their daily rates by 15 per cent. CANATUR president, Mauricio Ventura, asked 'Who is the winner in this?' and answered, 'The tourist' (Mesoamérica, 1996).

The Costa Rican Institute of Tourism's (ICT) claim that the country is a model of sustainable development now rings a little hollow. As Jeff Marshall asks:

Instead of promoting massive centralised tourism projects tied to foreign capital, why doesn't the ICT concentrate on the careful planning and development of a network of quality, locally owned and operated, small scale tourism businesses that are compatible with the natural environment and integrated within the existing structures of local communities and economies?

And from her 2001 analysis of land management and ecotourism in Costa Rica, Ana Isla concluded that:

sustainable development suppresses the human rights of local communities and the rights of nature in favour of the rights of corporations, and vulnerable local nature and local people have become connected to the international markets and the world economy on disadvantageous terms. Communities have had to surrender their safe local food system and their role as agricultural producers. Thus, local environments and communities are impoverished.

Sustainable development aggravated poverty and environmental destruction for the short term benefit of capital

... In Costa Rica, these acts of colonisation are called acts of 'sustainable development'.

The island of Bali, Indonesia's main cultural tourist draw, has long attracted foreign visitors. Increasing consumer demand has coincided with the Indonesian government's own targets for tourism, which have used Bali as a pivotal marketing tool. At the same time, the special nature of Bali's attractions and the assumed fragility of its cultural life have made it one of the earliest testing grounds for theories about cultural sustainability in the context of tourism development.

National policies to increase tourism were accompanied by a conscious attempt to maximise economic benefits and minimise unwelcome impacts on the island's culture and environment. A tourism master plan drawn up by French consultants and released in 1971 recommended that 'any changes should reinforce not detract from traditional Balinese social structures'. These were based on *banjars*, neighbourhood associations which controlled virtually every aspect of people's lives. As part of the strategy, tourism development was to be confined to the area around the airport, on the southern peninsula.

A new resort, Nusa Dua, was constructed there to cater for the luxury package market and the conference trade. From there tourists are taken to visit famous temples, see craftspeople and artists at work or watch dance performances, with the proceeds going into the treasury of the *banjar* involved. Elsewhere, the largely agricultural life of the islanders was planned to continue.

The plan's formula for sustainable tourism certainly increased visitor numbers and limited the spatial development of tourism. But it 'gave rise to undisguised criticism in Bali ... The Master Plan was a plan for tourism, but it clearly was not a plan for the development of Bali'. In practice, the new hotels needed skills and capital not available locally, thus bringing in outside investors, both Indonesian and foreign, and limiting the projected local employment benefits.

Moreover the planners had not reckoned with the huge

popularity of Bali among independent travellers and young people booking flight-only holidays - the 'new' travellers. By 1985, ad hoc, unregulated tourist enterprises of all kinds were flourishing alongside the planned new hotels and packaged cultural attractions.

With tourist numbers exceeding forecasts, international assistance from the UNDP was sought to help with the management, planning and control of tourism on the island. Meanwhile, concern at the growing imbalance of prosperity between the south and other parts of the island led to an apparent *volte face*. The authorities discarded the original vision of a tourist ghetto and instituted a Spatial Arrangement Plan in 1989 which identified sixteen centres for tourism development around the island as part of a dispersal strategy.

This move could be seen as reflecting the agenda of local government, answering local needs, rather than national government, intent as the latter was on preserving the tourism product. In effect, however, the Spatial Arrangement Plan's wider distribution of tourism's economic benefits served to reinforce the kind of power structure that is most damaging to Bali's cultural continuity.

In 1995, an Australian report highlighted disturbing patterns of ownership in new resort developments around the island. It confirmed that these are no more likely to be controlled by local Balinese than the resorts in the southern enclave. Powerful Javanese and foreign investment interests are now firmly entrenched in the island's tourism economy.

Sustainability for these investors is strictly a matter of sustaining profits and their concerns are more about the availability of land for golf courses and condominia than about local needs and the continuation of a flourishing cultural community. The provincial authorities appear helpless to prevent the construction of new attractions alien to Balinese culture; new hotels are sited on sacred land despite local protests; and rural land is transformed into tourist playgrounds.

The Bali Sustainable Development Project undertaken

jointly by academics at Canada's University of Waterloo and Indonesia's universities of Gadja Meja and Udayana has attempted to demonstrate an alternative vision to the process of relentless outside manipulation, setting out proposals for integrating tourism into the wider Balinese economy. Some of its conclusions have been incorporated into the Bali Planning Department's recent five-year development plan, which recognises the importance of maintaining a viable agricultural sector and of supporting village institutions.

Implicit in this is the need to maintain local autonomy. But its effectiveness will depend on the nature of its challenge to the prevailing power relationships, in which outside investors now appear to be dominant.

Aung San Suu Kyi's National League for Democracy (NLD) won 81 per cent of the parliamentary seats in elections in Burma (Myanmar) in 1990. The response by the generals of the SLORC (State Law and Order Council) was to imprison most of the newly elected parliamentarians and to turn the country into what Amnesty International has called 'a prison without walls'.

Since that time, the United Nations Commission on Human Rights has described the country's violations of human rights as:

> extremely serious, in particular concerning the practice of torture, summary and arbitrary execution, forced labour, including forced portering for the military, abuse of women, politically motivated arrests and detention ... important restriction on the exercise of fundamental freedoms and the imposition of oppressive measures directed, in particular, at minority groups.

The issue of tourism in Burma highlights a number of points of interest in this chapter. These concern not just the relationship of the Burmese government to the tourism industry, but also the relationship of First World governments and tourism-related TNCs to the Burmese government and the role and responsibilities of tourism more generally.

Since 1990, 'The SLORC has been wooing new investors - especially in the area of tourism and hotel development - with offers of ten year tax breaks and full repatriation of profits'. As Mahr and Sutcliffe point out, such investment from TNCs based in the First World lends the régime political legitimacy, which is confirmed by the arrival of First World tourists - international tourist arrivals increased steadily from 26,607 in 1992 to almost 200,000 in 1998 (WTO/OMT, annual).

The SLORC/SPDC declared 1996 the 'Visit Myanmar Year' and increased its efforts to profit from the tourism industry by aiming at a target of half a million visitors for 1996. To prepare for the expected increase in tourists, the SLORC/SPDC put its people to work - forcibly - as described by Mahr and Sutcliffe:

Whole communities have been forcibly relocated from their homes to make way for foreign hotels and to 'clean up' areas for the eyes of tourists ...

Thousands of people have been forced to work without pay on tourist sites - restoring the moat around Mandalay Palace, for example. Plans have been put into action to relocate the more 'picturesque' ethnic peoples to special villages where they can be visited by tourist groups in what amounts to a human zoo. Model villages for this purpose are under construction near Rangoon and some Padaung people have already been resettled to Inle Lake. There tourists can visit - for a charge - and take photos of 'long-necked' Padaung women.

These human rights violations have been documented in detail by the UK-based Burma Action Group and reported by Tourism Concern and increasingly in the western media. In 1996 Aung San Suu Kyi specifically asked visitors to stay away from her country until the military government hands over power to the NLD. Lonely Planet Publications, however, have been publishing their Burma guidebook since 1979 and have continued to do so since this call for visitors to stay away.

In May 2000, the Burma Campaign UK and Tourism

Concern launched a boycott campaign against Lonely Planet Publications because of its Burma travel guidebook written by Joe Cummings and Michael Clark. Under the banner 'There are times when travellers have to take a stand.

This is one: BOYCOTT LONELY PLANET', they asked consumers of travel guides to boycott all Lonely Planet publications until the Burma guidebook are withdrawn. Glenys Kinnock, European parliamentarian, in an article in the UK *Guardian* newspaper summarises the request behind the boycott thus:

Aung San Suu Kyi asks a simple thing ... She's asked for sanctions so that the junta will be starved out of existence. We can impose our own sanctions and not go on holiday to Burma. And we should certainly not buy from publishers that suggest that we should.

In a letter to concerned members of the UK parliament, Tony Wheeler, Lonely Planet publisher, retorted by accusing the two groups of censorship. The debate between the two has been joined with some heat ever since (Wheeler, 2000, 2001; Burma Campaign UK and Tourism Concern, 2000a and 2000b). In response to the boycott campaign's claim that visiting the country is tantamount to approval of the SLORC/SPDC, Wheeler claims that only a tiny proportion of tourist revenues will reach the illegitimate military government's coffers and that the Burmese people want to talk to outsiders.

The cartoon is one of many representations of the boycott campaign's view of the Lonely Planet attitude. Wheeler claims that the NLD voices asking for a boycott are those of NLD members living in exile who are not aware of the current reality in Burma. The debate also reached the UK BBC's Newsnight programme in October 2000 which revealed that the Sittwe Hotel, promoted in Lonely Planet's guide along with other government guesthouses in the area, is included in an International Labour Organisation report (ILO, 1998) as having been built with forced labour. Critics describe Wheeler's approach as one of arrogant defiance and stubborn self-certainty. In the UK *Observer* newspaper Nick Cohen used the debate to describe the attitudes of both the new tourists who are likely to visit Burma and the alternative guidebook publisher who is likely to benefit from sales to them:

The Burma spat has been distinguished by the extremism of the invective of bohemian travellers. Dea Birkett, a travel writer, whined rhetorically in the *Guardian* of all places: 'Aren't holidays supposed to be carefree times for suntans and self-indulgence? Is it really such a crime to seek out somewhere where you can simply enjoy yourself? Tourism Concern and the Burma Campaign's moral outrage is designed to make us feel bad about being good to ourselves. To restrict freedom of movement is the hallmark of totalitarian régimes.'

Forget her wheedling style for a second, and consider the implications of Birkett's words. The opponents of dictatorship, who fight without resources, international support or any military force which might defeat the junta on the field of battle, are totalitarians. Rich western tourists, by contrast, are the true victims even when they stay in Rangoon hotels built on the site of the homes of the Burmese poor - which were bulldozed without compensation - or travel on a moving staircase built by forced labour to catch the marvellous view at sunset from Mandalay Hill.

Only a sadist would want to make them 'feel bad about being good to ourselves' ... Though I'm all for boycotting Lonely Planet, the real significance of the argument is cultural. Discerning liberal consumers are now so self-confident and self-pitying that they pose, without irony, as the victims of Stalin and Hitler when anyone suggests they might make the tiniest moral choice. It says so much about them.

Whatever the pros and cons of the argument, few if any British tour operators can currently be unaware of the debate around the ethical grounds for not visiting Burma. New hotels are being built by TNCs from Hong Kong, Japan, Malaysia, Singapore, South Korea and Thailand, and French and Swiss interests are also involved. Companies such as Voyages Jules Verne, Coromandel and David Sayers Travel all run cultural or trekking tours to Burma. Coromandel describes its relation with Burma thus:

We are probably Britain's leading specialists for Burma, firmly believing that contact with the free world does more good than isolation. In spite of a number of good new private sector hotels and new airlines, Burma remains a destination for the traveller rather than the tourist, but the rewards are great, with splendid scenery, magnificent monuments, and a warm and smiling welcome from the Burmese themselves.

Explore, on the other hand, ceased covering Burma on its tours largely because of UK Foreign Office advice regarding the nature of the régime. Bales also ceased to cover Burma in their main brochure in 1999 for the same reason, although they are still willing to arrange tailor-made tours upon specific request.

Burma represents an attractive Third World destination for the new middle-class tourists. But more importantly from the standpoints of the First World corporate decision-makers, it represents an attractive investment opportunity for tourism businesses. And First World governments can and do assist in these processes of tourism investment and associated human rights violations.

The UK government's stated policy is not to promote investment in Burma because of the SLORC/SPDC's human rights violations. In 1996, however, despite its stated policy, the government's Department of Trade and Industry (DTI) allocated £50,000 travelling expenses to trade missions to Burma for the year. After the first mission at the end of February, in the words of Tourism Concern, the

Shadow Foreign Affairs Minister [Derek Fatchett] asked a parliamentary question about the DTI's plans for future trade missions [to Burma] and the reply was 'we intend to evaluate the results of this mission before deciding on supporting the second'. Civil service speak for 'oops - we've been found out'.

It can be assumed that First World governments would not try to cover up public knowledge of such trade missions if they believed that the development to be promoted by these missions could be portrayed as being ethically sound or in the interests of sustainability.

The example of Burma is indicative of the 'reality' to which governments and the industry work. It is a reality which they use to justify their actions and investments. If ethical considerations contradict this reality, then they must be hidden from view.

Tourism in Burma gives us an illustration of the way in which investment is used to serve specific interests, those of the Burmese government, First World governments, tourists and crucially tourism-related businesses. Other interests, those of the visited, the resettled, the majority of Burmese people, are decidedly not served by these investments and developments.

But whereas in many Third World destination countries the governments have to be coerced by First World governments, international lending agencies and TNCs, in the case of Burma the SLORC/SPDC actively enlists the assistance of these bodies. Power is still very much based in the First World, but with a willing partner in Burma's military and business elites.

Despite the clarity and documentation of the link between Burma's human rights violations and its exploitation of nature and cultural tourism, the brochures of some new tourism companies still extol its virtues. In such circumstances, then, it is hardly surprising that for many tourists the relationship between travel, tourism and human rights has remained rather nebulous.

Indeed, the occurrence of human rights abuses and their coincidence with perceived danger may actually act as a fillip to tourism in certain circumstances and among certain types of tourists.

It has been argued that an understanding of issues of power is essential to an analysis of tourism developments and the role of governments in this. The necessity for such an understanding is as great for analyses of new forms of tourism to Third World destinations as it is for mass tourism developments - perhaps even more so given the relationship of new forms of tourism to 'development'.

It is commonly perceived, especially from the level of the local community, that power rests with the national government. This may indeed be the case in some instances, but we have suggested that the actions and policies pursued by national governments are often circumscribed at best and are sometimes dictated by the influence of external organisations.

This includes both the inevitability that tourism must increase, as well as the contest over which form of tourism development should take place. It is especially so for Third World governments weighed down by a burden of debt - a burden that was largely foisted upon them by First World banks and governments as well as their own incautiousness resulting from the unseemly rush for western-style development.

For the most part, the outcome of this process of First World influence on Third World development has been government policies which increase the unevenness and inequality of development within national boundaries and which further widen the gap between First and Third Worlds. The policies pursued for the development of tourism are largely those most suitable to the profits and enjoyment of First World investors and tourists rather than those most beneficial to Third World communities and governments. This is not to say that there are no opportunities for positive and beneficial change. Our discussion of pro-poor tourism initiatives, for example, suggests that such opportunities may exist. But given the global analysis and the enormity of global poverty, the ability of tourism initiatives to tackle global inequality is slight.

We have tried to show how, even where governments have attempted to follow environmentally benign, socially and economically beneficial and culturally sensitive tourism developments, forces beyond their control have subverted the policies and have served only to emphasise the seemingly ever-widening gaps. In the process, government attempts to satisfy outsiders' views of the content of tourism have turned sustainable tourism into an item of political discourse.

In order to achieve this broader analysis, a number of key themes (new tourism, uneven and unequal development and the Third World) and key words (globalisation, sustainability and development) were identified. Summarises these positions and seeks to illustrate the relationships between the key words and key themes by drawing some examples from and questions raised by the book. Clearly the relationships summarised in the cells of the table are not exclusive and there is considerable overlap between both the key words and key themes.

Globalisation, sustainability and development, it was argued, were best thought of as key words as each is open to competing meanings and interpretations: to a backpacker the Third World may represent exotic cultures and environments and an endless world of adventure; to mass tourists in the USA, Europe or the Pacific Rim, the notion of the Third World may represent a threat, and a place either to avoid when holidaying or where a holiday needs to be carefully controlled, through all-inclusive enclave tourism, for example.

Arguably, the most important purpose for this book was to establish that these key words are hotly contested and that relationships of power underlie the construction, representation and implementation of these processes. So for example, this helps us understand the way in which new tourism seeks to differentiate and distance itself from mass forms of tourism and how sustainability does not have a fixed and agreed definition that is shared by everyone.

The first of the key themes - unequal and uneven development - was adopted as shorthand for indicating the inequality faced by certain nation states, regions, communities and individuals. The principal focus was on the way in which inequality is expressed globally through the First and Third Worlds, but clearly unevenness is also expressed, for example, in the way certain Third World destinations become tourist magnets while others do not. This is an explicit recognition that relationships of power must lie at the centre of tourism analysis. This necessitates a more nuanced and extended discussion of inequality and shows that power is transmitted in and through tourism.

This varies from the power wielded by private business consortia such as the WTTC, to the priorities of environmental sustainability, to the way in which new tourism draws in and controls new Third World destinations. As Hutnyk observes: 'social sciences have sometimes been complicit in maintaining distinctions and privileges among different classes of people, and between First and Third World, by choosing to investigate the conditions of "the poor" and "disempowered" rather than pursuing research into power' (1996:216).

We have traced these relationships of power and variable development through the Third World, though we have recognised that in itself the Third World is a socially constructed and contested entity that is inexorably related to development.

Our final theme is new tourism to which we return and recap below. At the outset we argued that this theme was a means or medium for analysing and understanding the broader scope of this book.

We have added 'tourism and geographical imagination' to the themes. The notion of tourism and geographical imagination seeks to emphasise that we are dealing with the nature of representation, how the context and meanings of words such as sustainability and development are socially constructed by host communities, governments, TNCs, smaller operators, environmental organisations and tourists. They are words whose meaning is open to interpretation and are continually contested between different interest groups - a point that is reflected in the examples provided in the final column.

NEW FORMS OF THIRD WORLD TOURISM

As the early chapters of the book argue and portray, they have arisen as a result of a wide variety of economic, socio-cultural and environmental factors. Factors such as a structural economic shift from a Fordist to a post-Fordist mode of production, accompanied by cultural shifts characterised as moving from modernism to postmodernism, and a growing environmentalism, help explain the increase in the number of new forms of tourism.

Independent travel has sought to distance itself from mass tourism, and a variety of benevolent terms (appropriate, alternative, acceptable, responsible, sustainable, and so on) have been employed in an attempt to assert that it is these forms of tourism that provide an ethical and practically acceptable response to 'development' and the structure of disadvantage of the Third World.

We have attempted to demonstrate a tentative link between the economic and cultural shifts in contemporary capitalism and the growth of the new middle classes. We suggested that it is these class fractions in particular (though not exclusively) that can be linked to the growth of new tourism. Furthermore, these new groups and their motives are more formally represented by the international NGOs which campaign around issues of conservation, ecology, pollution, human rights and cultural identity to which many of the new middle classes subscribe.

These organisations represent the vanguard of this movement to gain a moral base and a justification for their own definition of sustainability, which is often constrained by a restricted association with ecology. The subliminal promotion of a conservation ethic and the assured certainty of one form of sustainability are responsible for the emergence of attitudes which in some cases have been characterised as eco-colonialist.

Chapter 6

Tourism Trends and Career Prospects

The World Tourism Organization forecasts that international tourism will continue growing at the average annual rate of 4 per cent. By 2020 Europe will remain the most popular destination, but its share will drop from 60 per cent in 1995 to 46 per cent. Long-haul will grow slightly faster than intraregional travel and by 2020 its share will increase from 18 per cent in 1995 to 24 per cent.

Since e-commerce has taken off on the internet, tourism products have become one of the most traded items on the net. Tourism products and services have been made available on the net at bargain prices through intermediaries. In recent time, tourism providers (hotels, airlines, etc.) have started to sell their services through the internet.

This has put pressure on intermediaries from both the virtual and the traditional brick and mortar stores. Space tourism is expected to "take off" in the first quarter of the 21st century, although compared with traditional destinations the number of tourists in orbit will remain low until technlogies such as a space elevator make space travel cheap.

Technological improvement is likely to make possible air-ship hotels, based either on solar-powered airplanes or large dirigibles. Underwater hotels, such as Hydropolis, expected to open in Dubai in 2006, will be built. On the ocean tourists will be welcomed by ever larger cruise ships and perhaps floating cities. Some futurists expect that movable hotel "pods" will be created that could be temporarily erected anywhere on the planet, where building a permanent resort would be unacceptable politically, economically or environmentally.

BENEFITS OF TOURISM

Tourism is now the world's largest industry. The World Tourism Council estimates that travel and tourism provides employment for more than 100 million people world wide (that's one in sixteen workers) and is responsible for over 7% of world wide capital investment. In the year ended June 2003, there were 1,261,818 visitors to the Fraser Coast. Of these 67% were intrastate visitors (849,000), 17% were interstate visitors (214,000) and 16% were international visitors (198,818). In the same period 5,223,187 visitor nights were spent in the region. Domestic and International tourism contributed in net terms approximately $6 billion to the Queensland economy. Tourism generates $2.4 billion annually as an export earner, accounting for 11% of total Queensland exports overseas, second only to coal exports.

MULTIPLIER EFFECT

A tourist dollar is a new dollar injected into the local economy. A percentage of this new dollar is spent in the community by the recipient and this dollar is spent and re-spent creating a multiplier effect. The more new tourist dollars entering a local economy and the longer the percentage is retained locally, the greater the economic benefit.

EMPLOYMENT OPPORTUNITIES

Tourism is a labour intensive industry and creates many job opportunities, especially for young people and part-time and full-time workers. In the tourism hospitality and recreation industries alone there are 50 categories of employment and approximately 200 classifications of occupations.

DIVERSIFICATION

Tourism can provide diversification, making the local

economy less reliant on a traditional base e.g. agriculture and mining. This is particularly significant for regional rural communities.

OPPORTUNITIES FOR BUSINESS

Tourism creates opportunities for the establishment of new products, facilities and services and expansion of existing businesses which would not otherwise be justified solely on the resident population.

PRESERVATION OF THE ENVIRONMENT AND HERITAGE

Tourism highlights the need for proper management and, through effective policies and planning, can ensure that the environment, heritage and inherent character of an area is preserved.

THE CATALYST FOR RESIDENTIAL DEVELOPMENT

In many places visitors who initially travelled to particular areas as tourists, have relocated to those areas to become residents and acquire a better quality of life.

IMPROVED TRANSPORT SERVICES

Tourism can stimulate the establishment of new and improved transport services to and within a regional area.

A BROADER SOCIAL OUTLOOK

Tourism provides the opportunity for residents to interact with other people and cultures and brings new ideas into the community.

Tourism Costs and Benefits

Costs

Social Costs

- May attract visitors whose lifestyles and ideas conflict

with the community's. An example may be the visitors' use of drugs and alcohol.

- May change individual behaviour and family relationships.
- May lead to an increase in sexually transmitted diseases.
- Loss of traditional values and culture through imitation of visitor behaviour or cultural diffusion resulting from normal, everyday interaction.
- May create crowding and congestion.
- May compete with residents for available services, facilities, and existing recreation opportunities.
- May result in harassment of visitors perceived to be wealthy and an increase in crime.

Can involve violations of human rights. People have been displaced from their land and beaches have been reserved for hotel guests while access is barred to local people.

Benefits

Social Benefits

- Brings in outside dollars to support community facilities and services that otherwise might not be developed.
- Encourages civic involvement and pride.
- Provides cultural exchange between hosts and guests.
- Encourages the preservation and celebration of local festivals and cultural events.
- Facilities and infrastructure developed for tourism can also benefit residents.
- Encourages the learning of new languages and skills.
- Tourism related funds have contributed towards schools being built in some areas.

Environmental Benefits

- Fosters conservation and preservation of natural, cultural and historical resources.

- Encourages community beautification and revitalization.
- Could be considered a clean industry.

Environmental Costs

- May threaten specific natural resources such as beaches and coral reefs or historical sites.
- May increase litter, noise, and pollution.
- Brings increased competition for limited resources such as water and land, resulting in land degradation, loss of wildlife habitats and deterioration of scenery.
- Directly contributes to sewage and solid waste pollution.
- Emissions generated by forms of transport are one of the main environmental problems of tourism.

Economic Benefits

- Helps diversify and stabilize the local economy.
- Provides governments with extra tax revenues each year through accommodation and restaurant taxes, airport taxes, sales taxes, park entrance fees, employee income tax etc..
- Creates local jobs and business opportunities. These include those jobs directly related to tourism (hotel and tour services) and those that indirectly support tourism (such as food production and housing construction).
- The multiplier effect:
  - Brings new money into the economy. Tourist money is returned to the local economy as it is spent over and over again.
  - Helps attract additional businesses and services to support the tourist industry.
- Is labour-intensive.
- Earns valuable foreign exchange.

Economic Costs

- Tourism development of infrastructure (airports, roads, etc.) can cost the local government a great deal of money.
- May inflate property values and prices of goods and services.
- Leakages:
  - If outside interests own the tourism development, most of the economic benefits will leave the community.
  - Considerable amount of foreign exchange revenues leaks back out of the destination countries for tourism-related imports.
- Employment tends to be seasonal. Workers may be laid off in the winter season.
- Many jobs in the tourism industry are poorly paid. This is a particular problem in LEDCs where the local workforce lacks the skills to fill the better paid management positions.
- Tourist numbers can be adversely affected by events beyond the control of the destination e.g. terrorism, economic recession. This is a big problem in LEDC countries dependent on tourism.
- Tourism follows a "product life cycle", with a final stage of decline, where the destination no longer offers new attractions for the tourist, and the quality has diminished with the rise of competition and tourist saturation.

BENEFITS COMMUNITIES

Tourism is one of the most effective ways of redistributing wealth, by moving money into local economies from other parts of the country and overseas. It brings income into a community that would otherwise not be earned.

Economic Benefits

Economic benefits resulting from tourism can take a number of forms including:

- *Jobs*: Employment may be associated directly, such as tour guide or managerial positions; or in supporting industries like food production or retail suppliers.
- *Increased spending*: Increased spending in the community generated from visitors or tourism businesses can directly and indirectly promote the viability of local businesses.
- *Economic diversification*: Tourism operators can play a role in highlighting the broad prosperity that tourism can bring to a community and will contribute to a greater understanding and respect for the value of tourism.

Economic diversification is, for many communities, an insurance policy against hard times. By offering an additional means of income, tourism can support a community when a traditional industry is under financial pressure, particularly where that community relies heavily on a single industry.

Case Study: Farmers markets

The popularity of farmers' markets is increasing becoming a key driver of economic development in regional areas. Activities such as visits to farms and farmers' markets, fruit picking and agricultural farm accommodation may provide important supplemental activities to struggling rural areas. Some of the benefits of Farmers' Markets seen include:

- Showcases local produce and local products
- Encourage visitors from other areas
- Showcase the local and regional areas
- Allows for community events to be incorporated
- Provides distribution opportunities for small businesses
- Valuable contribution to the economic development of the area as money is spent locally
- Infrastructure

Infrastructure including roads, parks, and other public spaces can be developed and improved both for visitors and local residents through increased tourism activity in a region.

SOCIAL BENEFITS

Community identity and pride can be generated through tourism. A positive sense of community identity can be reinforced and tourism can encourage local communities to maintain their traditions and identity.

ENVIRONMENTAL BENEFITS

Providing financial or in-kind support for the conservation of the local environment and natural resources will enhance the reputation of any tourism business. Tourism, particularly ecotourism, can place a greater focus on the conservation of natural resources through the recognition of their importance to visitor experiences and their economic value to the local community.

CAREER IN TOURISM OPERATORS

Maximum benefit from community involvement for the tourism operator occurs when a tourism venture operates in harmony with the social and cultural aspirations of the local community. Involving the community in the development and subsequent operation of tourism projects will not only create greater local support for the operation, it also has the potential to:

- Increase business profits through improved word of mouth referral;
- Grow repeat business from improved experiences with the community; and
- Increase visitation through recognition of best practice standards.

Communities form the backdrop of any tourism product. They provide the support that tourism needs to survive and are often part of the reason visitors are attracted to a destination. Sustainable and responsible tourism is about ensuring a win-win for the community, economy and environment. The attitude, resources and strategic thinking of tourism operators is essential.

OUTLINE OF ADVANTAGES AND DISADVANTAGES

Advantage (depending upon implementation some of these can turn into disadvantages):

- Employment (1 emp/1000 tourist) (labour intensive, few administrative positions, little upward mobility.)
- Infrastructure development (roads, water, electricity, telecom and cybercom, but not necessarily local priorities.)
- Cultural preservation (economic incentives to preserve food, fashion, festivals and physical history, but these tend to be superficial elements of a culture.)
- Environmental protection (econ incentives to preserve nature, wildlife and urban cleanliness)
- Foreign exchange (generates resources to import food, pharmaceuticals, technology, consumer goods.)
- Development of health care services (those these aren't always available to local people.)

Disadvantages (depending upon implementation some of these can turn into advantages):

- Cultural destruction, (modernization (world mono-culture), freezes culture as performers, loss: language, religion, rituals, material culture.)
- Primary products (sun, sand, surf, safari, suds, ski, sex) (little value added, neo-colonialism)
- Environmental destruction (game drives, resorts: golf, ski, beach, desert, world as play ground, SUV.)
- Marginal employment (low skill, low wage, menial services, prostitution, drug trade, gambling, hustlers.)
- Low benefits (no job security, no health care, no organizing, no work safety rules or enviro standards.)
- Development of illegal and/or destructive economic activities (markets for drugs, endangered species, etc.)
- Outside hiring (skilled middle and senior management recruited out of the area and transferred in.)

- Concentration employment (walled resort enclaves.)
- Seasonal employment
- Outside decision making (decisions made outside of the area, corporate dollars corrupt government.)
- Unrealistic expectations (divert young people from school and brighter futures.)
- Anti-democratic collusion (industry support of repressive governments)
- Land controlled by the elite (people relocated, agriculture eliminated, prohibited from N.P.)
- Negative lifestyle's (STD's, substance abuse, begging, hustling)
- Diverted and concentrated development (airport, roads, water, electricity to tourist destinations, development not accessible to locals),
- Little forex stays in country (airplanes, vehicles, booze, hot air balloons, generally have foreign owners),
- Package programs
- Cruises (eat and sleep on board so the economic benefits to the ports-of-call is very thin and limited.)
- Unstable market (fickle, affected by local and world events, generally highly elastic)
- Health tourism (traveling to get medical procedure at lower cost) has it own set of unique challenges, which include: Determining the credential, skills and quality of the facility and personnel. Language communication challenges on topics requiring a lot of details, sometimes even when both parties seemingly speak the same language. Different cultural issues and expectations around health care and the body. Post-treatment complications, after the "tourist" has left the facility.

Solutions (for visitor):

- Act to support cultural diversity
- Engage in activities that add value to the community
- Don't do activities that deteriorate the environment

- Don't engage in illegal activities
- Act to disperse the benefits
- Patronize locally (community) owned enterprises.

Solutions (for the host):

- Support the traditional cultural legacy
- Training and education in local culture, history, natural science, etc.
- Select development and activities that draw from local traditions and add value to the community
- Don't promote activities that deteriorate the environment
- Don't engage in illegal activities
- Adopt a programme to disperse the benefits
- Patronize locally produced products and locally (community) owned enterprises.
- Make business and foreign exchange transactions transparent and efficient.

ECOTOURISM, RESPONSIBLE TOURISM AND E³ TRAVEL PROGRAMS

IBF has long been uncomfortable with the terms eco-tour and ecotourism because there is no accountability and they have been used to embrace ANY travel that includes "nature" — getting out of a city — even when getting there is by a gas guzzling SUV (sport-utility vehicle or four-wheel drive); ripping up the savannah in the process, and regardless of its impact — that is not us. Other not uncommon characteristics of "eco-tourism" can be; energy-intensive accommodations, encouraging gluttonous amounts of eating (with no reference to dining room waste, how food was produced, or where — a reliance of imported foodstuff and drinks,) prodigious amounts of promotional materials that are paper intensive, and other wasteful and/or energy intensive practices, and little client education on impact of cultural behaviour on the environment.

Consequentially we rarely use the term ecotourism in any of our publicity. "Responsible travel" is facing the same deterioration. It should be "(original) eco-tourism plus". Too often it is defined and practiced with a diluted focuses on cultural responsibility and economic benefit, and a general neglect energy intensiveness (i.e. motorization) and other sustainability issues.

As an alternative we measure programs by a "E³ Travel" standard (environment, economics and education). This is very similar to the triple bottom line concept of sustainable business (environment, social justice and fiscal), but we like to think of it as the top line for travel programs.

- Environmentally friendly (using primarily non-motorized transport, but reflecting all aspects of the projects including reducing printing and paper consumption, selection of energy efficient lodging, consuming local produced food and goods, and minimizing waste at all levels),
- Economic/equity benefits (supporting the decentralized, indigenous economy, including local produced food, goods and services, and local employment generator) and
- Educational/enriching/engaging (training guides and helping participants to explore the diversity and complexity of the local natural and human ecology.)

If you draw these as a triangle, each element reinforces the others:

- The use of non-motorized transports virtually mandates patronizing local business. In many parts of the world it is often impossible to bicycle from tourist enclave to tourist enclave in a day. The increased exposure to the local culture, local cuisine, local economy, local interaction, and environment inherently leads to enhanced education and more enriching experiences. But environmental issues go beyond choosing the mode of travel. It is worth bringing your environmental consciousness/audit to every aspect of your travel project: If you use a travel provider, is the advertising and back office side of the "eco-tour" company as environmentally friendly as they would have you thing that their programme is? Can you steer away from energy intensive and import intensive hotels and over-sized everything and steer toward local produced services and goods? Vacation is a time to pamper yourself, and you can still indulge yourself in quality, but you may want to pass on providers of lavish (and wasteful) quantity.

- Aiming for an enriching and well rounded educational experience, is a natural to get more into the community and supporting local business. This argues for eliminating the barriers of glass, steel and speed that go with motor vehicles. Walking and bicycling are great modes for picking up information, engaging with the community and environment around you and supporting the most-local economy.
- Including as a goal equity and supporting local suppliers of goods and service dictates increased interaction with the cultural and enriching experiences. The use of non-motorized transport virtually assures that the benefits will be decentralized and widely beneficial. Sort through you choices is not always easy: There are foreign owned businesses with excellent environments practices and who provide their employees and the surrounding community with excellent compensation and benefits. And, there are local owned business that exploit their employees, do very little to share there good fortune with the surrounding community, are energy and resource intensive, and materially wasteful (make no attempt to reduce, reuse or recycle.) It is hard to make hard and fast rules here, but the small businessperson in the community is usually pretty equitable and a contributing member of the community. The also likely to be fairly well interwoven in the culture and environmentally responsible.

Incidentally, in tourism E^3 product doesn't seem to be a gender thing: We have seen both male and female own travel specialist who were both good and bad. We have seen foreign owned, male and female, boutique hotel operators who were good and bad. And, we have seen locally owned, male and female service providers who were both good and bad on a E^3 audit.

Within the E^3 structure, an urban bike ride with a lecture on a historic district, a work project in a village and forest walk learning about ethno-botany and looking for primates all can come out on top, as we think they should. Traditional "S"-tourism" (sun, sand, sea, skiing, sailing, sitting, swimming, scuba, snorkel, safari, sitting, sleeping, sight-seeing) can be done in a E^3 way. It is not necessarily the location, the activity or the personnel, but it is how it fits together, the benefits and the costs. Help heal the world when you travel. Do the E^3 of defined activity guarantee sustainability? No, not if integral to getting to the activity is airplane travel by the participants.

Given current technology, even with carbon offsets, you are at best at a "second-best solution". The theory is that second-best solutions are never as good first-best, which in this case would forgoing the flying. A reasonable expectation of how people are going to get to the E^3 activity must be incorporated into the equation. The triple bottom line of responsible tourism is 3 E's: environmental sustainability, engaging in the local economic, and enriching your life from the culture. Actually, it is about the same for all life.

Tourism is the act of travel for the purpose of not only recreation, but also the provision of services for this act. It might occupy local services such as entertainment, accommodation and catering for tourists. It may seem, that tourism brings only benefits, but further consideration shows that it also has disadvantages. Firstly, many countries depend heavily upon travel expenditures by foreigners as a source of taxation and as a source of income for the enterprises. Therefore, the development of tourism is often a strategy tò promote a particular region for the purpose of increasing commerce through exporting goods and services.

Secondly, it provides direct employment for the people associated with occupations in bars and hotels. Thanks to it, the average standard of living of people increases well and at the same time unemployment is on the decrease. However, tourists cause environmental damage through forest fires, destruction of sand dunes and pollution. Consequently this serves negatively as increased pollution disturbs local residents and also it may discourage tourists from further entering the country.

After this, tourism undermines culture by commercializing it and this is often connected with increasing litter, graffiti, vandalism and noise - tourists do not always respect traditional cultures, which is sad but true. In general, tourism is an extremely profitable process in loads of countries, especially those in which the process of development continue to depend on this industry because this industry does not require a lot of literacy and also it yields maximum profits with less investment.

There are a number of benefits of tourism for both the tourist and the host destination. On a large scale it offers a good alternative to some more destructive industries for generating income both on nationally and privately. The tourism industry encompasses many different areas, so it also creates jobs in many different areas. With tourism comes hotels, resturants, car rental agencies, tour companies, service stations, souvenier shops, sports equipment rentals, and much more. All of this creates many different levels of employment for people in a given community.

In many places the introduction and development of tourism allows local people an opportunity for economic and educational growth that would not otherwise be available. In addition, it allows both the tourist and the local community a chance to experience other cultures, which broadens understanding. If properly used, tourism generated income can be tremendously beneficial to the host country and it's local communities. Tourism generated income can be used on a national and local level to better education, improve infrastructure, to fund conservation efforts, and to promote more responsible tourism.

INDIA IN THE PICTURE

Tourism in India has received a major boost in the past decade since the Indian Government realized the great potential of tourism of India during vacations. Tourism of India during vacations has grown by leaps and bounds with a great influx of tourists from throughout the. world who have been irresistibly attractive to the travelers. India has the right tourism potential and attractions to captivate all types of tourists whether it is adventurous tour, cultural exploration, pilgrimages, visit to the beautiful beaches or to the scenic mountain resorts, Tourism of India has it all for you.

Travel through Indian states and cities bring to light, the cultural and the geographical richness of India. We provide you a glimpse to the richness of tourism in India with information on all the major tourist destinations of India and tourism services of India that will take care of all your problems while you are in India. India, located in Asia. Is bounded by the Himalayan ranges in the north, surrounded by the Arabian Sea, the Bay of Bengal, and the Indian Ocean. In 2006, about 4 million foreign tourists visited India and spent US$ 8.9 billion. In 2007, India's 5 million international arrivals - out of 903 million worldwide - were the world's 42nd highest.

India's tourism sector lags behind less endowed countries. Among India's shortcomings are "stringent visa requirements and airport density, which rank poor 106 and 121" out of 124 countries on the *Travel & Tourism Competitiveness Report 2007*.India's expensive hotel rooms stand at the rank 113. "People's openness to tourism" ranking is 97. At the same time, India has great advantages: price competitiveness ranking was a high 6th, while safety and security was a good 39th. The tourism sector is growing at double digits. India has a huge advertising campaign "Incredible India". Travel and tourism contributes 5.3% to India's GDP.

TOURISM BY STATE

Andhra Pradesh

Andhra Pradesh has a rich cultural heritage and a variety of tourist attractions. The state of Andhra Pradesh comprises scenic hills, forests, beaches and temples. Andhra Pradesh is the home of many religious pilgrimage centres, one of them being 'Tirupati,' the abode of Lord Venkateswara, which is the richest and most visited Hindu temple in India. Hyderabad is known for its rich history, culture and architecture representing its unique character as a meeting point for North and South India, and also its multilingual culture, both geographically and culturally.

Also known as The City of Nizams and The City of Pearls, Hyderabad is today one of the most developed cities in the country and a modern hub of information technology, ITES, and biotechnology. Hyderabad offers many attraction to the tourists. It is famous for its delicious *Hyderabadi Biryani.It is india's second largest metropolitan.* Andhra Pradesh is the home of many religious pilgrim centres.

Tirupati, the abode of Lord Venkateswara, is the richest and most visited religious centre (of any faith) in the world. Srisailam, the abode of Sri Mallikarjuna, is one of twelve Jyothirlingalu in India, Amaravati's Siva temple is one of the Pancharamams, and Yadagirigutta, the abode of an avatara of Vishnu, Sri Lakshmi Narasimha. The Ramappa temple and Thousand Pillars temple in Warangal are famous for some fine temple carvings.

The state has numerous Buddhist centres at Amaravati, Nagarjuna Konda, Bhattiprolu, Ghantasala, Nelakondapalli, Dhulikatta, Bavikonda, Thotlakonda, Shalihundam, Pavuralakonda, Sankaram, Phanigiri and Kolanpaka. The golden beaches at Visakhapatnam, the one-million-year old limestone caves at Borra, picturesque Araku Valley, hill resorts of Horsley Hills, river Godavari racing through a narrow gorge at Papi Kondalu, waterfalls at Ettipotala, Kuntala and rich bio-diversity at Talakona, are some of the natural attractions of the state.

Kailashagiri is situated adjacent to sea in Visakhapatnam, it is one of the beautiful sight which shows the entire beauty of Visakhapatnam having other side sea. A Beautiful park is developed on the hill top of Kailashagiri, the city boasts of having a Park on hill top that has a luxurious toy train, ropeway and beautiful view of beach front into which Eastern Ghats merge into the sea.

Further, Visakhapatnam is home to many tourist attractions like INS Karasura Submarine museum (The only one of its kind in India), the most beautiful and the longest Beach Road in India, Yarada Beach, Araku Valley (Known as poorman's Ooty, a lot of movies are shooted here), VUDA Park, Indira Gandhi Zoological Gardens, etc. The weather in Andhra Pradesh is mostly tropical and the best time to visit is in November through to January. The monsoon season commences in June and ends in September, so travel would not be advisable during this period.

Places to visit:

- Hyderabad: The capital of AP, it is a melting pot of various cultures, known for its historical monuments as well as modern marvels. The places to visit are-Charminar, Mecca Masjid, Salarjung Museum, Hussain Sagar, Lumbini Park, Snow world, Ramoji Film city, Water world, Hitech city, Golconda, Paigah tombs, Falaknuma palace.
- Visakhapatnam: Undoubtedly the most beautiful city on the east coast, it boasts of natural and man-made beauties. It is fast emerging as the country's best tourist and party destination.The places to visit are-Kailashagiri, R.K.Beach, Rushikonda beach, Simhachalam temple, Vizag-Bhimili Beach Road,

Bojjannakonda, Thatlakonda, Appikonda Beach, Yarada Beach, Bhimili Beach, Gangavaram Beach, Borra Caves, Araku valley, Tenneti Beach Park, Ross hill church, Dolphin's nose mountain, Submarine Museum, Aquarium, Indira Gandhi Zoological Gardens, Duduma waterfalls and Red sand hills.

- Tirupati: India's most famous and richest temple. Lord venkateshwara temple, Tirumala, Deer Sanctury, Horsely Hills, Sri Kalahasti Temple, Lepakshi.
- *Vijayawada*: Commercial hub of AP. Places to visit are- Kanakadurga Temple, Gandhi hill, Prakasham Barrage, Krishna River bank, Mangalagiri Temple.

Assam

Assam is the central state in the North-East Region of India and serves as the gateway to the rest of the Seven Sister States. Assam boasts of famous wildlife preserves – the Kaziranga National Park (*pictured*) and the Manas National Park, largest river island Majuli and tea-estates dating back to time of British Raj. The weather is mostly sub-tropical. Assam experiences the Indian monsoon and has one of the highest forest densities in India. The winter months (October to April) are the best time to visit.

It has a rich cultural heritage going back to the Ahom Dynasty which governed the region for many centuries before the British occupation. Other notable features include the Brahmaputra River, the mystery of the bird suicides in Jatinga, numerous temples including Kamakhya of Tantric sect, ruins of palaces, etc.

Bihar

Bihar is one of the oldest inhabited places in the world with history of 3000 years. The rich culture and heritage of Bihar is evident from the innumerable ancient monuments that are dotted all over the state in eastern India. Bihar is home of many tourist attractions. Bihar is visited by scores of tourists from all over the World all the year round. .Around total 6,000,000 (6 million) tourist visits Bihar every year.

In the earliest day, tourism in region was purely based Educational tourism as Bihar was home of some prominent ancient universities like Nalanda University & Vikramaúîla University. Bihar one of the most sacred place of various religions like Hinduism, Buddhism, Jainism, Sikhism & Islam, Many tourist travel to Bihar to visit their pilgrimage. Mahabodhi Temple, a Buddhist shrine and UNESCO World Heritage Site is also situated in Bihar. Mahatma Gandhi Setu, Patna, is one of the longest bridge in the world.

Delhi

Delhi is the capital of India. A fine blend of old and new, ancient and modern in every stream of life is the soul of Delhi. A melting pot of cultures, religions and castes makes Delhi a diverse place. Delhi has been the capital of India from the mythological days. The rulers left behind their trade marks in the architecture. Delhi currently has many renowned monuments and landmarks such as the Tughlaqabad fort and the Qutub Minar, the Jama Masjid and the Bahá'í Lotus temple, the Humayun's tomb and the Red Fort, and India Gate and the Magnificent President's house (Rashtrapati Bhavan). Delhi is famous for its wide roads and crisp winters.

One of the few places in India where colours of nature changes with the seasons. From Kerala to Kashmir and from Gujarat to Assam all the mouth watering delicacies and shopping goods are found in Delhi. The cosmopolitan nature of the city has only added to the beauty and glory of it. Big gardens, wide roads, ancient structures, and power of politics is what Delhi is all about. Delhi is popularly known for its monuments. Most of them which are built by the Mughal Emperors.

Goa

The state of Goa is situated on the West Coast of India,

between the borders of Maharashtra and Karnataka and is better known to the world as the former Portuguese enclave on Indian soil. With the rule of the Portuguese for over 450 years and the consequential influence of the Latin culture, Goa presents a somewhat different picture to the foreign visitor than any other part of India.

The state of Goa is famous for its excellent beaches, churches, and Hindu temples. The Bom Jesus cathedral, Mangueshi Temple and Shantadurga are famous attractions in Goa. Recently a Wax Museum (Wax World) has also opened in Old Goa housing a number of wax personalities of Indian history, culture and heritage.

Himachal Pradesh

Home to the some of the most popular Hill Stations, and home also to some exquisite alpine & Trans-Himalayan destinations, the Indian state of Himachal Pradesh is a major product in the Indian tourism market. Himachal is famous for its sweet apples. Among the major crowd pullers in Himachal Pradesh are: Shimla, the states capital, Manali, Dharamshala, Dalhousie and Kasauli.

Jammu and Kashmir

Jammu is noted for its landscape, ancient temples, Hindu shrines, castles, gardens and forts. Hindu holy shrines of Amarnath and Vaishno Devi attract tens of thousands of Hindu devotees every year. Jammu's natural landscape has made it one of the most popular destinations for adventure tourism in south Asia. Jammu's historic monuments feature a unique blend of Islamic and Hindu architecture styles.kkkii

Tourism forms an integral part of the Kashmiri economy. Often dubbed "Paradise on Earth", Kashmir's mountainous landscape has attracted tourists for centuries. Notable places are Dal Lake, Srinagar Phalagam, Gulmarg, Yeusmarg and Mughal Gardens etc.. However, the tourism industry is severely affected by the insurgency. In recent years, ladakh has emerged as a major hub for adventure tourism. This part of Greater Himalaya interpreted as "moon on earth" comprising of naked peaks and deep gorges was once known for the silk route to High Asia with the sub continent.

Karnataka

Karnataka, the eighth largest state in India, is a veritable treasure trove of tourist delights. By virtue of its varied geography and long and rich history, Karnataka boasts of numerous spots of interest for tourists. Karnataka has been ranked as fourth most popular destination for tourism among states of India. With its 507 out of the 3600 centrally protected monuments, Karnataka has the second highest number of protected monuments in India, next only to Uttar Pradesh. Karnataka is famous for its waterfalls. Jog falls of Shimoga District is one of the highest waterfalls in Asia. This state has 21 wildlife sanctuaries and five National parks and is home to more than 500 species of birds.

Karnataka is a rock climbers paradise. Yana in Uttara Kannada, Ramnagara near Bangalore district, Shivagange in Tumkur district and tekal in Kolar district are a rock climbers heaven. Gol Gumbaz at Bijapur, has the second largest pre-modern dome in the world after the Byzantine Hagia Sophia.

Kerala

Kerala is a state on the tropical Malabar Coast of southwestern India. Nicknamed as one of the "10 paradises of the world" by the National Geographic traveller, Kerala is famous especially for its ecotourism initiatives. Its unique culture and traditions, coupled with its varied demography, has made it one of the most popular tourist destinations in India. Growing at a rate of 13.31%, the tourism industry significantly contributes to the state's economy. The Kerala Tourism Development Corporation, the government agency that oversees the tourism prospects of the state, has adopted the brand "God's Own Country" for its campaigns. The slogan holds global Superbrand status. Kerala is gifted with 42 rivers running as the life stream of the culture. This state has a variety of land scapes which can attract the tourists such as coastal regions, backwaters, Nilgiri mountaing on one side, malabar highlands, and so on.

Madhya Pradesh

Madhya Pradesh is called the "Heart of India" only because of its location in the centre of the country. It has been home to the cultural heritage of Hinduism, Buddhism, Sikhism, Jainism and Islam. Innumerable monuments, exquisitely carved temples, stupas, forts and palaces are dotted all over the State. Madhya Pradesh is also known as Tiger State because of tiger population in MP (Madhya Pradesh). Many Famous national parks like kanha, banthavgadh and pench are located in MP. The natural beauty of Madhya Pradesh is equally varied. Consisting largely of a plateau, the State has everything. Spectacular mountain ranges, meandering rivers and miles and miles of dense forests offering a unique and exciting panorama of wildlife in sylvan surroundings.

Maharashtra

Unlike most other states in India, Maharashtra boasts of a large number of popular and revered religious venues that are heavily frequented by locals as well as out-of-state visitors. It also boasts of the City of Mumbai with its Bollywood fame, ancient cave temples at Ajanta and Ellora, the Tuljabhavani temple at Tuljapur, the Mahalakshmi temple in Kolhapur, the city of Pune the seat of the Maratha empire, the fantastic Ganesh chaturthi celebrations and much more.

Orissa

Orissa has been a preferred destination from ancient days for people who have an interest in spirituality, religion, culture, art and natural beauty. Ancient and medieval architecture, pristine sea beaches, the classical and ethnic dance forms and a variety of festivals. Orissa has kept the religion of Buddhism alive. Rock-edicts that have challenged time stand huge and over-powering by the banks of the river Daya.

The torch of Buddhism is still ablaze in the sublime triangle at Udayagiri, Lalitgiri & Ratanagiri, on the banks of river Birupa. Precious fragments of a glorious past come alive in the shape of stupas, rock-cut caves, rock-edicts, excavated monasteries, viharas, chaityas and sacred relics in caskets and the Rock-edicts of Ashoka.

Orissa is also famous for its well-preserved Hindu Temples, especially the Konark Sun Temple. Orissa is the home for various tribal communities who have contributed uniquely to the multicultural and multilingual character of the state. Their handicrafts, different dance forms, jungle products and their unique life style blended with their healing practices have got world wide attention.

Punjab

Punjab is one of India's most beautiful states. The state of Punjab is renowned for its cuisine, culture and history. Punjab has a vast public transportation and communication network. Some of the main cities in Punjab are Amritsar, Chandigarh, and Ludhiana.

Punjab also has a rich religious history incorporating Sikhism and Hinduism. Tourism in Punjab is principally suited for the tourists interested in culture, ancient civilization, spirituality and epic history. Some of the villages in Punjab are also a must see for the person who wants to see the true Punjab, with their beautiful traditional Indian homes, farms and temples, this is a must see for any visitor that goes to Punjab.

Rajasthan

Rajasthan, literally meaning *"Land of the Kings"*, is one of the most attractive tourist destinations in Northern India. The vast sand dunes of the Thar Desert attract millions of tourists from around the globe every year.

Attractions:

- *Jaipur*: The capital of Rajasthan, famous for its rich history and royal architecture.
- *Jodhpur*: Fortress-city at the edge of the Thar Desert, famous for its blue homes and architecture.
- *Udaipur*: Known as the "Venice" of India.
- *Jaisalmer*: Famous for its golden fortress.
- *Barmer*: Barmer and surrounding areas offer perfect picture of typical Rajasthani villages.
- *Bikaner*: Famous for its medieval history as a trade route outpost.
- *Mount Abu*: Is the highest peak in the Aravalli Range of Rajasthan.
- *Pushkar*: It has the first and one of the very Brahma temples in the world.
- *Nathdwara*: This town near Udaipur hosts the famous temple of Shrinathji.
- *Ranthambore*: Situated near Sawai Madhopur, this town has one of the largest and most famous national parks in India.

Sikkim

Originally known as Suk-Heem, which in the local language means "peaceful home", Sikkim was an independent kingdom till the year 1974, when it became a part of the Republic Of India. The capital of Sikkim is Gangtok, located approximately 185 kilometers from New Jalpaiguri, the nearest railway station to Sikkim. Although, an airport is under construction at Dekiling in East Sikkim, the nearest airport to Sikkim would be Bagdogra.

Sikkim is considered as the land of Orchids and mystic cultures and colorful traditions. Sikkim is well known among trekkers and adventure lovers, as West Sikkim has a lot to give them. Places near Sikkim include Darjeeling also known as the Queen of hills and Kalimpong. Darjeeling, other than its world famous "Darjeeling tea" is also famous for its refined "Prep schools" founded during the British Raj. Kalimpong is also famous for its Flora cultivation and is home to many internationally known Nurseries.

Tamil Nadu

Tamil Nadu or "the land of Tamil" is a beautiful state nestled in the southern Indian peninsula, on the shores of the Bay of Bengal and the deep blue Indian Ocean. Many great· rulers including the Cholas, Pallavas, Pandyas and the Vijayanagara Empire ruled over parts of Tamil Nadu. The state is known for its cultural heritage and temple architecture. Tamil literature is amongst the oldest in India. Much of the ancient culture of Tamil Nadu is still alive. We have Carnatic music, an Indian classical tradition. Bharatha Natyam is its twin dance form, always accompanied by this music and the rich tradition of folk music continues to inspire people.

Attractions:

- *Chennai*: Capital of Tamil Nadu and also India's fourth largest metropolitan.
- *Coimbatore*: Industrial centre, Temples, Kovai kutralam waterfalls.
- *Mahabalipuram*: World famous for its shore temples.
- *Chidambaram*: Lord Shiva in the enthralling form of a Cosmic Dance.
- *Kanchipuram*: The Golden City of a thousand temples, Handloom Silk.
- *Kanyakumari*: Southernmost tip of India, where the Arabian Sea, the Indian Ocean and the Bay of Bengal meet.
- *Ootacamund*: Queen of southern hill resorts of India.
- *Madurai*: Oldest cities of southern India.
- *Rameswaram*: Well-known pilgrimage in India.
- *Thanjavur*: The rice bowl of Tamil Nadu.
- *Tiruchirapalli*: City on the banks of river Cauvery.
- *Auroville*: International Utopian city being built, Aurobindo Ashram Associations.
- *Mudumalai Wildlife Sanctuary*: Wildlife sanctuary.

- *Kodaikanal*: Princess of hill stations in southern India.

Uttarakhand

Uttaranchal is the 27th state of the Republic of India. Blessed with magnificent glaciers, majestic snow-clad mountains, gigantic and ecstatic peaks, valley of flowers, skiing slopes and dense forests, this Abode of Gods includes many shrines and places of pilgrimage. *Char-dhams*, the four most sacred and revered Hindu temples: Badrinath, Kedarnath, Gangotri and Yamunotri are nestled in the Mighty Himalayas. Haridwar which means *Gateway to God* is the only place on the plains.

A picturesque state, with a breathtaking panoramic view of Himalayas, Uttarakhand promises its tourists a visit full of fun and unforgettable moments. It contains the most fascinating and beautiful part of the Himalayas and provide watershed for Gangetic River System spanning 300Km from Satluj in the west to Kali River in the east. Nanda Devi (25640 Ft) is the second highest peak in India after Kanchenjunga (28160 Ft). Dunagiri, Neelkanth, Chukhamba, Panchachuli, Trisul are other peaks above 23000 Ft. It is considered abode of *Devtas, Yakashyas, Kinners*, Fairies and Sages. They all are present here on glittering peaks, roaring rivers, beautiful hills slopes and valleys in one or another form. It boasts of some old hill-stations developed during British era like Mussoorie, Almora and Nainital.

Uttar Pradesh

Situated in the northern part of India, Uttar Pradesh is important with its wealth of monuments and religious fervour. Geographically, Uttar Pradesh is very diverse, with Himalayan foothills in the extreme north, the Gangetic Plain in the centre, and the Vindhya Mountain Range towards the South. It is also home of India's most visited site, the Taj Mahal, and Hinduism's holiest city, Varanasi. The most populous state of the Indian Union also has a rich cultural heritage, and at the heart of North India, Uttar Pradesh has much to offer. Places of interest include Varanasi, Agra, Mathura, Jhansi, Prayag, Sarnath, Ayodhya, Dudhwa National Park.

West Bengal

Kolkata, one of the many cities in the state of West Bengal has been nicknamed the City of Palaces. This comes from the numerous palatial mansions built all over the city. Unlike many north Indian cities, whose construction stresses minimalism, the layout of much of the architectural variety in Kolkata owes its origins to European styles and tastes imported by the British and, to a much lesser extent, the Portuguese and French. The buildings were designed and inspired by the tastes of the English gentleman around and the aspiring Bengali Babu (literally, a *nouveau riche* Bengali who aspired to cultivation of English etiquette, manners and custom, as such practices were favourable to monetary gains from the British). Today, many of these structures are in various stages of decay. Some of the major buildings of this period are well maintained and several buildings have been declared as heritage structures.

Chapter 7

Career Opportunities and Essential Prerequisites in Tourism and Travel Management

It was again the Ministry of Tourism which took the initiative to introduce training programmmes in tourism and travel management. In 1982, it established the Indian Institute of Tourism and Travel Management (IITM), a registered society, as a centre of excellence for education and training in the field.

It started functioning in New Delhi, and the main campus of the Institute has since been shifted to Gwalior in its own sprawling campus, Thereafter, universities started introducing courses in travel management at various levels. Some universities have also constituted Departments of Tourism Studies.

Several Polytechnics in some States have also introduces three-year Diploma programmes in the subject. The AICTE is also the regulatory authority in respect of education and training in tourism and travel. In 1995, the IITTM introduced a full-time Diploma Course in Tourism and Travel Management of fourteen-month duration. The course is also offered at its Eastern Centre in Bhubaneshwar established in 1997.

Eligibility criteria are a graduate degree in any discipline and age not more than 28 years. Selection is made on the basis of an entrance test held in several centres. The test is intended to assess the candidate's general knowledge with particular reference to history, culture, geography and places of tourist attractions in India, reasoning and English. IN addition, the IITTM conducts a Diploma in Destination Management (DDM) programme in collaboration with Air India, and National Institute of Water Sports (Goa). The Institute has five in Calcutta, Delhi, Guwahati, Lucknow, and Thiruvananthapuram.

The Business Management, offers a regular Postgraduate Diploma in Travel and Tourism Management. The course has been designed by the IITM which evaluates the answer scripts, declares the results and awards the diploma. The Thiruvananthapuram Chapter called the Kerala Institute of Tourism and Travel Studies conducts a full time PG Diploma in Tourism and Travel Management of one-year duration. The programme consists of three modules of four months each with emphasis on tour operations and guiding, travel operations, and front office management. Besides the management course, several Chapters also offer short-term programmes in foreign languages (French, Spanish and German), Air Travel, Fares and Ticketing, Computerised Reservation System.

UNIVERSITY COURSES

As of now, as many as 40 universities have introduced travel management courses at the certificate, PG Diploma, Bachelor Degree, and Master's Degree level. Many universities have permitted their affiliated colleges also to offer it as one of the subjects in the first degree programmes. The subject is also offered as a vocational subject in many colleges. Travel Management course is also offered through distance learning mode. The Bachelor Degree course is of three-year duration leading to the award of Bachelor of Tourism Administration (BTA) or Bachelor of Tourism Studies (BTTM).

The Postgraduate Diploma in Tourism Management (PGDTM) is of one-year duration and is open to graduates in any discipline. The Master's degree programme of two-year duration leads to the award of Master of Tourism Administration (MTA) or Master of Tourism Management (MTM). The nomenclature of the award of the Banaras Hindu University, the Kakatiya University, and the University of Madras is MA (Tourism). The Admission requirement is Bachelor's degree with tourism as one of the subjects or BTA/BTS degree.

Sri Chandrasekharendra Saraswathi Viswa Maha Vidyalaya (Kancheepuram-631561), a deemed university, offers a unique programme, BA (Indian Culture) of three-year duration. Oriented to tourism, the course covers three areas, viz., Archaeology, Tourism, and Culture, Eligibility is a pass in 10+2 examination. The university also offers a limited number of scholarships for deserving students admitted to the course.

DISTANCE LEARNING PROGRAMMES

Distance learning courses in tourism and travel management at certificate, first degree, postgraduate diploma and postgraduate degree levels have been introduced by Indira Gandhi National Open University (IGNOU), Karnataka State Open University, Kota Open University, UP Rajarshi Tandon Open University and schools of distance education attached to several universities.

The package of courses offered by IGNOU comprising Certificate in Tourism Studies (CTS), Diploma in Tourism Studies (DTS), Advanced Diploma in Tourism Studies (ADTS), Bachelor of Tourism Studies (BTS), and Master of Tourism Administration (MTA), is the most comprehensive one. The CTS (six months), DTS (one year), and BTS (three years) courses are open to candidates who have passed the 10+2 examination. However, candidates without this qualification are also eligible if they have successfully completed the Bachelors' Preparatory Programme(BPP) of six-month duration.

Only candidates who have passed the DTS examination are eligible for the ADTS course to one year duration. The

MTA course of two year duration is open to two categories of candidates, viz., (i) holders of BTS and BA (Tourism) degrees or PG Diploma in Tourism, and (ii) holders of any Bachelor degree or Diploma in Tourism. However, all candidates in the second category are required to clear four additional courses during the period of study. UP Rajarshi Tandon Open University offers BTS, DTS and CTS courses. The MTA programme is offered only by the Madurai-Kamaraj University. Other institutions mostly offer PG Diploma Courses.

IATA/UFTAA TRAINING COURSE

Founded in 1945, the International Air Transport Associations (IATA) is the world organisation of scheduled airlines. The IATA, in collaboration with the Universal Federation of Travel Agents' Associations (UFTAA), launched in 1972 an International Travel Agents' Training programme to meet the growing demand for well-trained staff in the travel industry. The IATA/UFTAA Diploma has become a hallmark in the travel industry.

It guarantees excellent standards in training and has gained worldwide recognition. The training programme is operated under the authority of Passenger Agency Training Board. IATA's Agency Training Service located in Geneva (Switzerland) oversees general administration, course contents and conducting of examinations. In each country or area, there is a local coordinator who is responsible for the promotion of the course, distribution of training kits and organisation of examinations locally. The Air India is the coordinator in India.

The training programme is basically a self-study course. There are, however, Authorised Training Centres (ATCs) in many countries which prepare students for the examination. The ATCs are authorised to use the IATA-UFTAA course material. Before taking admission to any ATC, the students must verify the authorisation number allotted to it. There are two courses viz., Standard (Entry level) and Advanced

Course. Candidates desirous of taking the Standard Course should have passed the secondary school or its equivalent examination and should be proficient in English. They should also have good knowledge of world geography and basic mathematics.

The Standard course examination consists of two papers-Paper 1: General Travel Knowledge (21/2 hours) and Paper 2: Air Fares and Ticketing (3 hours). Examinations are held every year in March and September. Students must register themselves three moths before the examination. They can take both papers on the same day or separately (e.g., Paper 1 in March and Paper 2 in September). To qualify for the Diploma, the candidates must score at least 75% marks.

CAREER OPPORTUNITIES

Hotels and Catering: Several factors have been contributing to the fast growth and development of the hotel and catering industry. The number of foreign tourists is steadily increasing. Internationally business traffic following the liberalisation of the Indian economy is also registering similar growth. More number of Indians than before now travel within the country on business or for pleasure. All these factors are giving a boost to the hotel and catering industry. Further, for various reasons, eating out is no longer limited to affluent only. Hotels and catering establishments are being increasingly used for social and family events and occasions. Hotels are also being frequently used by business and industry for board meetings, and sales and executive conferences.

Besides, holding seminars, workshops, conferences, conventions and exhibitions in hotels has become a regular feature. Most of the big hotels are geared up to meet such requirements. All hotels, therefore need qualified manpower to manage their various departments. Bigger the size of a hotel and higher the "star" rating, more are the number of departments and clearly defined jobs. In others, the number of staff is relatively less, each performing a number of tasks.

Various estimates about the manpower requirements for hotel industry suggest the demand for trained and qualified persons for exceeds the supply. It is, therefore, not surprising that the representatives of a large number of hotels throng to the campuses of reputed institutions of hotel management for recruiting suitable candidates.

Sensing market demand for qualified persons, training institutions have sprouted in various parts of the country. But not all of them offer quality programmes. It must be noted that like any other institutions offering technical education, establishing hotel management institutions involves considerable investment in infrastructure facilities in terms of adequate space, equipment and gadgets and qualified teachers. Students must be enough opportunities for gaining practical experience.

They should also be exposed to hotel environment. Obviously, students qualifying from reputed training institutions have an edge over the run-of-the-mill ones. Choosing a good institution is essential for making a successful career in the profession. The number of students recruited through campus interviews by reputed hotels could be a good index.

A rudimentary knowledge of some of the Indian and foreign languages is an added advantage in the profession. Those who aspire to make a career in hotels must take a conscious decision based on a clear understanding about the nature of the job. The work is both physically and mentally strenuous. It will be rewarding to go through the book titled Careers in Hotel Management by Arun Agarwal and Mamta Agarwal (Caring, 1997) to get a realistic idea about hotel environment and the kind of aptitude required for a successful career in the profession.

Tourism and Travel: Professionally qualified persons having good knowledge of history and geography of the country, its culture, customs and tourist sites will certainly find a career in tourism and travel both exciting and rewarding. Career opportunities are gradually opening up following the liberalisation of the economy. Not only more and more foreign tourists visit India, travelling and holidaying abroad are also becoming a passion for many Indians. The number of advertisements in newspapers about package tours indicates this growing trend.

The travel agencies, tour operating companies, cargo agencies, big hotels, airlines and tourism departments offer a wide variety of job opportunities. Freelancing as tourist guide is yet another option. Tour operators and local tourism departments often employ professional guides possessing comprehensive knowledge about the history and culture significance of the place. Those possessing entrepreneurship qualities may venture to start their own tourism concerns after gaining adequate experience. Candidates who can speak some of the Indian and foreign languages stand in good stand in the profession.

Travel and Tourism is the world's largest industry in terms of employment and second to oil industry in terms of turnover. It is a service-based industry and requires professionals and specialists skilled in various disciplines. The industry broadly covers the following areas:

- Hotels, restaurants and tourist complexes
- Travel agencies, tour operators
- Transport facilities for tourists
- Amusement, entertainment and sports units for tourist
- Units providing cultural, adventure and wildlife experiences to tourist.

The Department of Tourism under the Central Government is the nodal agency for the formulation of national policies and programs and is assisted by the Director-General of Tourism, with offices in India and abroad. The State Directorates of Tourism are responsible for the publicizing and promoting travel within India for domestic tourists. The Tourism Finance Corporation of India has been set up to meet the loan requirements of the tourism industry.

The work in the industry essentially involves providing

services like boarding, lodging and travelling to people who are away from home, either on business or on holiday. The two most important activities related to the industry are therefore accommodation and travelling i.e. hotel industry and travel trade. The Hotel Industry has been discussed separately. Under travel trade we would be looking at the major tasks or duties performed by Travel Agents and Tour Operators.

Career prospects in Travel and Tourism are extremely encouraging. The number of international tourists has increased from 70 million in 1960 to 700 million by the year 2000. As per World Tourism Organisation estimates it is going to hit 1.5 billion in the next 20 years. India share is abysmally low at half per cent. In 1999 India got 2.5 million international tourists and this is expected to rise up to six million by 2010.Annualy the industry earns Rs 14,000 crore in foreign exchange for the exchequer.

EDUCATION QUALIFICATION

Simple graduates, with the requisite personal attributes can gain entry into this industry. However, with the growing professionalism in every field including travel and tourism, aspirants for a career in this field should take specialized training, so as to give themselves an edge in the job market. There are a number of good institutions, which offer training courses in different aspects of travel and tourism. The Indian Institute of Travel and Tourism Management (IITM) is one such institute, which runs a 24-month diploma course in Tourism Management at Gwalior.

Graduates of not more than 28 years of age are eligible to enroll in the course after qualifying the entrance exam. Other courses offered by the institute include destination management, language courses, wildlife tourism management etc. The IITM through its chapter at Delhi, Lucknow and Thiruvananthapuram has been conducting management development programs. The Delhi chapter of the institute also offers many short term courses like Basic Course on

Computer Application in Tourism and Travel Agency; Basic Course on Air Travel Fares and Ticketing; Basic course in Airlines, Travel Agency and Tour Operation Management and Foreign Language Courses.

Two year PG courses and one year PG Diploma (part time or correspondence) are available at various universities/ institutes. Indira Gandhi National Open University conducts Bachelor in Tourism Studies through distance education for 10+2 pass. Jamia Millia Islamia Delhi offers two-year PG diploma programme in Cultural Heritage and Tourism. Number of Universities like Delhi University offers tourism as a subject.

You love travelling. You travel frequently and extensively. The sights, smells and sounds of a new place fascinate you. Palaces, forts and historical monuments transport you in time to a different era, a different world. Travelling for you is not just another physical activity. Your heart's in it. Every journey is an eye-opener. Every journey enriches you from within. Well, if you are a victim of wanderlust, then maybe a career in tourism is just the thing for you.

The tourism industry creates jobs and earns foreign exchange which leads to the economic well-being of a nation. Tourism may bring about commercialisation of the natural beauty and resources of a country, but it also helps people broaden their minds, helping them learn from other cultures and enjoy the benefits of improved transportation, civic amenities, better communication, hospitality and recreation facilities.

SCOPE IN TOURISM

People usually travel on business and pleasure, but over the last decade, the nature of tourism has developed in scope and direction, away from these traditional activities to a wide range of new activities such as sports and leisure, adventure tourism and eco-tourism. Today people travel also for medical/health reasons (medical/health tourism), for pilgrimage (spiritual tourism), to learn and experience wildlife (wildlife tourism), learn about art, culture, architecture (cultural/heritage tourism), about political situations (political tourism), for going back to nature (nature/eco tourism) or learn/experience festivals, cuisines and crafts.

The friendly and informal atmosphere in a travel and tourism organisation attracts people with excellent interpersonal skills. Major opportunities are in customer service, sales, and travel management. A tourism job demands excellent organisation skills, imagination and creativity in solving problems, excellent customer service, strong communication skills, attention to detail and the ability to meet deadlines and coordinate schedules under stressful conditions.

For tourist guiding and tourist escort services, individuals should be willing to work long or unusual hours and on holidays; they should be tuned to social customs and etiquette and be good coordinators. Interpreters must possess excellent language and communication skills, in addition to the general skills necessary for the travel and tourism industry.

TRAINING

Starting with ticketing and reservation or hotel management or destination management courses for school leaving students (class 12 th/10+2/equivalent) to postgraduate diploma and degree courses for graduates in travel and tourism management and international qualifications offered by IATA and City Guilds, there is a wide variety of courses for people with different aspirations.

Fine artists, crafts persons, dancers, musicians, theatre artists and various performers also work in this industry offering tourists a view of the traditional arts and crafts of the nation. Graduates passionate and knowledgeable about the country's history may train to be travel guides while those trained in adventure sports, wildlife care, or event management can work in providing specialised tourist activities and experiences. Photographers and travel writers, museologists and curators and interpreters are also a part of the tourism experience.

Travel and tourism represents a broad range of related industries and services such as hotels, restaurants, retailing, transportation, travel agencies, tour companies, cruise lines, tourist attractions, leisure, recreation, and sport and cultural organisations. The travel and tourism experience in India offers religious spots for Hindus, Sikhs, Buddhists, Jains etc. So religious/pilgrimage tourism is a major opportunity. India already has health tourism in the form of yoga, massages and traditional ayurvedic medicine. Kerala pioneered health tourism in India through Ayurveda.

A clutch of state-of-the-art, but relatively low-cost hospitals like Escorts Heart Institute and Research Centre (New Delhi), Apollo Hospital (Chennai), P D Hinduja National Hospital and Medical Research Centre (Mumbai) and Indraprastha Apollo Hospital (New Delhi) have become centres of the booming medical tourism industry. At least a dozen more including Wockhardt, Breach Candy, CARE etc. are considered equally good. Many more are ready to jump on the bandwagon.

The department of tourism, Government of Karnataka, has ambitious plans for the state in medical tourism. The Federation of Indian Chambers of Commerce and Industry, Western Region Council (FICCI-WRC) has set up a task force for the promotion of health and medical tourism in Maharashtra. A study by CII and McKinsey has estimated that medical tourism could bring Indian an additional 50 billion - 100 billion rupees in annual revenue by 2012.

The Ministry of Tourism has identified 40 locations in rural areas for development and promotion of tourism. Examples are Pochampalli in Andhra Pradesh for its traditional weave saris and Raghurajpur village in Orissa for its crafts and Odissi dance. The concept of rural tourism will help in giving knowledge about traditional ways of life, arts and crafts, boost employment opportunities in rural areas and offer a ready market to rural artisans.

Trade experts from the travel industry point out that along with Europeans, Americans, Japanese, Chinese and Britishers, travellers from Russia, Hungary and Iran are also coming to India. Domestic tourists are increasingly adding to the travel business.A host of ancillary service providers like masseurs, tour guides, handicraft makers, car rental operators, restaurants, service apartment developers and even roadside eateries are getting a boost with the Indian tourism industry being on the roll. Careers in travel and tourism offer job satisfaction and excellent growth opportunities.

CAREER PROFILES

As mankind moves further into the 21st century the excitement of travel and the spirit of place inspire people to explore and discover the world as never before. Tourism delivers the experience of elsewhere. Whether it is caviar and vodka in a Russian hotel or beer and whitebait with the locals in a Hokitika pub, travellers revel in the magic of new experiences.

Governments and businesses are involved in making the magic happen on a large scale, creating jobs, wealth and opportunities for diverse cultures to understand each other. But it is not as simple as waving a wand. Tourism competes for resources and business. It affects people and the environment in a variety of ways. The industry is constantly addressing these issues.

A GLOBALLY GROWING INDUSTRY

Increasingly people have more disposable income to spend, while air travel allows the speedy displacement of massive numbers of travellers. In 2005 the tally of tourists arriving at international destinations reached a record 808 million. In addition, millions more domestic tourists travelled within their own countries. These visitors need services and infrastructure to welcome, accommodate and entertain them. Their hosts need skills to welcome the paying guests and to refresh their goods and services through innovation.

Typically, where masses of people are involved in prolonged and diverse activities, there is a need to study, analyse, and monitor human behaviour, to predict trends and foresee consequences.

The World Travel and Tourism Council has established a 'New Tourism' strategy. The strategy advises governments worldwide to manage the growth of industries, employment, and the environment. Tourism impacts on global and national economies, on human cultures, societies and natural environments. To ensure sustained growth in the industry, tourists, their hosts, governments and commercial enterprises work to protect the environmental and cultural attractions that draw visitors to their countries. In 'clean, green' New Zealand, whose varied and wonderful landscapes attract so many travellers, the environment is a primary consideration.

Tourism is an exciting area of growth, commerce, research and innovation. Degrees in tourism tend to be vocationally oriented. Domestic and global opportunities for employment are excellent. As the sector grows and becomes more complex it needs a well trained workforce that understands its working, management and marketing. A degree in tourism provides background knowledge of the industry, and transferable skills that can be applied within a range of public and private sectors. Careers in tourism contribute signifi cantly to the economy, to increased understanding of human behaviour and to building relationships with other countries.

TOURISM IS CONSUMER DRIVEN

Whether they are inbound, outbound, or domestic, tourists travel for a variety of reasons: holiday; recreation and leisure; education; business; a change of weather or routine; to visit family and friends; to experience something different, exciting or challenging. An emerging group of savvy travellers are becoming an important target market for New Zealand. This group of people like interacting with the destination they visit. They travel regularly, have a tendency to spend more than other visitors and participate in a wide range of tourism experiences. They actively participate in the natural environment, are environmentally and culturally aware and seek authentic, new experiences. These tourists are an important target market for the New Zealand tourism industry.

Niche tourism is a growing area and this accounts for the emergence of specific types of tourism: heritage; garden; wine; lighthouse; film site; pop-culture; gambling; disaster; pilgrimage; sport; ancestry; adventure; ecotourism and more.

As mankind moves further into the 21st century the excitement of travel and the spirit of place inspire people to explore and discover the world as never before. Tourism delivers the experience of elsewhere. Whether it is caviar and vodka in a Russian hotel or beer and whitebait with the locals in a Hokitika pub, travellers revel in the magic of new experiences.

Governments and businesses are involved in making the magic happen on a large scale, creating jobs, wealth and opportunities for diverse cultures to understand each other. But it is not as simple as waving a wand. Tourism competes for resources and business. It affects people and the environment in a variety of ways. The industry is constantly addressing these issues.

Increasingly people have more disposable income to spend, while air travel allows the speedy displacement of massive numbers of travellers. In 2005 the tally of tourists arriving at international destinations reached a record 808 million. In addition, millions more domestic tourists travelled within their own countries.

These visitors need services and infrastructure to welcome, accommodate and entertain them. Their hosts need skills to welcome the paying guests and to refresh their goods and services through innovation. Typically, where masses of people are involved in prolonged and diverse activities, there is a need to study, analyse, and monitor human behaviour, to predict trends and foresee consequences. The World Travel and Tourism Council has established a "New Tourism" strategy.

The strategy advises governments worldwide to manage the growth of industries, employment, and the environment. Tourism impacts on global and national economies, on human cultures, societies and natural environments. To ensure sustained growth in the industry, tourists, their hosts, governments and commercial enterprises work to protect the environmental and cultural attractions that draw visitors to their countries. In "clean, green" New Zealand, whose varied and wonderful landscapes attract so many travellers, the environment is a primary consideration.

Tourism is an exciting area of growth, commerce, research and innovation. Degrees in tourism tend to be vocationally oriented. Domestic and global opportunities for employment are excellent. As the sector grows and becomes more complex it needs a well trained workforce that understands its working, management and marketing. A degree in tourism provides background knowledge of the industry, and transferable skills that can be applied within a range of public and private sectors. Careers in tourism contribute significantly to the economy, to increased understanding of human behaviour and to building relationships with other countries.

Whether they are inbound, outbound, or domestic, tourists travel for a variety of reasons: holiday; recreation and leisure; education; business; a change of weather or routine; to visit family and friends; to experience something different, exciting or challenging. An emerging group of savvy travellers are becoming an important target market for New Zealand. This group of people like interacting with the destination they visit. They travel regularly, have a tendency to spend more than other visitors and participate in a wide range of tourism experiences.

They actively participate in the natural environment, are environmentally and culturally aware and seek authentic, new experiences. These tourists are an important target market for the New Zealand tourism industry. *Niche tourism* is a growing area and this accounts for the emergence of specific types of tourism: heritage; garden; wine; lighthouse; film site; pop-culture; gambling; disaster; pilgrimage; sport; ancestry; adventure; ecotourism, and more People have different values and interests, which motivate and energise them. Aligning values with an appropriate industry and organisation is important to make the most of skills and abilities and ensure job satisfaction.

Tourism-related industries:

Tourism impacts directly upon a range of sectors. Tourists need information; transport; attractions and activities; accommodation and food. Industries include:

- Hospitality (catering; accommodation, luxury to budget)
- Transport (air, land, sea)
- Tourism Operations (tour wholesalers, inbound operators, travel agencies, tourist information centres)
- Attractions and activities (adventure tourism; events; sightseeing; wildlife viewing; wine tourism; theatre; museums; art galleries; art and crafts)
- Conservation/Environment
- Wine Industry

Careers within the tourism sector offer the opportunity to meet and work with a fascinating mix of people, to travel within New Zealand and overseas. First off most graduates can expect to work in assistant type positions. Experience on the ground is often necessary, but with a qualification, skills and industry knowledge acquired during degree studies, graduates can rise quickly to higher-level positions.

PRIVATE SECTOR

Private sector positions for tourism graduates, depending on prior industry experience may include: marketing assistant/manager; customer services assistant manager; event organiser/assistant; conventions and conference organiser;

hotel/motel assistant manager; staff supervisor; business manager/assistant; tour guide/interpreter; holiday or theme park assistant manager; human resources adviser or manager; tourism consultant; travel agency

consultant or manager; marketing advisor/manager; information/relationship officer/manager; public relations assistant/manager; tour manager; visitor services coordinator; visitor information consultant; museum activities officer; as well as those positions listed under public sector.

Tourism Industry Association of New Zealand (TIA) represents a membership of more than 2000 tourist operators. The Association is committed to business best practice and Qualmark, the industry's official quality mark. TIA has four main areas of activity: advocacy; events; industry development; working with other organisations. Based in Wellington with a staff of 14, TIA roles that are likely to interest graduates are in the areas of communications, IT, policy and events.

There are about 16,000 tourism related companies in New Zealand. Through research, networking and informational interviewing graduates will find the employer for them, or even start their own enterprise.

Tourism Holdings Ltd is the second largest tourism company listed on the New Zealand Stock Exchange. The company has on the ground operations in New Zealand, Australia and Fiji. Maui and Britz Motorhomes, Fullers Bay of Islands, Milford Red Boats, Kelly Tarlton's Antarctic and Underwater World, and Kiwi Experience are some of THL Ltd's well-known brands.

The company employs 1000 people and a high proportion of these are frontline staff. General Manager HR, Len Hatton, says that there are opportunities over the summer for customer service and support roles. The company provides development opportunities for staff by advertising positions internally first. Once people are in and have demonstrated their ability, they will be on the spot to apply for supervisory and management positions. *"We look for good all rounders with a positive attitude and the ability to help people have a great time,"* says Mr Hatton. Agrodome in Rotorua sells multiple products, stages agricultural shows and offers high action to passive adventure experiences. Agrodome is one of New Zealand's largest family owned tourism businesses. By the end of 2007, CEO Warren Harford says they will be receiving 50,000 visitors. 90% of staff is frontline, so the company wants people with sales skills who can talk well and interact with a multi-cultural clientele.

A foreign language is an advantage. Mr Harford says he runs an "upside down pyramid" management structure and values input from staff. Graduates employed by Agrodome have done very well. *"They start at the frontline and learn very quickly, applying what they have learned in their degree," he says. Karori Wildlife Sanctuary* offers a world-first conservation attraction.

At the Sanctuary domestic and international tourists can experience a bush walk with the opportunity to see rare native wildlife. Of the 16 full time positions those suitable for tourism graduates include tourism coordinator, marketers and guides. Tourism co-ordinator, and Victoria graduate, Phillip Stuart says he chose a commercial position because he is a people person and interested in tourist distribution channels.

James Cook Hotel Grand Chancellor, Wellington is one in a chain of 24 Grand Hotels International in New Zealand, Australia, Malaysia and Singapore. HR manager, Marissa Martin says the hotel looks to employ people with passion for the hospitality industry. The hotel may consider graduates with experience for positions such as food and beverage supervisor; duty manager responsible for the hotel at night; HR coordinator; sales/marketing support.

Reception work is useful entry-level experience that can lead to the role of duty manager. Candidates must be reliable, versatile and able to lead others of the same age as themselves. A career path tailored to individual interests is possible for stand out employees.

Totally Tourism Queenstown wants people with initiative and commitment. Managing director, Mark Quickfall, advises new employees to make themselves so valuable the employer doesn't want to let them go. The company owns eight aviation and adventure tourism businesses from helicopter tours to rafting and Kiwi movie experiences. Much of the work is operational. Those who have attitude and perform well can rise to supervisory positions running customer services and sales operations.

"It's rewarding to see young people come into the company and progress," says Mr Quickfall.

Public Sector Public sector positions for graduates at national, regional and local levels include: policy analyst; researcher; communications adviser; market analyst; marketing assistant; business analyst; passport & visa administrator; export trade assistant.

Government Tourist Organisations: *Ministry of Tourism* provides tourism policy advice to the Minister of Tourism. The Ministry works with other government departments on key tourism policy, and tourism events related issues. The Ministry also carries out research and provides tourism related statistics.

Tourism New Zealand (TNZ) is the Crown entity responsible for the international marketing of Destination New Zealand. The organisation employs staff to develop, implement and promote strategies for marketing New Zealand's tourism industry.

Regional Tourism Organisations: Regional Tourism Organisations (RTOs) are responsible for marketing their regions domestically and internationally. The 26 RTOs throughout New Zealand include Positively Wellington Tourism, Destination Queenstown, Venture Taranaki, Destination Rotorua Tourism and others. Along with city councils they are potential sources of job opportunities for graduates with an interest in marketing or communications.

Tourism Auckland's mission is to develop sustainable economic growth in tourism for the Auckland region through integrated marketing and industry development. Opportunities exist for graduates in areas of the business, such as international and domestic marketing, conventions and incentives (business tourism), media services and visitor information centre staff. *Positively Wellington Tourism* is the capital city's Regional Tourism Organisation.

It operates a marketing office and i-SITE Visitor Centre, employing 35 staff in full-time and part-time positions. A range of areas and skills are represented in Positively Wellington Tourism, including marketing; research and product development; conferences and events; communications and sales.

Several staff members completed a Bachelor of Tourism Management at Victoria University of Wellington and gained industry experience before joining the organisation. *Visitor Information Network (VIN)* is made up of 130 tourist information offi ces throughout New Zealand.

They provide tourist information to domestic and international visitors. Other Government Organisations: Policy advice, research, consumer marketing, business development, management and corporate communication skills gained from a degree in tourism are relevant but not limited to work in: Department of Conservation; Ministry for the Environment; Local and Regional Councils; Land Transport NZ; Department of Internal Affairs; NZ Customs; NZ Trade & Enterprise; Sport & Recreation NZ; Creative NZ and Museum of NZ Te Papa Tongarewa.

On the ground TIA says that private sector employers are looking to recruit people with the following base line personal attributes and skills: warmth and friendliness; interpersonal communication; people and selling skills; ability to work effectively in teams; cultural awareness; leadership qualities. Moving on up Other key skills for now, and the future include: diverse language skills; computer/IT/software skills; sustainability knowledge/awareness; awareness of compliance requirements; management/planning and business skills. Getting academic A degree in tourism studies develops students' skills in social and environmental analysis. This leads to an understanding of the environmental, economic, and social impacts that result from tourism.

A degree in tourism management has an applied focus. Students learn to evaluate and apply concepts associated with the operational and strategic nature of financial, human and physical resources. Through degree training graduates develop intellectual skills that will add value to the sector. Skills include the ability to analyse, think critically, evaluate and synthesise information. Research skills The ability to access and evaluate information is vital in a commercially oriented, knowledge economy. During their degree students learn to apply a range of strategies and tools. They examine different aspects of the research cycle and approaches to tourism research.

While research into the study and management of tourism enhances industry related knowledge and skills, the skills are transferable to many areas of work. Tourism projects cover a range of investigations such as the structure and function of tourism channel distributions; studies of visitor behaviour; marketing special event tourism and many more. Analytical skills Analytical or critical thinking skills are necessary for effective decision-making and problem solving. Analysis includes the ability to identify a concept or problem, tease out its components, organise and evaluate information and to draw appropriate conclusions.

These skills are acquired through academic work and are useful in research, policy, and business roles with high levels of responsibility.

COMMUNICATION SKILLS

The ability to communicate clearly is paramount in a complex global economy. Through their studies graduates learn to present their work logically and clearly in oral and written forms and to use language and presentation tools appropriately. Through relationships with partner organisations, sponsors and relevant authorities, students develop liaison and negotiation skills. Degree courses also develop listening and discussion skills. Being able to speak another language is an advantage. Relationship management skills In a service intensive sector the ability to manage relationships is key to sustainability and success. The relationships can be complex and varied when a number of stakeholders are involved.

Stakeholders include tourism customers; goods and services providers; regional authorities; sponsors; associations; cultural, conservation and lobby groups. Tourism graduates acquire understanding of relationship dynamics in commercial and non-commercial settings. They may apply these skills and knowledge during fieldwork, and group discussions.

MANAGEMENT SKILLS

Through tourism management course work students gain an understanding of the principles of management across public and private sectors. Management includes understanding processes of policy and planning and applying this through fieldwork. Self-management is also a skill graduates develop through course work as they plan, design, implement and communicate about their projects.

The ability to be self-reflective is sought after in managers and leaders in many industries. Tertiary study fosters this skill and enhances employability. Marketing skills Marketing is a critical business function that identifies customer needs and wants through a variety of activities.

Businesses use the information to create, plan, communicate and deliver value to identifi ed target markets. Graduates who have specialised in marketing will have an understanding of strategic customer/client relations, research and marketing planning in tourism.

Globalization is not a buzzword solely associated with international business. It has translated into a booming new career possibility: Expanded services in the travel and tourism industry. According to the World Travel and Tourism Council

(WTTC), the industry already is responsible for more than 10 per cent of global employment. Brian White, PhD, director of the WTTC's Human Resources Centre in British Columbia, says the field is incredibly diverse and comprised of seven major areas:

- Airlines/transport
- Conferences and conventions
- Arts and culture
- Hotels, food and beverage
- Ecotourism
- Outdoor recreation
- Ancillary services associated with tourism.

With all this opportunity, where should you concentrate your efforts? Focusing on market demands may lead to more job openings. On the corporate side, according to a piece on Hoover's industry trends online, the travel and tourism industry is in consolidation mode.

This means that smaller companies are merging or being acquired by big players like American Express, Marriott and Carlson Wagonlit. So it might make sense to begin your career with one of the larger corporations, where you can gain exposure to many facets of the business while having relative job security.

CHARACTERISTICS FOR SUCCESS

This is a service industry, first and foremost, so you must have patience, flexibility and excellent interpersonal skills. Cultural sensitivity and awareness are critical, as tourism professional's deal with different countries and cultures. Senior-level executives generally have MBAs and develop skills and competencies that can be transferred across sectors.

Midlevel professionals need a mix of practical experience and academic credentials, according to White, who also teaches in the field. For example, individuals might work full-time in the travel sector while going part-time for an advanced certificate in travel and tourism.

PROS AND CONS

One obvious benefit of working in the travel and tourism industry is the opportunity to actually hop on a plane and see many locales at low prices, or even gratis. Another benefit is the fact that it is an international field that changes along with global trends. One of the downsides to the business, especially the hotel and restaurant side, is the long hours. Management must often work evenings and weekends. Individuals are often asked to move to a new location without much notice.

ETHICS AND TOURISM

White reminds us there is a strong set of ethics required in the field of tourism, noting the industry has profound economic implications for a country's economy and people. It is important for individuals to consider their responsibilities, he adds. Tourism is about more than making a profit; it involves benefiting local communities, creating jobs that provide fair wages and not exploiting the environment.

Travel and Tourism are necessary for broadening our horizons, and thus for living a life harmoniously and meaningfully. These also boost financial incomes of the travel and tourism departments of the States and country. The advancements of the science and technology have enhanced the global tourism also resulting in the income of huge foreign money, better foreign relationship, and the trades. Thus, travel and tourism field is an extensive, lucrative, and enriching one. There are several departments in any travel or tourism company, for various arrangements and its management. So, there are millions of job opportunities in this travel and tourism sector, in the various parts of any country and abroad.

Work in the travel and tourism industry is essentially concerned with providing services for people who are away from home, on business or holiday. Travel can be leisure travel involving package tours, pilgrim travel, and adventure travel etc or purely business. Work at every functional level in the industry involves dealing directly with people. Travel agents assess the needs of tourists and businessmen and help them make the best possible travel arrangements from the many travel options available. Also, many major cruise lines, resorts, and specialty travel groups use travel agents to promote travel packages to the millions of people who travel every year.

We restored a 1930's British built bungalow within our smallest estate - Talayar at Munnar, Kerala and took our first baby steps into Eco Tourism. We believed then as we do today, the enormous capacity of tourism to uplift the local social economy. The bungalow, which came to be known as the Talayar Valley Bungalow, had all the trappings of the British era. Wrought iron bath tubs, Doulton wash basins, Shanks flush tanks, in built fireplaces in all rooms, brass adjustable light holders - all within large rooms and even larger bathrooms. The experience was subtle and non hotel in every sense. The success was dramatic and astounding. More importantly the guest comments were hugely motivating.

Today we have spread the Eco Tourism word with our brand Briar Tea Bungalows across all our tea holdings. Being among the largest tea plantation companies in South India, we decided to restore and share as many bungalows with guests as we can and currently have a total of 20 rooms spread across Kerala and Tamil Nadu, in Valparai, Meghamalai, Nilgiri - Wyanad and Munnar, amidst lush forests in the Western Ghats.

The Western Ghats are amongst the 25 biodiversity hotspots that the world recognizes. This chain of hills is not only rich in its historical and cultural heritage but is also home to endemic plants and animals. At least 40% of the 10,000 or more species of living organisms that live in the Western Ghats are found nowhere else in the world.

The private forests surrounding the Briar Bungalows are a wildlife mecca, home to at least 9 species of amphibians,

18 species of reptiles, 66 species of birds and 29 species of mammals. Many of these are endangered specie protected under Schedule I of the Wildlife Protection Act. Among amphibians are 5 species endemic to the Western Ghats, including Melanobatrachus indicus, a species rediscovered recently after nearly 100 years. Among reptiles are 14 species endemic to the Western Ghats, including the flying lizard Draco dussumeri and the shield-tail snakes (Uropeltis spp.). Of the 49 species of rainforest birds, three are endemic species, including the Malabar Grey Hornbill and Nilgiri Flycatcher.

Other rare and endangered species including the Great Hornbill and the Spot-bellied Eagle Owl have been sighted. Of the mammals, 3 endemic species occur - Lion Tailed Macaque, Nocturnal Brown Palm Civet and the Malabar Spiny Dormouse.

The Nilgiri Langur, Asian Elephant, Wild Dog and Leopards use these fragments too. The New Garden Forest area is unique, as it is home to two troops of lion-tailed macaques numbering a total of 82 individuals who use the rainforest and adjoining tea garden area in our Puthutotam Estate, Valparai. We have been singularly focused on achieving our Eco Tourism goals - training local estate workers in hospitality skills, maintaining conservation practices by creating bio – diversity areas and wildlife corridors within our gardens, educating estate workers in preserving a plastic free atmosphere and most importantly, never forgetting the 'big' picture - the welfare and happiness of each and every worker within our plantation.

THE PROSPECTS OF A CAREER

It has a number of sectors or smaller 'industries' as it were, that work in collaboration. Each sector is an important branch of the main industry and have their own special characteristics. Commercial Services - Government & Travel Agencies Government: Apart from working at the airport (an expansive topic on its own), there do lie other opportunities at the - Customs Department where special officers are in charge of checking all luggage for illegal goods or items that are liable for duty. Guides - young graduates who have an interest in history and languages find this profession quite intriguing, since it gives them opportunities to meet new people, enhance their research skills, get good salaries etc. Knowledge of other languages is generally preferred.

The Indian Institutes of Travel and Tourism Management (IITM) offer short-term courses in this field. -Immigration Department where a tourist is first given service. Special training courses have started in some universities for learning about immigration procedures, since both the industry and the Government feel that there should be a separate cadre for this purpose.

Travel Agencies: Planning vacations or business trips to new places can be quite tiring and strenuous without the help of a travel agent. They have answers to all possible questions concerning the shortest route to the destination, travel mode, the important documents that will be required (visa, passport, vaccination certificates etc.), suitable places to stay, current exchange rates, tourist spots to visit, climate and they will plan the trip keeping in mind the clients' preferences, budgets and special needs.

A great deal of work is done on the computer where the latest information on flight schedules, departure/arrival timings, hotel ratings etc. can be obtained. Agencies may involve themselves in special discount packages, slide/movie presentations on various places and other promotional work to attract customers.

The four departments of a travel agency are - Accounts (handles the billing for individuals and groups) - - Tours (deal in in-expensive packaged tours, with the accommodation, food, transport etc. all taken care of) - Travel (provide detailed information on routes, costs) - Cargo (covers the booking and recovery of all cargo from the destination points connected by either Air, rail or road) The Department of Tourism in the Government does major amounts of work for the international market, in formulating policies, developing centres to attract tourists, providing adequate transport, advertising the different spots and publicizing the various experiences, providing accurate information on all possible tourist areas.

HOTELS

The hotel sector is one which requires a large amount of manpower, with a wide variety of skills from housekeeping to computers. People with specialized training for food and beverage, recreation, marketing, accounting, security, fire-fighting, public relations and so on are much needed. There are many institutes that offer hotel management and candidates from institutes like the one at Pusa, Delhi have good future prospects. Many hotels also offer overseas training opportunities, which allow young people to gain promotions rapidly. Employment in foreign countries for Indians is also very encouraging. In India alone, about 1, 80,000 vacancies are expected to be filled within the next decade.

TRANSPORT

As we know, transport can mean anything which takes us from one place to another - by air, road, railway, sea etc. The two main areas we will discuss are air and road transport. Travel by air - Post Second World War saw a tremendous change in travel, with the increased access to air travel. People got more opportunities to see other places and tourism advanced at a high pace.

Working in an airline, whether on the ground staff or in flight is an exciting option for many people these days. Foreign airlines like Aeroflot, British Airways, Royal Jordanian have all been granted new land rights and additional flights. Many of the top airlines like Cathay Pacific, ones based in Hong Kong, Emirates offer attractive salaries and numerous benefits to their flight attendants. The jobs in airlines are challenging ones but worth the struggle. Travel by road - Coaches, tourist cars employs numerous people every year. This arena has the added advantage that there is scope for self-employment. Presently, drivers with good conversational skills, who are educated, bi- or multi-lingual are much in demand. Bank loans are available for those wishing to invest in vehicles for this purpose.

Since this industry has so many areas, the requirements for each field will naturally be different. In general, most candidates enter the field through a travel agency or a tour-operating company. For the government positions, advertisements are usually given in the newspapers regarding the vacancies.

Candidates for these positions are only selected after passing a written exam, interview and medical examination. Most private sector companies are flexible in their choosing - focusing more on interest, aptitude and personality rather than academic achievement. Experience is definitely an advantage, but on-the-job training is also given to new entrants. The higher the post one seeks, the better should be the qualifications.

This industry is highly competitive and finally, those with better education in the field of travel and tourism are more likely to move ahead faster. The basic needs are a school-leaving certificate (10+2) for those seeking a position, upto the tourist guide level while candidates aspiring for managerial positions, need a graduate degree, in any of the fields dealing with history, art, languages, geography etc.

The hierarchy that exists in the Travel & Tourism industry is as follows: Counter Clerk/Counter Assistant - deals with designing itineraries, handling ticketing, reservations, suggesting suitable routes etc. Senior Assistant - supervises the counter clerks' work Junior Executive - In charge of counter work as well as certain marketing and sales projects of the agency services District Sales Manager - Regulates the marketing and sales of all the agencies in a particular zone or region Deputy General Manager - Assistant to the GM of the department or agency General Manager - manage the agency or departments in a particular company Vice President - Executive head of agency or organisation; designs policies in consultation with the managers, devises plans and projects to expand the agencies' services; has a responsibility towards the other employees and is answerable to a Board of Directors.

THE ELIGIBILITY AND TRAINING

It is relatively easy to enter courses designed for Travel & Tourism. The main areas such as travel agencies, transport, jobs at hotels, airline work all have good institutions that give training for about minimum 1-2 years with an adequate amount of practical training. The institutions run on the guidelines provided by the Indian Institute of Travel and Tourism Management and accurate information can be obtained by contacting the institutions directly. Some of the admission criteria is given in the Information on Institutions section.

ELIGIBILITY

Students can enter the undergraduate courses with a Higher Secondary Certificate while the post-graduate courses, require graduation in any field. The Indian Institute of Travel and Tourism Management This a reputed National centre for the education, training and research in the 'travel and tourism' management field. It is an autonomous organisation on the Ministry of Tourism, Government of India. It gives substantial amounts of help to graduates, directly and also via the Universities to enter the careers dealing in tour operation, leisure management, transportation, accommodation and interpretation services. It aims at reaching complete professionalism of all human resources involved in tourism, through the academic courses.

The Institute works in collaboration with the International Institute of Tourism Studies at the George Washington University and receives lot of academic support. Programmes are being developed with many international universities

(Univ. of Calgary in Canada, New School of Social Research, New York and many more) for the purpose of faculty-exchange programmes, sharing of facilities and knowledge which will benefit students and faculty equally.

Eligibility & Requirements to enter these courses: graduate degree; - age should not be more than 28 years SC/ST/OBC/Ex serviceman + 5 years; - an entrance exam needs to be given at the specific places - Bhubaneshwar, Calcutta, Chennai, Delhi, Gwalior and Mumbai, which consists mainly of General Knowledge questions and secondly, an interview. Number of seats available at each centre is quite limited - only 50 - which makes entry very competitive.

OTHER OPTIONS IN TOURISMS

Space Tourism is the term that's come to be used to mean ordinary members of the public buying tickets to travel to space and back. Many people find this idea futuristic. But over the past few years a growing volume of professional work has been done on the subject, and it's now clear that setting up commercial space tourism services is a realistic target for business today.

The first steps will just be short sub-orbital flights, like Alan Shepard made in 1961, since these are easier than getting to orbit. But the technical know-how to make passenger launch vehicles and orbiting hotel accommodation is available, and there is enormous unsatisfied demand - market research has revealed that most people, at least in the industrialized countries, would like to take a trip to space if it was possible. This gives huge scope for reducing the cost of space travel by large-scale operation like airlines.

The main obstacle is simply the conservatism of the space industry as it is today. Since Sputnik was launched in 1957 most space activities have been funded by governments. And this "cold war" pattern of space activities has created an image of space that colours everyones' thinking about it - writers, journalists, politicians, scientists and engineers, and the general public. Even science fiction writers assume as obvious that most space activities will always be government activities.

As on Earth, so in Space:

On Earth governments provide a number of services, defence, police, a legal system. But most activities are private - done by individuals and companies. Well, it's going to be the same in space. The Cold War is now over, and space agencies' budgets are being cut. True, so far, instead of using their huge funding to try to develop a profitable business like space tourism, the agencies are continuing the same activities - even though taxpayers aren't so interested any more. However, the general public are very interested in traveling to space for themselves. So after some false starts in the 1950s, 60s and 80s, work towards realizing space tourism is finally starting to gather some momentum. And the reasons why it is going to happen this time include:

- Because people want it
- Because it's a realistic objective
- Because it's the only way in which space activities can become profitable
- Because it's the quickest way to start to use the limitless resources of space to solve our problems on Earth
- Because living in space involves every line of business, from construction to marketing, fashion, interior-design and law

And not least,

- Because it will be fun!

Please note, developing low-cost passenger launch vehicles is not just to create a pastime for the rich. In business, the companies that make big money are the ones that serve big markets. Like tourism on Earth, there will be a small expensive segment for the rich - but the great majority of space tourists will be middle-class customers - the greater majority of us. But utilizing space depends on access. Until access is cheap, we can't make use of the limitless resources available in space to solve the problems of our ever-more-crowded Earth. But once access is cheap then we can. And to make it cheap we need large turnover. Tourism can generate the large-scale launch activity needed to reduce costs sufficiently to start to use space resources - and so it's one of the most important projects in the world today.

That is, commercial space activities today include satellites being used for communications, broadcasting and photography (remote sensing). But these are small businesses - no more than a few $billions per year - that will never need humans in space. So "commercial space activities" today are not leading towards space tourism. Consequently specific efforts need to be made to set up space tourism services, because they won't happen as a natural consequence of present-day space activities.

Some people say "Developing space tourism is very difficult, so it'll take a long time. Leave it to the government space agencies." But the agencies already spend $25 billion per year on "space activities" - and they are not trying to develop launch vehicles that could open space up to the public. Barely 2% of their budgets are used for this purpose - although even just one year of their huge funding would be plenty! So Space Future is playing its part by collecting all the work that is going on, and making it accessible, to help people to understand that *this is the way to the space age.*

PHASES OF SPACE TOURISM

Like any other business, once space tourism gets started it will develop progressively. It can be helpful to think of it as going through several phases. Starting with a relatively small-scale and relatively high-priced "pioneering phase", the scale of activity will grow and prices will fall as it matures. Finally it will become a mass-market business, like aviation today.

Pioneering Phase

The phrase "space adventure travel" has been suggested

by Gordon Woodcock of Boeing, and is a convenient one to describe the first phase. Customers will be relatively few - from hundreds per year to thousands per year; prices will be high, $50,000 and up; and the service will be nearer to "adventure travel" than to luxury hotel-style. Orbital accommodation will be safe but "spartan".

Mature Phase

This will see demand growing from thousands of passengers per year to hundreds of thousands per year. Tickets to orbit will cost less and flights will depart from many different airports. Orbital facilities will grow from being just clusters of pre-fabricated modules to large structures constructed in orbit for hundreds of guests, permitting a range of orbital entertainments.

Mass Phase

Ticket prices will fall to the equivalent of a few $ thousand, and customers will from hundreds of thousands to millions of passengers per year. Apparently unthinkable to most people in the space industry, even 1 million passengers per year is just 8 hours of aviation! And aviation is still growing fast at today's level of 1 billion passengers per year. So there's no reason to suppose that space travel will ever stop growing. There's certainly no limit to the possible destinations. And the access to space resources that low cost launch will bring about will ensure that economic growth needn't end for a few more millennia at least! Space tourism is an idea whose time has come. It's going to start soon, and it's going to grow rapidly, generating the funds needed to open up space to a wide range of human activities.

TOURISM OR TAXES

Until space tourism becomes a substantial business space activities, including particularly all crewed space activities, will remain a burden on tax-payers - that means *you*. No other activity than tourism offers similar promise of turning space activities into profitable commercial activities in the foreseeable future.

Suppose the taxpayers of the world were to ask: "For how many more decades are we going to have to pay $25 billion per year (the current level of government space spending!) before space activities become financially self-supporting?" Since the space agencies of the world currently have no plans to develop passenger-carrying launch-vehicles, this would be at least 30 years - just $750 billion. Why should the public agree to pay this? Especially since the agencies are not doing what they want?

In the last few years space activities in Russia have shrunk by about 90% - because they have little commercial value. And currently Russia must concentrate its resources on activities that are commercially valuable and contribute to economic growth. The budgets of NASA, ESA and several national space agencies have started to be cut recently. It's quite possible that government budget cuts in the rich countries will lead to continuing cuts in space spending there too, since they have little public support. The only way to ensure the growth of space activities is to put them on a commercial basis - and that means developing a space tourism industry.

It's possible to go even further and argue that until space tourism becomes a major new profit centre of the aerospace industry, economic growth in the rich countries will remain sluggish. Over the past few decades' governments have invested approximately $1 trillion in space activities, but this investment is still far from earning a commercial return. By normal business standards a $1 trillion investment should be earning annual profits of $100 billion or more by now - but annual turnover (let alone profits) of all commercial space activities is still only in the billions of $$. Large-scale profits can arise only from large-scale space activities - which can be achieved only by making much more effort to develop economical passenger launch-vehicles.

During the last decades of the 19th century and the

first decade of the 20th century "Buffalo Bill's Wild West Show" toured throughout the USA and Europe to enormous popular acclaim. No doubt Bill Cody was mocked by his previous colleagues saying "Entertainment's no job for a real cowboy". But "Buffalo Bill" created a great deal of wealth; he became world-famous; and he entertained and educated tens of millions of people about the "Wild West". (He also went on to play an important role in the development of aviation). By comparison, being a cowboy became relatively less and less well-paid.

Today it may be fun as a hobby, but as a way of life such manual labour has its limitations - unless you're in a cigarette commercial! It would surely to right to say that Bill Cody read the times correctly. So, instead of expecting taxpayers to keep paying colossal sums for their expensive - and elitist - interests, astronauts and space agency staff should learn from Bill Cody and start to develop an orbital hospitality industry.

This will not only be hugely popular with the public around the world, but it will also enrich the space industry and other participating businesses, and the economies of those countries which play a major role in it, and it will stimulate world economic growth.

For as long as the space industry does not take this path, then space activities will remain a tax-payer funded activity. As such they surely don't have a very bright future. Who'll pay $500 billion to watch a few people walk on Mars? - when instead they could spend a few tens of $ billions (at most) and get a space tourism industry? As the choice becomes clearer it's easy to predict what taxpayers will choose - if their opinions are asked!

These are some suggestions we've received but for which we don't yet have any write-ups. If you're familiar with any of them, let us know: If you have any nominations for this page, please send them in. Remember, good *and* bad examples of space tourism in science fiction qualify! "Space tourism" is the term that has come to be used to mean members of the public traveling to and from space by buying tickets like an airline. It's a distinct category of "space travel" which also includes travel in space for work purposes - to date, mainly by government staff.

In recent years it has become increasingly recognised that, although government space agencies are not interested in space tourism, it is a legitimate objective of space development - and it is likely to generate substantial investment funds that will help to develop space.

Indeed NASA itself published a report "General Public Space Travel and Tourism" in March 1998 which endorses the idea of space tourism; points out that it is going to start quite soon in the form of sub-orbital flights; and argues that it is likely to become a much larger market for launch systems than satellite launch.

Although space tourism appears in a number of science fiction stories, it's very striking that in almost none of them is tourism portrayed as more than a small-scale activity greatly overshadowed by government space activities - military operations, scientific research, defence, etc. This seems to be a good example of how the Cold War pattern of space activities paralyzed the public's imagination.

That is, government monopoly organizations carrying out "missions" in space ostensibly for the benefit of the taxpayer created a fixed image of what space activities are, which has dominated the imaginations of engineers and scientists, the media, politicians and the general public for several decades.

This effect has been so strong that even most science fiction writers became unable to imagine anything different - although they are generally thought to be some of the more imaginative members of society! Yet, search as you may, almost no stories set within the next 50-100 years feature near-Earth space tourism at all, and in those that do it is an economically and socially minor activity.

Space Future disagrees firmly with this collective image, and maintains that space tourism will become the main economic activity attracting commercial investment into space and thereby financing space development - within as little as a decade or two. That is, far from being a small-scale activity of just a few rich people, tourism in space will grow like air travel to become a mass market available to the middle classes, and will dwarf other space activities.

Encouragingly, the objective of space tourism is gradually coming to be more and more widely accepted. Compared to that coming reality, today's long-term projections by government space agencies (which are generally accepted by the media and appear in much science fiction) that in 50 years the sum total of human space activities will comprise a handful of scientists working at bases on the Moon and Mars, and perhaps a hundred in Earth orbit - will come to seem astonishingly blinkered.

In the following we discuss a number of examples of space tourism activities appearing in science fiction stories - both short stories and novels, and also film and video. The authors would be grateful for any references and (better still) excerpts from other stories, in order to make this survey as complete as possible.

Space Tourism in Science Fiction

- Space Tourism in Books and Short Stories
- Passing Mentions of Space Tourism
- Space Tourism in the Movies

Space Tourism in Books and Short Stories:

The idea of tourism in space is the central story line in a number of well-known and not-so-well-known science fiction stories. It also plays a significant part in a number of other stories, and gets some sort of mention in even more. In the following we discuss a number of these.

"The Menace from Earth"

A good place to start seems to be Robert Heinlein's wonderful 20-page story "The Menace from Earth", first published in 1957 by Fantasy House Inc, and more-or-less continually available in one or other edition of a short-story collection of that name. It's about a 15 year-old school-girl,

Holly Jones, a 3rd-generation lunar inhabitant, whose hobbies are designing star-ships and flying in "Bats' Cave", a natural cavern two miles wide and half-a-mile high which is Luna City's air reservoir and is also used for recreational flying. (With weight 1/6 of that on Earth, almost anyone can fly like a bird on the Moon.)

The story concerns a rich tourist from Earth, Ariel Brentwood, who temporarily mesmerizes Holly's boyfriend, Jeff Hardesty, to Holly's discomfort. The heart of the story concerns Holly helping Ariel to try out flying in "Bat's Cave".

Realistically, Heinlein depicts tourism as being an important part of the lunar economy, and the flying scenes are wonderfully described. The theme is certainly a realistic possibility for early in the 21st century - quite soon now - and Heinlein takes his usual pleasure in working out the engineering details correctly. Holly describes her custom-made wings to the reader:

"They're lovely! - titanalloy struts as light and strong as bird-bones, tension-compensated wrist-pinion and shoulder joints, natural action in the alula slots, and automatic flap action in stalling. The wing skeleton is dressed in styrene feather-foils, with individual quilling of scapulars and primaries. They almost fly themselves."

A great bit of foresight, and a charming story as well, which captures the mood of 1950s USA at its best - something like the atmosphere of Norman Rockwell's paintings - fresh, optimistic, a little naive, but confident and going places - especially out into space, of course!

Also a great example of Heinlein's skill as a story-teller with a clear idea of how the future of space activities could really be. (It's perhaps more correct to call him a "story-teller-engineer", in the same tradition as Nevil Shute, the airship and aircraft engineer and novelist.)

"Skyport"

Another particularly striking story from the same era is "Skyport" by Kurt Siodmak, reprinted as a Signet paperback in 1961. This contains what must be (at least for Space Future types) the truly classic scene:

"Just tell me the general idea you have in mind - the idea Sven and my daughter keep so mysteriously to themselves. What is this thing that's so revolutionary and so daring? Fantastic and at the same time logical? I'm quoting, of course, my daughter." He looked steadily at Lee. His eyes brightened as if an inner light had been turned on. Lee glanced at the architect and the girl. He found response in their faces. "I need your assistance in building a hotel in outer space," he said artlessly.

"Skyport" contains what now seem funny scenes due to some technical misunderstandings, but these are excusable given that it was published between Sputnik 1 and Gagarin's first flight. It's essentially a realistic story - largely concerning boardroom wheeling and dealing between business rivals trying to get control of the orbital hotel as a pawn in their empire-building - unconcerned by its cosmic significance.

It also contains some excellent discussions about space law, interior design in zero-gravity, marketing and other subjects as they relate to a space hotel. It seems fair to say that Siodmak had a good idea of how extremely popular such a project would be, and how it would lead on to growth of space activities.

"A Fall of Moondust"

In the second rank of tourism stories, Arthur C Clarke's 1961 novel "A Fall of Moondust" (republished most recently by Bantam Books 1991) concerns the misadventure of a party of lunar tourists whose vehicle sinks in a crater full of dust.

However, in the world in which it's set, there's a research station between the Moon and Earth, and another on the Moon, and it's clear that only very rich people get to be tourists, and they're a very small part of what's going on in space - so we're back in the traditional space paradigm.

Having said that, lunar tourism is always going to be considerably (perhaps 10 times?) more expensive than tourism in low Earth orbit, due to the Moon being 1000 times further away.

However, there's no reason to suppose that lunar tourism won't grow to a large scale, and even become the dominant activity on the Moon - though it may be a close thing in competition with ice-mining for export to hotels in low Earth orbit..

"Picnic on Paradise"

Joanna Russ's excellent 1968 novel "Picnic on Paradise" (republished most recently in 1979), is set much further into the future when interstellar travel is common. It concerns an unfortunate party of tourists who get caught up in a civil war while visiting a distant planet.

They seem to be something like "adventure tourists" since they have a tour guide with them. The drama arises because she's fiercely aware that they're most likely all going to die very soon, and she's profoundly irritated with her idle rich clients and their hopelessly unrealistic ideas about what to do. A great read.

Charlie and the Great Glass Elevator

In 1973 the childrens' fantasy story "Charlie and the Great Glass Elevator" by Roald Dahl, was first published by George Allen & Unwin. It opens with Charlie and his parents and grandparents flying skywards in a glass elevator (it's a *children's story*, remember!). They continue upwards until they reach orbit where they come across the subject, titled "Space Hotel U.S.A."

"...Two days before, the U.S.A had successfully launched its first Space Hotel, a gigantic, sausage-shaped capsule no less than one thousand feet long. It was called Space Hotel 'U.S.A.' and it was the marvel of the space age.

It had inside it a tennis-court, a swimming pool, a gymnasium, a childrens' playroom and five hundred luxury bedrooms, each with a private bath. It was fully air-conditioned. It was also equipped with a gravity-making machine so that you didn't float about inside it. You walked normally."

There's then some discussion of the rich and famous people who are going to stay in the hotel - one offering $100,000 per day for the "honeymoon suite", and it continues:

"...but you cannot send guests to an hotel unless there are lots of people there to look after them, and that explains why there was yet another interesting object orbiting the Earth at that moment. This was the large Transport Capsule containing the entire staff of Space Hotel 'U.S.A.' There were managers, assistant managers, desk-clerks, waitresses, bellboys, chambermaids, pastry chefs and hall porters."

The story subsequently turns into a battle with aliens, but even these short sections show that the author was thinking through the idea of orbital hotels rather clearly (leaving aside the gravity making machine, at least).

"Satellite City"

This book is set in the near future where taxes in the United States consume almost all wealth. The rich and the Mafia have set up a 'Las Vegas in Space' for tourists and the tax-sheltered wealthy. The story revolves around a private detective whose case takes him to the station and forces him to confront its founders.

From the context of the story, it is pretty clear that a vacation in the huge resort platform was expensive, but not out of reach of reasonably wealthy tourists, and the hotel residents were not extremely surprised to be visited by the not very well-to-do private detective. At the least, it shows an expectation that resorts in Earth orbit would be expensive and exclusive commercial vacations, but no more so then high end cruise ships.

"Galactic Tours"

A very different sort of book is the picture-book "Galactic Tours", by the space artist David Hardy and writer Bob Shaw, which illustrates a range of tourist possibilities with sweeping imagination - from lunar and Martian holidays and skiing on Europa (one of the moons of Jupiter) in our solar system, to weird and exotic far-future possibilities in other star systems.

To stick to reasonably predictable matters, it's clear that lunar tours will become a big business. Once low-Earth orbit is routinely accessible to tourists, the 3-day trip each way to the Moon and back (using no more than Apollo-era technology) makes a 2-week trip a very realistic "package".

One day too, tourists will travel to Mars and go skiing on Europa - at least a few early explorers should within a few decades from now. However, the journey times of a year or so needed to get to another planet from Earth make such trips much less promising as tourist destinations. It's a lot less realistic to imagine large numbers of people taking a few years off work than a couple of weeks, whatever the price. But for these trips and the even more far-out ideas, it's worth remembering the striking effects of compound economic growth: at less than 2.5% per year, incomes grow 10 times per century - that means 100 times in 200 years! - and 1000 times in 300 years!! So however expensive you want to assume interstellar travel will be, it won't be more than a few hundred years before it will be economically feasible - a short time even in human history - let alone in cosmic evolutionary terms!

"Rim"

A more recent addition to science fiction about space tourism is "Rim" (sub-titled A Novel of Virtual Reality) by Alexander Besher (first published in 1994 by Harper Collins West, and reprinted by Harper Paperbacks in 1996). Much of the action takes place either in Japan or in cyberspace, but about 50 pages (out of about 300) are devoted to action in and around the 350-room "Station Seven Intercontinental" hotel that occupies the top 20+ floors of "Space Station Seven" and is described as the "the first orbiting luxury hotel in the world".

The description unfortunately contains a number of technical errors such as stating that the hotel is "...in geosynchronous orbit 280 miles above Neo-Tokyo" (!) - which are rather less forgiveable today than they were in the 1950s. But such remarks as that the hotel "...was a special favourite of Japanese honeymooners, who were prevented from traveling abroad by the New Nippon quarantine..." ring truer.

There's also unexplained artificial gravity, and no real thinking through of orbital hotel design - nor any scenes of ordinary guests enjoying the pleasures of staying in orbit - so Besher still can't be said to be describing the (relatively near) future that Space Future is promoting - but "Rim" is definitely "getting warmer"!

Encounter With Tiber

"Encounter with Tiber" starts with a near-future history of how space gets opened up to the general public - and space tourism is given a major role (though it takes up only a few pages out of more than 500). The scene is set with a second space shuttle accident, which poses the problem *how* is the money to be raised to pay for a new generation of fully reusable space vehicles?

Sig Jarlsberg, (something of a modern-day Delos Harriman, the businessman-hero of Robert Heinlein's classic story "The Man Who Sold the Moon") founds an ecological travel company for the rich and famous, 'Planet Vision Adventure Tours' which grows into "Share-the-Planet Tours .....a giant in the burgeoning industry of low-impact, high-priced tourism". In 1999 Sig assembles a group of super-rich clients (including the names of some of today's more famous billionaires) and convinces them to invest in a space tourism business venture:

"If you want that better world, we need to see space tourism take off right away, and it can't be as a plaything of a tiny group of super-rich people. It's got to have broad-based popular support and enthusiasm right from the start.

And for that, ladies and gentlemen, I propose - ShareSpace Global".

Buzz Aldrin is himself a strong supporter of space travel for the general public, and is currently promoting the *real* 'Sharespace', a lottery to finance a number of reusable launch vehicle projects collectively. So he's obviously trying to follow the maxim of predicting the future by making it happen! In the following years the suborbital "Skygrazer", the reusable booster "Starbooster" and orbital "Starbird" upper stage are developed which reduce the cost of passenger travel to orbit.

The main story of "Encounter with Tiber" then takes over as messages arrive from intelligent extra-terrestrials and stimulate governments to finance more space activities. As a result, by the early 2010s there are 9 government space stations - 2 French, 2 Russian, 1 Chinese, 1 Japanese, 1 US and 2 international ones - with a total of 35 permanent staff.

At that time the then still young hero of the novel makes his first visit to the new international station 'Starport' as "the first kid in space", and there's some discussion of a plan to buy 4 space shuttle External Tanks to be linked together into a 'space hotel', one to be "...just an empty padded space that people can use as a gym".

Space Future's vision of how things are going to work out differs in considering that governments are *not* likely to build any more space stations. That is, the International Space Station will be the last, at least until space flight has become much cheaper than it is today.

The hero describes the impressive view of Earth, and the fun of living in zero-gravity: "Swimming through the air to the other window was a lot of fun" and "...we played an odd game the Japanese had devised, Ping-Pong inside a Plexiglass cylinder that they had shipped up for some now-forgotten reason (to get the ball "over the net" you had to get it through the central hole)".

Finally he opines "As soon as there's enough room up here..... there's going to be a *real* tourist trade. This is more fun than skiing and skydiving at the same time. If there were just room enough, think of what you could do." (The action then switches to 2075 for the encounter with the aliens.)

Realistic in giving space tourism a major role in raising the investment needed to develop space, "Encounter with Tiber" is also interesting in describing the leading role that a single visionary individual with enough resources behind them can play. The development of low-cost passenger space vehicles is certainly at a stage today at which wealthy individuals can and are playing a very significant role - as they did in the early days of aviation. (A few more would be welcome!)

"Not the Only Planet"

In 1998 Lonely Planet Publications, the Austrialia-based publisher of books for travellers to out-of-the-way places, published the book "Not the Only Planet" as part of their new "Lonely Planet Journeys" fiction series. This is a collection of 10 stories by known science fiction writers, which might seem to offer a good chance of getting a vision of tourism in space.

But no such luck. The objective of the collection is stated as being stories that "...in some special way caught the experience of travel". However, only two of them are space travel stories of what might be called the reasonably near future, involving visits to Mars and Venus respectively - and even this is being generous.

The first, while technologically feasible, sfaces the problem that Mars is unlikely to be a significant tourist destination for a very long time - for the reason that it takes a year to get there. The second story involves major futuristic prosthetic surgery to put up with Venus' hideous climate! Joanna Russ gets closest to the feeling space tourism in her alien phrase book - but that too is looking rather far ahead!

The rest of the stories are all more-or-less surrealistic (for want of a better word) - involving time travel, parallel worlds, psychological and far-future mind-bending. This isn't a criticism: the editor selected them from hundreds, as he explains "...it isn't difficult to find of tales dealing with travel...... Science fiction and travel have always gone together....."

Having said that, lunar tourism is always going to be *near-term space travel by the general public.* Collectively they just don't have a vision of an interesting and convincing near-future world of human space activities centring on tourism.

To put it differently, science fiction writers haven't painted a clear picture of how space is going to be opened up - the growth of space tourism leading to the development of more and more exotic orbital hotels, and lunar development based on exporting ice and other materials to these orbital facilities.

But this isn't because they've considered the possibility and decided it isn't interesting - it's primarily because they aren't aware of the possibility. The image they mostly have of near-future, near-Earth space activities is that they're going to be more of the same - government technology development projects - and hence boring, not material for new and interesting stories.

But the facts remain that most people want to go to space; and NASA has confirmed in print that space tourism is feasible, near-term and could grow into the largest business activity in space. Space Future's scenario not only leads to an interesting and fun future in space, but it's the only scenario that does so.

For that reason it's going to happen, and the signs are that it's going to start fairly soon now. It's just sad that science fiction writers haven't started drawing this future to the attention of the public yet.

PASSING MENTIONS OF SPACE TOURISM

In a rather different category, tourists get a passing mention in quite a lot of science fiction stories. For example Ben Bova devoted a few pages of his "Moonbase Orientation

Manual" to tourism on the Moon 40 years from now. However, the tourists are clearly not seen as important characters - just a few rich people visiting a government base, while taxpayers are expected to pick up the main tab for the serious work being done.

This category is the largest, and more examples will be added as they are brought to our attention. Suggestions please!

Space Tourism in the Movies

While there are plenty of movies from far in the past about space travel, we are unaware of any in which space tourism is a major business activity, or in which realistically portrayed orbiting hotels play a major role. Nevertheless the concept of tourism turns up here and there - just enough to show how the coming reality of space tourism has not been foreseen at all clearly in the movie industry.

Overall, it's probably lucky that zero gravity can't be faked (except in 20 second bursts inside an aeroplane). So Hollywood is going to *have* to build a studio in LEO to make all the great zero-G scenes that are imaginable! That should help to raise money for space hotels. Note, an orbiting film studio was one possibility investigated in the Commercial Space Transportation Study.

"2001: A Space Odysey" (1968)

The famous rotating low Earth orbit station in "2001" is sometimes quoted as an example of a space hotel. In the story, part of it is said to be a hotel, and people do apparently stay there while waiting for their connecting flights to and from the Moon.

However, it seems fair to say that it's not a "real" space hotel. For example there's no sign of anyone having any fun - and there are no women or children. Flights are very few, and the activities seem to be exclusively governmental rather than commercial (as they would more-or-less have to be being operated on such a very small scale).

Furthermore, the activities on the Moon are clearly government ones - classic NASA-types doing "research" and making serious decisions that will affect humans' destiny etc etc in solemn tones. Very strongly influenced by the "ruling paradigm" of the Cold War era, "2001" seems to have been made on the assumption that that pattern would continue indefinitely into the future. Present-day budget cuts at government space agencies, and growing interest in commercial space activities and space tourism are showing the way to how mistaken this was.

"The Fifth Element" (1997)

At perhaps the opposite end of the spectrum, a large part of the action in "Fifth Element" takes place inside what is said to be an orbiting "hotel", which actually looks very like a huge cruise liner. It's spoiled by the fact that the story is very average 1990s nonsense, and there's no attempt at showing either zero-G scenes or Earth and space viewing lounges - which are surely the major reasons why people are going to go to space hotels. It looks little different from a gaudy and noisy Las Vegas hotel.

"Moon Zero Two" (1969)

"Moon Two Zero" came out around the same time as "2001" and featured space tourists prominently in the plot. The film is set in a lunar resort city. The protagonist is an ex-astronaut, the first man to land on Mars and owner of his own spaceship, with which he makes a living scavenging dead satellites. Prices are not mentioned much, but in one scene a lunar visitor offers him $10,000 to take her to the far side of the Moon in his ship.

The rest of the movie concerns a mad tycoon's plan to crash a pure sapphire asteroid on the far side of the Moon (illegally of course), and the hero must to cooperate, or else. Regrettably, the film is not offically available now and hard to find, but copies may turn up on Ebay from time to time.

The travel bug begins to bite as summer approaches

and children get their holidays. Keeping this in mind, we cover careers for those inclined towards travel and adventure. With domestic and international tourism picking up, many careers can indeed be made in this sector. We describe some opportunities though many more may exist in related areas. We also talk to a company which employs young people as 'Holiday Consultants'. If you like meeting people, love adventure and have a pleasing personality, you can look for careers in a fast growing sector. The travel and tourism industry is growing very fast.

Once confined to families taking an annual LTC trip, today more people are venturing out of their homes and look for quality vacations where they can relax and also do something new and interesting.

Sports like river rafting and hang gliding are slowly catching on and there are many jobs that are available for a person who can arrange good holidays for the domestic as well as the international tourist. India earned $ 2753 million from international tourism in 1995. The total numbers of arrivals were 21.22 lakhs, and the figure is increasing every year.

With the growth of tourist traffic, travel-related jobs are increasing by the day. These relate to various related services facilitating travel, such as travel agencies, banking, hotels, guides, airlines and other services. Some of them may be seasonal, limited to the tourist season from September to March but others are permanent in nature. In this sector, girls are in as much demand as males and are even preferred for certain jobs.

Travel-related jobs are best suited for individuals who enjoy meeting people and make them comfortable. They are for those who love adventure and travelling. True, some are desk jobs, but even these jobs entail understanding the needs of the traveller and making the best arrangements possible for him. Many agencies are diversifying into travel services.

These include foreign banks and vacation companies

which offer this as an added service to their clients. For example, American Express has its Travel-Related Services Unit to provide assistance to clients. With the travel sector opening up and foreign timeshares and vacations becoming popular, tourist traffic is expected to increase manifold. Much of the traffic depends on internal stability of the country; fortunately that has existed in India. The government too recognises it as an industry.

Some of the areas where careers can be made are described here:

Travel Agencies: Facilitating travel and related services are travel agencies. They require people to deal with customers, guide them as they plan holidays and finally offer tickets for the best routes or offers. They also help in foreign exchange and visas. To join a travel agency, one can do a diploma in travel and ticketing from a polytechnic or an institute.

This is usually a short-term course (3-6 months) and will help gain entry into an agency. Some travel agencies and airlines offer this course. Short-term courses are also offered by Delhi Tourism. Freshers without a diploma can also join and learn on the job. The requirements are a pleasing personality and the ability to deal with customers. Of course a knowledge of destinations and procedures help a great deal.

Tour Operators: There are many companies operating tours for the domestic as well as the international tourist. Some may be for the usual destinations like hill stations but others are for unusual activities like river rafting, hang gliding, rock climbing and camping. Tour operators need people for selling the concept and then to accompany the groups to the destinations. For foreign groups, the agencies prefer girls, who are friendly and helpful. For domestic groups, males are preferred.

Again, the qualities required are a pleasing and outgoing personality, knowledge of the activities and often participatin in them with the tourists. A person hoping to work with a tour operator must be able to travel with the groups and know people at the destinations to make the tours pleasant for the client. Though one may do a course of tourist guide for this purpose, people with a knowledge of the activities can easily join tour operators. The jobs could be seasonal in some cases.

Tourist guides: The Ministry of Tourism grants licenses to three categories of tourist guides: regional, state level and monument guides. This is a three-month course followed by a test, after which the license is granted. For 12 years after 1984, no licenses were granted as the license holders had taken a stay.

People have thus been working even eithout a license. A guide gets about Rs 1,600 per day for outstation tours but they also get tips from clients and commission from hotels, restaurants and shops.

The best guides and those who are in demand are those who offer clean deals and are able to get the maximum advantage for the tourists. Guides must be in touch with foreign agencies who send groups to India. A fixed itinerary is offered and guides take the groups to those areas which they are familiar with.

Apart from the activities mentioned above, wildlife safaris are also becoming increasingly popular. During the season, a guide can hope to earn a six-figure sum but a person has to be good and understand the foreign tourist and his needs.

The job is exciting and satisfying and the earnings during the season are enough to see one through the off season as well. The age limit for a guide is 50 years but young and energetic persons are preferred.

Holiday consultants: This is a new concept, the idea being that the tourist gets all the details of travel and itineraries from one source. The holiday consultant will sell the holidays, plan out the itineraries, help in travel plans and arrange for ticketing and other details as well. Knowledge of the destinations and the activities available is a pre-requisite.

Index

F

G

I

M

P

R

S